THE COMPLETE
Job-Search
HANDBOOK

Howard Figler, Ph.D.

THE COMPLETE
Job-Search
HANDBOOK

Everything You Need to Know to Get the Job You Really Want

✦ **THIRD EDITION** ✦

AN OWL BOOK

HENRY HOLT AND COMPANY ✦ NEW YORK

Henry Holt and Company, LLC
Publishers since 1866
115 West 18th Street
New York, New York 10011

Henry Holt ® is a registered trademark
of Henry Holt and Company, LLC.

Library of Congress Cataloging-in-Publication Data

Figler, Howard E.
    The complete job-search handbook : everything you need to
know to get the job you really want / Howard Figler.—3rd ed.
        p.   cm.
    "An Owl Book."
    Includes bibliographical references and index.
    ISBN 0-8050-6191-6 (pb.)
    1. Job hunting.   I. Title.
HF5382.7.F54   1999   99-27570
650.14—dc21   CIP

Henry Holt books are available for special promotions
and premiums. For details contact: Director, Special Markets.

Designed by Victoria Hartman

Printed in the United States of America

10 9 8 7 6 5 4 3 2 1

The author is grateful to the following publisher for permission to reprint
previously copyrighted material: From *PATH: A Career Workbook for Liberal Arts
Students* by Howard Figler: copyright © 1979 by Howard Figler. Reprinted
by permission of the Carroll Press, Cranston, Rhode Island.

To Mom,
who encouraged my career
when I needed it the most

Contents

Acknowledgments

A writer works alone, but he does not write alone. This edition was inspired by people in career counseling who have given me insights, encouragement, and support that have nourished my writing of this edition from start to finish. These special individuals are Richard Bolles, H. B. Gelatt, Janice Klar, Betsy Collard, Helen Scully, Astrid Berg, Kathy Worgul, John Krumboltz, Patrick Ferris, and Constance Stevens.

I'd also like to warmly acknowledge Bob Entwistle, who pushed me to write this book in the first place, and Howard Stoker, who encouraged me in graduate school, before I had even tried to write anything.

I would like to thank my publisher for supporting all three editions of this book so fully and consistently with strong distribution and promotion. Their confidence in the book helped establish its place in the market.

My editors, Elise Proulx and Jen Charat, have been superb and congenial in every way. Elise gave me significant help in the early structure of the book and many welcome recommendations about sharpening the content. Jen provided key reorganizations of the book, many observations that improved its form and style, a final structure that made great sense, and a keen editorial eye that spotted and reshaped every unnecessary, foggy, or obscure sentence that I tried to slip past her gaze.

Finally, I want to acknowledge the ongoing parade of job searchers who endure bumps and bruises, anxiety, and the indignities of job hunting in exchange for the eventual rewards. I appreciate your bearing with us authors who think it's all supposed to happen just the way we write about it. Your day is coming. You will triumph and it will be worth your effort.

Introduction

People are always blaming their circumstances for what they are. I don't believe in circumstances. The people who get on in this world are the people who get up and look for the circumstances they want, and if they can't find them—make them.

—George Bernard Shaw,
Mrs. Warren's Profession

Some people in this world can advance their careers simply by declaring they are available. Like blaring trumpets, their credentials speak for themselves, announcing the presence of persons who are obviously suited to perform particular jobs. Such people are renowned for certain public achievements, or possess advanced degrees that automatically qualify them for certain work, or have rare or outstanding talents, or can measure their previous accomplishments on dollar scales that preclude the need for further certification. These individuals have career opportunities dropped into their laps. They represent about 1 percent of all job hunters. What about the other 99 percent?

If you have not won awards for your past work performance, are not famous, cannot announce your potency in terms of dollar sales, you are a mere mortal in the career-search process. There is no magic available for you. The success of your search will depend on how well you understand the process of finding better work.

For most ordinary folk, comfort, peace of mind, and self-assurance in the career search derive not from knowing that you possess one great talent to depend on, but from knowing you possess the appropriate skills to find other work if this talent should dissipate or lose its natural market.

Those 99 percent who possess average college grades, have no great accomplishments, graduated from nonprestigious universities, receive little recognition on the job, have checkered career patterns, are plain-looking, or are otherwise inheritors of ordinariness actually can, and do, turn the tables on the privileged by learning to acquire job-search skills from the very start. By having to survive, they learn to be superior survivors. The ordinary folk become stronger; the inheritors of great career wealth lose their potency when they can no longer receive automatic appointments based on their appearance, credentials, or birthright.

I know the hordes of job competitors you imagine make you highly anxious, but you can turn this anxiety to your advantage. So many talented and untalented people depend on luck, magic formulas, handouts from family or friends, or whims of the marketplace that a little initiative and focused effort can yield a greater gain. While they are wasting their energies looking for handouts, your knowledge of the secrets of the job-search process will pay off.

You Have Been Told to Work Too Hard

Despite the value of career skills, many in the vast middle class of job hunting are discouraged by well-intentioned friends or counselors who say: "Job hunting is hard work, so push yourself, make an all-out effort"; or "Know *exactly* what you want before making an application"; or "Exhaust yourself."

These are empty messages. They serve more to frustrate you than stir you to action. Admonished to work hard, work harder, know thyself, drive, drive, drive, you wonder what you are supposed to do first.

You do not want to embrace a philosophy of job seeking that sounds as if it were written for Superman. You want a job-search strategy that will not rip your life apart or double your anxiety level in one swift stroke.

In all likelihood, you have already devised a homemade strategy for your job search and have built it into your daily routine. You are making some progress on your wits and common sense, without having to spend a fortune on career consultants or have your palm read for further clues. In short, you are doing a decent job of job hunting on your own. However, you need a few hints about what you are doing wrong. These clues should suggest where you can make adjustments in your search while not disturbing the life routine to which you have become accustomed.

It has been said that getting a job is harder than any job you will ever do. Don't let that scare you. Landing a job is easier than you may believe. You can use this book to decide which skills you have been neglecting. You will see that you are already using many career skills very effectively and will be encouraged to perfect your own methods.

The Blessings of the Job Search

While you are pleased to know there is hope for those who seek better work, there is another part of you that says the job search is the curse of the employment misfit, or your penalty for being so untalented that no one notices you, or simply a bigger pain than anything else imaginable. It is a mistake to believe that a job search is a punishment for past failures. What may appear to be the curses of an extended exploration for better work are truly blessings in disguise:

✦ The curse of having to make the rounds of many employers, endure many interviews, and read numerous career materials before you decide becomes the blessing of reaching a large number of professional people who are acquainted with you and your work and can thus serve as your present and future contacts.

✦ The curse of struggling to identify your hidden talents—your subtle, not easily labeled abilities—becomes the blessing of discovering that you have many qualifications and skills that are marketable in a wide variety of employment contexts.

✦ The curse of not knowing exactly what your future will be, of living with unknown options and uncertain timetables, becomes the blessing of being secure enough so you don't jump at the first job opportunity; you enjoy playing with the many creative possibilities on your career landscape and trust that the mysterious plot in your career story will be resolved in your favor.

✦ The curse of having to ask many people a lot of questions and ask for their valuable time becomes the blessing of learned interview skills so you can elicit information and attitudes from anyone in a way that makes the interview even more pleasing to the other people than to yourself.

✦ The curse of having to explain yourself to everyone, justify your reasons for even wanting to talk about career matters, becomes the blessing of having the skills to portray yourself clearly, creatively, and in terms that are marketable without being pretentious or self-conscious.

✦ And the curse of taking on a task that seems to be a job in itself becomes the blessing of learning that most elements of the career search are already entwined in your daily routine of work and play and need only be improved or emphasized by a more conscious and focused effort on your part.

Perhaps the greatest blessing of job-search skills is that they can be used long before you are interviewed for your next job. You begin your search for your next position the very day you are hired in your present one.

There is a prevailing myth that all judgments of you as a job candidate are held in suspense until you arrive for the formal interview. That is why so many interviewees practice trying on new clothes and muttering magic phrases they hope will capture the interviewer's attention. This sort of preparation is self-defeating; if you believe that key words, manner of dress, or significant glances during a job interview will make the difference, you will find it extremely difficult to be your natural self. You will be one more victim of interview anxiety.

But if you take advantage of job-search skills long before the formal interviews, you will already know a lot about your target employer, who will also know a lot about you. As you will see in the forthcoming chapters, you can assess yourself, detect the available jobs, become expert about prospective employers, practice your communication skills, establish a network of helpers, and spend many hours with the people for whom you would like to work long before you decide to announce your intentions.

Whom and What This Book Is For

This book is for career changers, returning workers, midlife-crisis and second-career people, and any others who feel they deserve better careers than they currently have. I assume you have opened this book not for casual reasons, but because you need some immediate help with your special career predicament. Career decisions probably are not new to you. You already know a lot about the subject. You may be curious to see if anything new can be said. You are open to a new approach, anything that will dislodge you from your present rut.

If you are like most people, you prefer not to read a whole book to extract the information you need. To accommodate your desire to get information quickly, I have organized this volume so you can see at a glance what topics are covered. You can skip around in this book, read the parts you like best or need most. I wrote it to be used that way because you are probably already doing many things right in the career search. You are also doing a few things wrong and want to know what they are and how to correct yourself quickly.

How is this book different from other books on job hunting? First of all, it does its best to illuminate the entire *process* that occurs when a person seeks better work. This book spells out every skill you need to conduct a successful job search.

Second, I propose that most of your job-search activity can and ought to be initiated long before the formalities of résumé preparation and job interviews.

Third, most job-search skills are connected to certain generic life skills that you already use to solve other life problems. You have been using job-search skills every day, probably unconsciously.

Thus, this is a book that focuses on the twenty-seven skills that come into play whenever an individual seeks a new job.

While I encourage you to identify your job-search problems in terms of several skills that seem appropriate, I caution you not to expect a cookbook solution. I cannot tell you what to do in ten easy steps. You must decide the best sequence of events for yourself.

The twenty-seven job-search skills are presented in Chart 1 (page 6). They begin with understanding your uniqueness (self-assessment skills). Specific methods of information gathering and developing networks of relationships (connecting skills) then enable you to connect with a number of target organizations and become knowledgeable about them.

The skills of interpersonal exchange (communication skills) are vitally necessary for the many occasions when you talk with or write to individuals who have career possibilities for you. Skills for selling yourself are then used as you seek to fit your talents to the needs of the employer. Interviewing skills help you to focus on the special characteristics of job interviews and how you can best present yourself.

The chart allows you to see the entire job-search process as an organic unity, reminding you that the several parts of job exploration are interconnected and that proficiency in one job-search skill undoubtedly helps your progress in all the others.

The Twenty-eight Skills of the Job Search

The twenty-eight skills discussed in this book fall into five categories: self-assessment, connecting, communication, selling yourself, and interviewing. Each skill is briefly discussed below.

Self-Assessment Skills

1. *Values*. Identifying and clarifying the highest-priority rewards and satisfactions you hope to obtain in your career, discriminating among competing alternatives.

2. *Money*. Evaluating the importance of financial security and high earnings in your career equation. Deciding how money will rate compared to other sources of career satisfaction.

3. *Intuition*. Tapping into the many things you "know" are true about yourself that you cannot explain. Accessing intuition fully in your career imagings and decisions.

4. *Skills*. Identifying and labeling your most prominent strengths or abilities and choosing the ones you most enjoy using in work situations.

5. *Imagination*. Learning to envision new and previously unimagined career possibilities by using a variety of creative thought processes and methods.

The Twenty-eight Skills of the Job Search

Self-Assessment Skills	Connecting Skills	Communication Skills
Values	Jobs Are Everywhere	Listening
Money	Network of	Questioning
Intuition	Relationships	Initiating
Skills	Information	Writing
Imagination	Interviewing	Public Speaking
Reality Testing	Avoiding Networking	
Self-Reliance	Mistakes	
	Walk-In Method	
	Interim Jobs	
	Library/Internet	

Skills for Selling Yourself	Interviewing Skills
Sell with Dignity	Give Reasons to Want You
Ask Without Pushing	Show Rather Than Tell
Make Offers Come to You	Irrational Interviewers
Sell Yourself Long-Distance	Find Out Blind Spots
	Eight Factors of Every Interview

Lessons from the Front—Characteristics of Successful Job Hunters

Hide Your Résumé	Get Rid of Self-Defeating
Maximize Face-to-Face Contact	Beliefs
Shyness Is No Excuse	Always Have Backup Plans
What to Do If You Believe You're Not	Deal with Your "Bright but
Qualified	Scattered" Ambitions
Overcome Telephone Torture	Avoid Anger
Don't Exaggerate, Inflate, or Lie	Don't Fall Back on Easy
Don't Give Up Too Soon	Income
Treat the "Little People" with Respect	Value Your Liberal Education
Quit Doing Things That Will Make	Deal with Personal Flaws
Sure You'll Fail	Jump-Start Your Job Search

6. *Reality Testing.* Acquiring experiences that enable you to compare your expectations about a career with firsthand exposure to the actual field of work. Participating in a career setting without having to make a commitment to it.

7. *Self-Reliance.* Concentrating on your own career preferences and keeping others' opinions and attitudes in a secondary role; ultimately, making the choice that represents your best interests.

Connecting Skills

8. *Jobs Are Everywhere.* Recognizing that there is a myriad of job opportunities, widely unpublicized but broadly available. Building a list of people, organizations, and situations that offer the kinds of work you desire.

9. *Network of Relationships.* Learning how to create contacts for yourself by establishing relationships with people who can refer you to other people who can help you.

10. *Information Interviewing.* Obtaining information and insights directly from people in careers you may desire to enter; learning what questions to ask and how to conduct the entire exchange.

11. *Avoiding Networking Mistakes.* Learning to minimize the five negative behaviors that are so characteristic of many job hunters.

12. *Walk-In Method.* Approaching prospective employers on a walk-in basis, without previous appointments. A rationale for using this unconventional approach and how to use it effectively.

13. *Interim Jobs.* Accepting stopgap employment that allows you to survive financially but also makes it possible for you to continue exploration of your career goals.

14. *Using the Library and the Internet.* Using materials readily available in print and on the Internet to quickly obtain data about a target employer, a field of work, or an entire industry.

Communication Skills

15. *Listening.* Attending fully to another person's words, feelings, hidden messages, and subtle meanings; learning how to detect when you are not listening effectively.

16. *Questioning.* Using questions in ways that encourage the other person to talk freely and offer information that will aid your exploration; learning effective and noneffective methods of questioning.

17. *Initiating.* How to conduct a proactive job-search process; learning nonaggressive methods to interest people in talking with you and provide you with assistance; using initiative to your best advantage.

18. *Writing.* Using written forms of communication effectively; writing letters to prospective employers that convey your motivations and spark personal responses; the importance of spelling, clarity, conciseness, and other features of writing.

19. *Public Speaking.* Learning to speak comfortably in a variety of situations where you have informal audiences, such as group meetings, project teams, and presentations.

Skills for Selling Yourself

20. *Sell with Dignity.* "Selling" yourself and your services to others without resorting to manipulation or deceptive methods; presenting yourself in a fully honorable manner.

21. *Ask Without Pushing.* "Closing" a sale, asking for the job, with ease and conviction; being comfortable in asking for money.

22. *Make Offers Come to You.* How to place yourself in a variety of situations where you may receive job offers without asking for them.

23. *Sell Yourself Long-Distance.* Practicing your job-search skills when you're far away from your target geographical area; deciding how to conduct job hunting at a distance and when to move to the target area.

Interviewing Skills

24. *Reasons to Want You.* Presenting prospective employers with clear reasons why they will benefit from using your services.

25. *Show Rather Than Tell.* Ways of demonstrating during job interviews the skills that you will be using on the job; showing the employer samples of your work.

26. *Irrational Interviewers.* Applying your understanding that hiring decisions are often nonrational; tuning in to these factors during the interview so that the employer best appreciates what you have to offer.

27. *Find Out Blind Spots.* Detecting ways in which you may be undermining your own interview presentation, and developing ways to counter these problems.

28. *Eight Factors of Every Job Interview.* Acquiring the skills necessary to deal with the eight-item agenda for every job interview; understanding what interviewers look for.

Five Key Assumptions

Several assumptions pervade the recommendations given in this book; collectively they make up an attitude about the career search that is different from the view that job hunting is dreadfully hard work, highly competitive, and pressure laden. I believe it is important to bring these central assumptions into the open so that you can understand the attitudes and emotional tone of this volume.

The Job Search Is Fun. As long as you regard looking for work as drudgery or as punishment for leaving your last job, you will try to terminate it as quickly as possible and will accept the first thing that comes your way. I assume throughout this volume that the career search is an activity you can look forward to and become enthusiastic about. I believe it will become enjoyable for you about the moment you realize that you do have many options, that you can turn down an offer, safe in the assurance that you will find a better one. You can look forward to a job interview, instead of dreading it, because you will regard it as a chance to learn new ways of presenting yourself, rather than as an all-or-nothing situation.

The Job Search Involves Exploring, Not Hunting. Job seekers lose their patience and will because they are too single-minded about the task at hand. They may become anxious and frustrated because they are trapped by the mentality that says: "If I don't get what I want the next time around, I will stop trying." Anything short of a job offer is interpreted as a failure.

People make the mistake of *hunting*, rather than *exploring*, for their work. Hunting implies the direct pursuit of quarry, zeroing in on a known target. Exploration, by contrast, is a process you conduct in a carefree, information-seeking manner designed to satisfy your curiosity. Hunting is excessively serious; exploration is for fun.

Multiple Skills Are More Important. One of the complaints most frequently heard from job seekers is the no-talent refrain: "I don't do anything especially well, so why hire me?" Many people believe that a single prominent talent is necessary to attract employers; if you are not a financial wizard, an exceptional speaker, a skilled artist, or a persuasive writer, you may fear you are destined for mediocrity.

The power of a highly visible talent is overrated. Very few jobs exist that permit a person to depend solely upon one talent for success. It is far more commonly true that *multiple competencies* are necessary in any job for highest-level performance. For example, an effective insurance salesperson must possess persuasiveness, competency with numbers, and long-range planning ability when discussing estate matters with clients.

In most cases, the combination of competencies is more powerful than any single talent could be. Please recognize that all your strengths can be put to use.

The Job Search Depends on Detective Work. I assume throughout this volume that the job search calls for detective skills, that a large part of one's effort should be devoted to *finding* the right work situations. For every promising job you have found, another two remain undiscovered. The wise individual understands this and looks further. About 50 percent of your time should be devoted to the seek-and-ye-shall-find motif, which incorporates four of the skills categories; the detective attitude is at work in self-assessment, identifying job leads, communication skills, and selling yourself.

Detective work is a state of mind. Once you adopt this attitude, you will regard your career as a complicated mystery story and become absorbed in following the clues and looking for new evidence; you will enjoy being the Perry Mason of your own career.

You Need Time on Your Side, Not Against You. Time works against you if you force yourself to make an instant career decision. Your strategy requires time, and you can buy time by either staying in your present situation or acquiring an interim job (see Chapter 13). Time allows you to maintain the search at a comfortable level and to let informal contacts begin working in your favor. The harder you look for work, the more it may elude you. Instead of mounting a campaign worthy of Sherman's army, let your search take a more leisurely course. The lower your desperation quotient, the easier it is for you to exchange views with a potential employer on a level of parity. Therefore, I assume in this volume that the job search is best conducted many months before you must actually make a change; if you practice these skills before your situation becomes urgent, they will work doubly well for you when you embark on actual job interviews.

The Job Search Is an Everyday Thing

Looking for better work is rather like learning to tie your shoes by yourself. You have to do it several times before you get it right, but once you have it, you wonder how you ever allowed anyone else to do it for you.

We have tried desperately to make a science of career decision making, and have succeeded in making a mystique of it. In fact, choosing a career is the most obvious of functions, relying on the natural rhythms of self-reflection and human interaction. An army of career-choice "experts" has mobilized because of people's inability to recognize their own opportunities for career exploration. The less we do for ourselves, the more we assume that expert advice, outside consultation, and placement assistance are necessary. It is time to restore the natural order of things. Job seeking is as natural as any other kind of social interchange. By turning matters over to the pseudoscientists, we have assumed that (1) we know nothing or little about ourselves, (2) no one in our own circle of acquaintances can possibly be helpful, and (3) job getting requires a sophisticated set of techniques known only to the select few.

The more you believe that your ideal job is hidden away in a cave that can be discovered only by an experienced guide, the more helpless you will feel. Helplessness will lead you to desperation and a willingness to accept any employment as good fortune. By contrast, if you recognize that the skills of the work search are ordinary life skills and that they are available to anyone who cares to practice them, you can attend to the task yourself.

Looking for better work is fun. You can do it by yourself. It is relatively easy. Often it is a very enjoyable thing to do with your time. Why is it necessary to state that the career search is pleasurable, self-propelling, and not complicated? Because of the way you may have interpreted your previous job-seeking experiences. When you have obtained a job, you may have assumed that your success was largely a matter of luck, fortuitous circumstances, or being in the right place at the right time. When you were not successful, you blamed bad luck, waited to see if your luck would change, and when it didn't, set about the chore of job hunting. And what a chore you made it! You laboriously typed application letters, sent out hundreds of résumés, spent hours scanning classified ads in the newspapers, and underwent interviews with potential employers to demonstrate your dedication to the Great American Work Ethic.

Let's take a closer look at the first part, the "I was lucky" statement, often used to interpret a previous job-seeking experience.

> *Example:* After Eileen's children completed their schooling, she decided to reenter the work force. Because she had not been in a paid job for twenty years, she didn't know where to begin looking. While at the beauty salon, she sought the advice of her hairdresser and asked if she knew of anyone looking for part-time help. "It just so happened" that the director of placement at a local college had confided to the hairdresser that she was "terribly busy—her assistant had just left." The hairdresser made a personal reference to the director. Eileen followed this up with a telephone call and her résumé and got the job. Later, the job was made into a full-time assistant director's position. Eileen feels she was lucky in getting the job.

Was it just "lucky" that Eileen stepped into her new career as a function of her visit to the hairdresser? Or was she smart enough to take advantage of a natural referral network that exists simply because people are curious about each other and enjoy passing information around? What would have happened to Eileen if she had followed only formal channels in her efforts to find work? Only her hairdresser knows for sure.

> *Example:* Bob wanted a job with a youth recreation group, so he hung around and helped out the local YMCA with its basketball games, its field trips, and anything else. He got to know Jane, one of the leaders,

pretty well and showed her how the program could be expanded to include kids in his neighborhood. One day Jane invited him to a staff meeting; after the meeting there was a picnic. One thing led to another; a man was there from out of town who needed an assistant leader in his recreation center. Jane mentioned Bob's name, and he was hired a few weeks later. "All in all," Bob said, "I was pretty lucky."

Lucky, my foot. The young man in this example practiced naturally many of the skills outlined and detailed in this book. He found the target employer, asserted himself to become involved in its activities, used a personal referral to learn about a job opportunity, did information interviews with staff people, and observed the activities of the center. No doubt he also used many self-assessment skills to decide that the YMCA was a good target employer and many communication skills in talking with the staff there.

People meet their employers and associates in the strangest places. Exactly what implications does this have for you? It means simply that all your life activity can contribute to your work search. It means that your typical ways of getting together with people can support your job search. It means you can have your fun and profit by it, too.

Stop Making Excuses for Yourself

Like the child who can think of a thousand reasons for going outside, or ten thousand reasons for not doing his homework, many people have bottomless wells of excuses for their fear of getting involved in searching for better work. It probably requires only one of the following to arrest any work-seeking behavior, and chances are you can lay claim to several.

I'm Too Old. A person my age doesn't do all that running around looking for a different job. It takes too much foolish energy that I must be careful to conserve. Furthermore, I think it's a little undignified to admit I made a mistake in the past and go around confessing it to everyone.

Answer: Older folks look for new challenges because they have already licked several tough problems and want new ones. Changing work is not the confession of a sinner, but the spirit of a missionary who has something good to offer and wants to pass the wealth around.

I Can't Do Anything Else. I must admit, if you press me, that I am afraid there's nothing else I can do as well as what I am currently doing. I'm afraid of getting caught in the middle, losing my present work, and being unable to make the grade elsewhere. I was lucky to get my present work and am not so sure I'd be that lucky again.

Answer: The major currency in your work experience is transferable skills, which are abilities that can be marketed in numerous contexts. For example, if you have been an effective organizer in your present office, church, or community, you can carry these abilities to different work settings and put them to use without starting all over again.

I'd Better Hang on to What I've Got. There is no sense in building a record of good work and then throwing it away by looking for something new. Maybe my work isn't the greatest, but I should capitalize on the progress I have made, and not dismiss it for some uncertain future. I can't afford to surrender the experience I've accumulated.

Answer: No one is asking you to start over at the bottom. When you find a setting where your skills are transferable, you can reasonably request an appropriate level. If you are bored with your current situation, you must look for something more stimulating.

My Job Takes All My Time. My work doesn't give me time to think about doing anything else. I would have to take three weeks off just to explore this subject and would undermine my present responsibilities in the process. It's too large a price to pay for just shopping around in the dark.

Answer: Take a close look at the people you encounter routinely in your work and ask yourself how they might lead you to others. Whom do they know in other fields of work? Don't be so busy painting yourself into a corner that you fail to look for a way out.

I Don't Like Rejection. I would rather not push myself in situations where I am probably going to be turned away. No one likes that kind of treatment, and I am no exception. Why walk into a buzz saw when you know it's there? That sort of experience will only tend to reduce my confidence.

Answer: When you set about the work search, it is *you* who are doing the choosing, not the other way around. Perambulate through the work search as a data gatherer and let the job offers take care of themselves.

Let Fate Take Over. I would prefer to trust that the unseen hand, the mysterious flow of events that has been my life so far, will continue to shape the story of my career. I like surprises and have faith that good things will happen, that whatever comes my way, I can handle it and adjust to it. Going out to make my own changes is too much like tampering with a higher-order process.

To my vocation I will be called. I believe opportunities will cross my path and I will be wise enough to know which ones are marked for me.

Answer: If you are so closely in touch with divine powers that you prefer not to develop a conscious strategy, then play it your way. However, allow me to suggest it is not fate that guides you, but your sensitivity to yourself and your willingness to trust your instincts.

I Am Just a Complainer. I am really a chronic malcontent. It's just a lifestyle with me. I really don't want to change, but would simply rather complain, moan, attract sympathy, and just stay put where I am.

Answer: There are better ways to entertain yourself than whining. I believe people who grouse about their work are in need of help but don't know how to ask for it. If you are sinking in vocational quicksand, please call for a rope and pull yourself out.

The Alternative Might Be Worse. What I like about the miserable work I've got is that at least I know what sort of misery to expect each day. Whatever job I might get in exchange could be worse, even more debilitating. I am comfortable in a perverse sort of way with my present situation.

Answer: Risk is the tariff for leaving the Land of Predictable Misery. Secure a temporary visa—give yourself permission to roam the countryside and look at what other people are doing. If the alternatives demand too high a price in uncertainty, you can still come home again if you insist on it.

It Doesn't Hurt Enough Yet. I really cannot change because my present work is tolerable. I have nothing much to look forward to, but I can keep the pain to a minimum by dodging around, doing a little something different, and fantasizing that it will get better. I'm sure other people have it much worse, so I can put up with my share of discomfort.

Answer: Is the pain really tolerable or is your head just numb from repeated encounters with the wall? When *will* it hurt enough—when your children talk about what a kind, calm, and likable person you *used* to be?

I Don't Want to Shake Things Up. Life is comfortable and predictable, even if it is not exciting and filled with challenges. If I look around for a change now, I will have to unsettle myself, my entire family, and everything that is orderly in my life. That's an awful price to pay in search of a rainbow that might not be there. I will not take chances with my family's security.

Answer: Yes, the emotional health of you and your family is more important, but you may not know how they would react to your changing jobs. Ask your family members first before you make assumptions about how they would regard a shake-up.

Nothing May Turn Up. Then what? Suppose I pour myself into a search for something better and then discover, after all that turmoil, that nothing is available, that I must stay where I am after all? Wouldn't that be a terrible waste of effort? Why even expose myself to that possibility? At least when I go to a store, I know I will usually find merchandise. Job hunting is shaky business. I don't like the odds.

Answer: Sure, and there may be no trout in the stream, no friends at the golf course, but you still go there hoping something will occur. Charles Kettering's well-known saying about luck is especially apt here: "No one ever stumbled across anything sitting down."

No One Encourages Me. I am not being cheered on by those around me. My family and friends really don't know how I feel about my present work, so they see no great urgency for me to change. Besides, it is more comfortable for those close to me if I stay put. They won't have to adjust to my new ways or ideas.

Answer: You probably have not allowed them into your secret chambers. Any person with whom you share your struggle will cheer you on, because he or she wants the same attention when getting up the courage to move in a new direction. Don't suffer in silence; you will become your own worst critic.

I'm Already Set Financially in My Present Job. I'm earning a good income, so why should I mess with the thing? It would seem foolish to look for some other job when this one is reasonably secure. After all, I have to survive first, and then worry about job satisfaction.

Answer: This is an OK strategy for many people who like their work, but it can turn to mush if you're seriously bored or turned off by your job. Even if you're drawing the paycheck, if you hate getting up in the morning to do it, it's time for you to look at something else. You won't "survive" long in a job that is unsatisfying, heavily stressful, or both.

Conclusion

Of course, you have looked for work before. You probably did so, however, as an adolescent might seek to break into a strange social group. Job hunting has much the flavor of a ritual dance in which the initiate must perform in certain prescribed ways. The dance is a passionless affair because the individual does as told—send your forms here, sit there, talk now, go have this or that examined, cross your fingers, breathe deeply, wait . . . and wait some more. Ritual dances, with employers calling the tunes and job seekers dancing to them, will remain the dominant rites until work seekers learn to orchestrate their own methods.

You cannot depend entirely on college degrees, reference letters, other people, good fortune, or paper qualifications to get the job that is best for you. You must exert more active control over the process and take initiatives as often as possible.

Your success will depend heavily on your ability to use many skills of the job-search process. Without these skills, you are at the mercy of other people's arbitrary judgments and whims. You will also need to be aware of the pitfalls of job hunters, described later in the book as lessons from the front.

Job-search skills are lifetime skills. They can be used repeatedly in a person's life and work history. By possessing these skills you can reduce your fear of the career search because you can take better control of the search process.

You are most likely to regard the career search as enjoyable and effective if you put the skills to use many months before you have an urgent need to change your employment or your career direction.

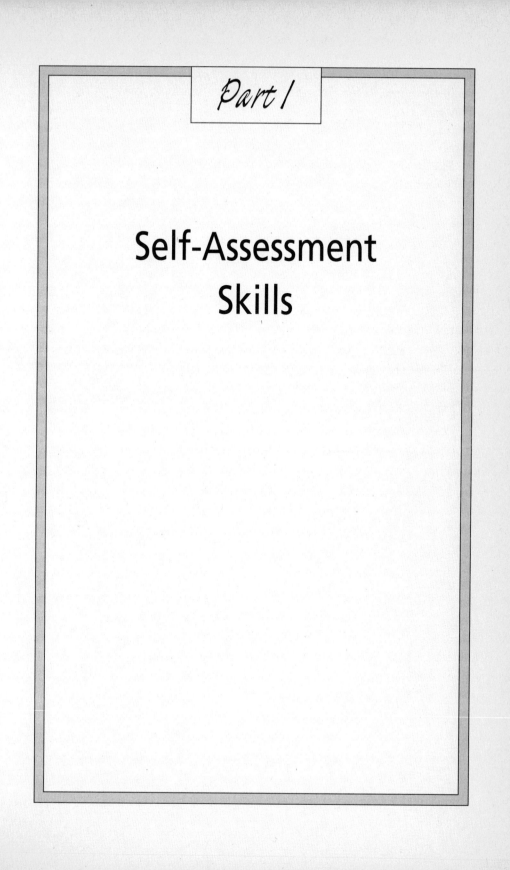

Part 1

Self-Assessment Skills

Express Your Values

What we call "creative work" ought not to be called work at all, because it isn't. . . . I imagine that Thomas Edison never did a day's work in his last fifty years.

—Stephen Leacock

Your reason to live is being needed.

—Victor Frankl

Values are the emotional salary of work, and some folks are drawing no wages at all.

+ "I can't quite put my finger on it, but I feel empty all the time on my job."
+ "I can't figure out why I'm doing this; it all seems to add up to so much nothing."
+ "It's just a job. Why should I expect anything more? So what if there are no fireworks; it's a living . . . but I'm not living very much."

And so we defend ourselves against criticism or regret about job choices we have made that defy the laws of emotional gravity, jobs we took because they were there, jobs devoid of purpose and redeeming virtue. The choice seemed reasonable at the time: "I had to do something, and this seemed as good as anything else."

As used in this chapter, the word *value* has a personal meaning: it reflects how you feel about the work itself and the contribution it makes to others. Your selection of one particular kind of work from among the thousands available must reflect what you regard as important, worth doing, inherently valuable. If you do not value the work you do, then no other incentive can possibly compensate for your lost sense of being significant, important, part of something you value. On the other hand, if you value the work you have chosen, then neither small office, nor lack of recognition, nor poor working conditions can stay you from your appointed rounds or dissuade you from your objectives.

Many folks dance the Safety, Security, Seniority, Longevity Polka. Security is the usual trade-off for work a person regards as dull, routine, and meaningless. "I would have quit long ago, but the paychecks keep coming in." "I put up with this place because they don't make you fight for your job every week." How many unhappy people do you know who buttress their positions with arguments of that kind? How much mediocrity, ennui, and routine acceptance of things as they are masquerade as job security?

Why Work?

When everything else about a job is stripped away, the Values remain. "Why do this job? Why work in the first place?"

Values are at the center of every career decision. This is not just a matter for social-service types to think about, but bankers, government workers, accountants, real estate salespeople, urban planners, oceanographers, retail clerks—everyone. Why *this* job and not any other? Is it just a matter of what is available at the time? I hope not. Will your choice be the best reflection of what you think makes work worthwhile (your values), or the lowest common denominator—you work just because everybody else does?

What Everyone Wants from a Job

No matter who you are, what you do, or how much ambition you have, you want the same things from your work that everyone else does: (a) work that is interesting for its own sake; (b) work that we can be respected for, because we do it well; (c) work that has some value for others. If your work does not fill any deeper need than survival, it will grate on you and make the rest of your day unrewarding too.

Values can be assessed by every job seeker along four dimensions:

Material. How much will I gain from this job? Will I earn a lot? Will I make a comfortable living? Will the pay and benefits help me get the things I want in life? Will those I live with be comfortable? The chapter on money (Chapter 2) discusses how you can incorporate financial questions into your overall career decision.

Social. Are these people I work with the ones I want to be part of? Do I like their company enough to be around them every day? Will I develop friendships here that will carry over to my personal life? Will I enjoy the companionship as much as the work?

Emotional. Will I enjoy the work itself, the experience of doing it? Will I look forward to being involved with the problems of the job, and feel challenged by trying to solve these problems? Will this enjoyment be strong enough to counter the frustrations that will inevitably appear on the job?

Spiritual. Will this work contribute to the greater good? This question is not just for people in the helping professions; it applies to every kind of work. "Does the bank provide services I feel are worthwhile?" "How do I feel about these singing telegrams that I do?" "Do my customers appreciate the work I am doing?" "How much would my work be missed if I were not here to do it?"

Few people will embrace these four Values dimensions equally, but all four are part of every job or career choice. Why is it important to highlight them? Any dimension that is ignored completely will come back to haunt a person. For example, if you're satisfied on the Material, Emotional, and Spiritual dimensions, but the Social is lacking, the job will eventually become a problem. You'll only be able to stand the people in it for so long, before you want out.

People think that getting a job is the hard part: not so. Staying interested enough in the job to do it well and with enthusiasm is the real challenge. That's probably why you are reading this book—you've been through a few Doggy Jobs already and don't care to find any more.

It's one thing to have a job, get paid, come home, go to work again, and join the car pool parade with little sense of anticipation. Ho hum. It's quite another to be doing something you value, affecting the world around you, and feeling involved in a worthwhile goal.

Regardless of the job you have, there are three things you can do to change it if it does not satisfy you:

1. *Change the job from within.* Ask for responsibilities that fit your abilities better. Volunteer for tasks that you find interesting. Get involved in things you think are worth doing. Seek out the coworkers you'd like to know better. If your job is boring, create a challenge for yourself.

2. *Define a new job, and seek it.* So you've done what you could to change the job, and it wasn't enough. Before you hit the streets to find a new one, shape a concept in your mind's eye of what you want that next job to look like. What will you be doing—can you see it? When it comes into focus, start looking for people who do this kind of work. Do *not* apply for such a job until you meet at least five people who are in that line of work.

3. *Seek unpaid work experience.* In some cases neither the old job nor the new job will satisfy you. Don't set out looking for another job too quickly. Instead, ask yourself: "What am I not getting from this job that I could seek outside of paid employment?" Is it use of a certain skill? Or involvement with certain kinds of people? Or a sense of challenge that is missing? Or is there certain subject matter that you want? Whatever it is, look for an opportunity to pursue it on a voluntary basis. This is a necessary safety valve, because few jobs will offer all the things you want. So what? Do them anyway.

Who would want to work and not get paid for it? You do it all the time, in the community work you do, the sports teams you play on, the organizations you belong to, the gardens you cultivate, or the projects you have around the house. Unpaid work serves three major purposes:

1. Unpaid work satisfies needs not met by your paid employment. Jobs may be dull or frustrating no matter what we do to spice them up, so we need other work to keep us fired up.

2. Unpaid work may provide a foundation for future paid work. Unpaid activities can grow into careers, either second careers or replacements for your primary work. Part-time involvement allows you to accumulate knowledge without risking the family fortune. One day you may want to market what you know, if you get fed up with your present job.

3. Unpaid work enhances your paid employment. Writing books and articles in a professional field . . . serving on community boards . . . giving free service to friends (tax accounting, car repair, etc.) . . . research projects . . . conducting free clinics (sports, health, etc.). These are examples of work that pays little or nothing but, in terms of the skills we develop, the knowledge we acquire, and the experience we accumulate, helps us do our primary jobs better.

Most dream careers start with unpaid work. If there is a career you've dreamed of having, you've probably already been doing it, and thinking about it, and reading about it, long before you ever get paid for it, whether it's being a rock guitarist, a writer, a counselor, or an entrepreneur with an idea for a new business.

As you take steps toward starting your dream career, you are going to experience risk—risk of failure, risk that you will be disappointed in yourself, and the risk of unforeseen factors and events. Risk is the price of admission. Be a risk taker. It's the only way you will find out what you have to offer and how much value your work has for others. People who sit around wondering where to find the forty-year no-cut contract will probably immobilize themselves, because they are afraid of making a mistake. Those who look for the sure thing do not make good workers.

Spotting Your Key Value

Many readers will recognize that the four Values dimensions mentioned earlier are often clustered together when they find a job that really fits them. Often this is because the job captures an underlying value that is of special appeal.

Many of us have one Key Value, a theme that is so appealing, a subject matter that is so interesting to us, or a work environment we find so irresistible that we are naturally attracted to it. Examples of key values include:

+ Working with disabled people
+ Being around big-money deals
+ Being in the center of activity for a town or city
+ Competing with others verbally
+ Being around athletic events
+ Teaching
+ Being involved with dancing
+ Helping children to grow up
+ Getting to talk with as many different people as possible
+ Working with plants and flowers
+ Involving myself in social change
+ Making decisions with numbers
+ Selling ideas

> *Example:* Joan is a person whom no four walls can contain. She feels imprisoned when she is sitting down for more than an hour. She works as a counselor in a community college. The job is all right, and most of the people are, too, but Joan's one key value involves being outside, being physically active, and indulging in a love of nature. What can she do about it?
>
> *Solution:* Joan tried backpacking on weekends for a while, but that was not enough. She kept the counselor job for security reasons, but eventually found her way to long-distance running, which gave her an excuse to be outside almost every day of the year. Today she is an ultra-distance runner, and probably spends as much time per week "working" outdoors as she does in the counseling office. Joan is in touch with her one key value and is doing pretty well in acting on it. Her next step may be to become a mountain guide . . . or perhaps buy a cabin in the foothills . . . or maybe design programs for the college

that involve outdoor activity . . . or find some combination of these that fits her life situation best.

I Just Wanna Earn a Living

There are those who will say: "Never mind Values. I just want to work so that I can produce an income, feed a family, and live comfortably. I entered the restaurant supply business because it is a good way to make money—that's it. There is nothing interesting about it." The one key value for these folks is to stay close to the market and do what is necessary to earn a comfortable and predictable income. However, I would bet that these people still have the four Values dimensions taken care of. Obviously the Material draws their attention. But also, they manage to work around people they like pretty well (Social). They find it reasonably enjoyable and a challenge to keep producing income (Emotional), and they believe their work gives others a decent product or service (Spiritual). If they were not getting some satisfaction in these four areas, I believe they would have gotten out a long time ago and looked for a different place to "just earn a living."

A Word on Behalf of Social Consciousness

For some, career choice is focused on helping others or making a contribution to society. Counselors, ministers, social workers, probation officers, teachers, etc., come to mind. Most others think that social consciousness is for do-gooders, not for them. They would claim it is not a part of their career choice. But every career choice affects other people in some way. The dental hygienist can affect my attitude toward dental care; the person who answers the phone can make me not want to do business with a particular store; my tax accountant can affect my life in a hundred ways.

Work has no meaning at all unless it creates value. The work that you do will not be honored or respected, nor will it earn the money you want, unless it has value for others. We pay to hear songs sung, to have walls painted, to have parklands protected, to buy vehicles to carry us around, and for anything else we value. We pay you to provide us something we want and cannot provide for ourselves. Without us, your career does not exist.

I say this because "values" in career choice are often interpreted to mean, What can *I* get out of my career? Yes, your enjoyment, challenge, and lifestyle are important, but they are possible only if you consistently create something of value for others. Career choices that focus on just you and your needs eventually become empty and unsatisfying. People who reach levels of success and ask "Why am I doing this?" or "Is this all there is?" have lost their core reasons for working.

Social consciousness can be considered by everyone in contemplating various careers:

+ Will I be helping people with these bank loans?
+ Do I believe the services that this company offers are valuable?
+ How do my graphics make these publications more readable, and thus educate people better?

The best jobs and careers are those in which the individuals *believe* in the value of what they are doing. They believe the product is a good one. As a result, they sell it better, invest more money in it, persist with it, and attract others to work with them.

Every successful career has a theme of social consciousness about it. A new tool won't sell unless it does someone some good. Government programs work best when they answer a need; teachers work best when students learn; and new businesses don't get very far unless people want what they are offering. So, don't think that social consciousness went out with the sixties. It is and always will be a factor in career choice.

A Sense of Purpose

Have you ever wondered what keeps people going in difficult jobs: years on a research project . . . struggling through the thickets of politics . . . running a restaurant for ninety hours a week . . . building a house . . . coaching a team of deaf athletes . . . writing a book for which the audience is uncertain . . . supervising a much-maligned police department . . . starting a program in the face of community opposition?

It's not the money. It's not the glory either. It's not even the promise of a successful outcome. It is the hope that something good might happen, and underneath that is a sense of purpose, a belief that the work is worth doing, a goal that lies outside the needs of the person working toward it.

In her long-range study of people and their careers, Gail Sheehy writes:

> What first emerged from the surveys and interviews was an outline of that enviable creature, the person who enjoys optimum well-being. . . . The person of optimum well-being is best characterized by the ten statements of self-description that follow. . . . 1. "My life has meaning and direction." This is the characteristic that correlates most closely with optimum life satisfaction. People of high well-being find meaning in an involvement with something beyond themselves; a work, an idea, other people, a social objective.[1]

I would suspect that this could be confirmed in any sample of people who are happy in their work, professional or otherwise. "Purpose" gets us involved in the big, ambitious projects, the goals not yet reached, the search for new discoveries, the quests that are exciting; it keeps us going in the face of repeated setbacks. "Purpose" can be more enticing than money, security, and status because it deals with living problems. If your work does not affect anyone, then why do it? If your work does touch someone, then what more reason do you need?

How Your Values Are Exhibited

All methods for identifying values yield one or two essential kinds of information: (1) *past experience*—what you have already done in your life that you have valued, and (2) *future desires*—what you hope to do in the future that you would regard as highly rewarding.

Past experience is a rich source of your work values because your behavior is strong evidence of your preferences. Even if you are young, twenty years of personal choices can yield many clues about your prominent motivators.

Future choices are expressed in daydreams, fantasies, and plans, which cannot be verified by actual behavior. Hence, the values they reflect may be more tentative. Dreams, however, are powerful forces when they are vivid enough to be imagined in great detail. Often they are harnessed to your understanding of your past experiences. When you shape past values in the light of your presently unfolding and changing needs, you can forge a powerful vision of a desirable future.

Mattson and Miller, in *The Truth About You*, assert that your key values can be determined by a thorough review of your peak life experiences—occasions or periods when you have exerted yourself strenuously, have performed successfully, and have been pleased with what you accomplished. These occasions can be studied for the presence of values, and, Mattson and Miller claim, your one or two most prominent values appear consistently in these life experiences.

> ***Example:*** Won spelling bees at age twelve. Wrote essay on psychoneurosis at age sixteen. Wrote and presented a show for children at age eighteen. Edited a sports section and wrote column at age nineteen. Wrote songs for a camp show at age nineteen. Edited book manuscripts at age twenty-four. Read poetry at age twenty-six. (Values: personal recognition, use of words.)

An individual typically expends far more effort than the minimum required to earn a paycheck when it is possible to satisfy prized values. The individual climbs a personal Mount Everest not only because it is there, but also to satisfy a compelling personal need.

Because people's needs change with age, you may have some career aspirations that are linked only marginally to your past experiences. Future desires can also be examined for the presence of consistent themes.

> *Example:* I would like to: build bookcases, understand decisions made on the commodity exchanges, buy and sell antiques, study American folklore, collect historical anecdotes about the Civil War, raise farm animals for profit. (Key themes: interest in historical America, manual activities, and the farming business.)

Of course, these aspirations must be tested in the crucible of life experiences, but dreams should not be damped down by skepticism or taken too lightly. Effective dreams grow from your being in close touch with past successes and especially with failures. The strongest drives often result from earlier disappointments or half-successes that were affected by circumstances.

You may protest that dreams and values are fine, but few people get a chance to fulfill career fantasies in their lifetimes. Most of us are stuck, you say, with marginally satisfying jobs. Changing your dull job for someone else's will not help matters.

The mistake in this reasoning is in viewing jobs as finished landscapes. Of course, values will not magically appear once you have discovered them. And employers may frustrate your dreams. However, knowing what the dream looks like will help you piece it into your current situation. Finding even one source of value in a sea of boredom is a powerful antidote to a dull job.

✦ If you dream of architecture but are only a mechanical draftsman, try designing your best attempts at floor plans during your spare time and ask the professional staff to evaluate your work.

✦ If you can barely tolerate your job but see no way out, find a source of stimulation incidental to the job that will allow you to endure it, such as joining the company bridge team, starting a local investment club, or organizing theater trips.

✦ If the only enjoyable part of your present job is public speaking, but your boss lets you do precious little of it, look for another department that might want to borrow your services.

✦ If you want a job with complete independence, but the only available ones are too risky financially, decide how much security you are willing to surrender in exchange for some autonomy. Perhaps a part-time source of income where you have decision power will help you to tolerate submission in your regular job.

• If you love exercising control over budgets, but have little authority to do so, try seeking an outside source of funds for your organization (government grant, foundation money, or other) and then put yourself in charge if your proposal is successful.

Values of Significant Others

How do your family and friends feel about the career choices you are considering? How do you feel about their opinions regarding what kinds of work might be best for you? You are not likely to reject everyone else's values entirely, but neither must you be a mirror image of the people around you. How would your mother react if you told her you were going to become a motorcycle racer? a sewage inspector? a chicken plucker? Inevitably, people will try to influence your choice. Your job is not to ignore them but to take their thoughts and feelings into account, and then make your best decision based on your own judgment and preferences.

Values-Clarification Exercises

The data for discovery of your values are all around you. Your values weave through the fabric of everything you do. The kinds of work to which you are attracted and the forms of play that exhilarate you are revealing. Those activities you regard as both work and play say even more about where your values lie. Building a toolshed, watching horror movies, plotting the course of a caterpillar, digging with your hands for seashells, listening for little harmonies in sounds of the night—any of these activities has value to the person who does it.

Here are a few exercises you can do to clarify your values further.

• *Exercise One*
You may find important clues to your career values in how you view the work of those closest to you. Unless you choose to, you need never feel obligated to carry on the occupation or profession chosen by a significant relative; however, you should notice which parts of that work appeal to you in a natural way and take this as evidence of your own preferences.

Try making a list of your family and friends, and put the occupation of each person beside his or her name. *Occupation* is here interpreted broadly to include the major way in which the person spends his or her time, including student and other nonpaid activities. Which single part (activity, task, subrole, duty) of that person's job do you find the most appealing? Try your best to find at least one part of the occupation that represents a value you appreciate. Identify the aspect of the job you would choose for yourself and the value it represents.

> *Example:* Friend, barber: meets many people (friendliness)
> Friend, carpenter: builds houses (body use/seeing results)
> Mother, schoolteacher: supervises class (decision making)
> Father, accountant: has steady income (security)
> Uncle, banker: handles money (responsibility)
> Aunt, dress designer: makes new designs (creativity)
> Minister: exhibits concern for others (compassion)
> Neighbor, treasurer: controls finances (responsibility)
> Neighbor, professor: keeps knowledgeable (learning/reading)
> Brother, coach: physically active (health)

Once you have identified all these separate values derived from the occupations of family members and friends, try making a composite occupation from the values you have identified. Be creative. Don't worry about whether such a career actually exists or whether you could enter it. Just try to stitch the values together into a coherent whole.

> *Example:* Values: friendliness, body use, seeing results, decision making, security, responsibility, creativity, compassion, learning, reading, health
>
> Possible composite careers: health director for a summer camp, physical fitness consultant for private industry, forester or range manager or other outdoor administration

✦ *Exercise Two*

It is often even more revealing to witness an event with other people and then compare what each of you valued in it. By exploring the differences among you, you may see your own values in sharp relief, because others have seen the same event in different ways.

Choose another person with whom to do this exercise, a person who will help you focus on your values by participating in the exercise with you.

1. *Recall an experience that made you happy.* Recount to your partner an experience that gave you a good feeling, made you happy, or left you feeling better than when you started. Try to distinguish between something you *thought* was good and something that *felt* good inside. Your feelings are more important than your ideas in this case.

Example: I felt good about the summer weekend I organized for my cousins.

2. *Provide details.* Describe the experience in as much detail as you can. What exactly did you do to make it happen? Try to remember as much of the sequence of events as you can, including not only what you did but also how you felt about it each step of the way.

Example: I arranged a preliminary meeting of the group at a restaurant during the winter to see if they were interested. We had a lot of laughs, recalled old times, and told stories. I told the most. Then I proposed a summer weekend and outlined how we would plan for it.

3. *Identify a value.* Of course, there will be more than one value involved in the experience, but start by clarifying only one key value. What one aspect did you like about what you were doing? What seemed worthwhile about the experience? For what purpose did you expend this time and energy?

Example: I suppose the biggest satisfaction was doing something to keep a family and its bonds together, arranging an event that would make it possible for the cousins who were once close to revalidate a family tie.

4. *Reach deeper.* Once you have stated a value to your partner, the two of you can take an even closer look by asking: "What in particular was satisfying about this?" It will seem you are repeating the original question, but you are actually reaching deeper to another layer of meaning. In fact, the question "But what did you really like about that?" might be asked several times until the deepest layer of meaning is reached.

Example: Well, I guess I like to be a catalyst, a person who brings other people together. I really enjoy recognizing a situation in which a group of people would like to fortify their bonds, but haven't been able to do so because of circumstances. I really enjoy being the person who makes it happen.

5. *Check with partner.* At one or more points in the process of describing your experience and identifying the values inherent in it, you should ask your partner to use his or her own words to help clarify what you were trying to say. Ask this person to restate in different words the value(s) you seemed to be

expressing so that the two of you can arrive at the sharpest possible definition and label of your particular value.

> *Example:* Partner: You seem to get a kick out of arranging things, giving people a chance to reach each other on an informal basis. Yes, you seem to have a definite preference for informality in the things you set up. You seem to believe that informality is the best setting in which to give people the freedom to get closer, enjoy each other better.

It is important to be able to place your own labels on your values and to derive and label these values by reviewing your own experiences. This exercise gives you an opportunity to practice examining your experiences and discovering values in them. This most basic form of value clarification can be used with any sort of experience, big or small. More important, it *should* be used with all sorts of experiences, because values may be revealed in even the tiniest of events. Your more enduring values are especially likely to be hiding in tiny, obscure life events because such events occur naturally and unconsciously without your thoughts, shoulds, or oughts intruding. These are the kinds of life experiences you can include:

+ Teaching your little sister how to tell time
+ Knocking over the bottles at the county fair
+ Cleaning out your files till you know where every last item is located
+ Keeping a shell collection
+ Seeing how fast you can add up the restaurant check
+ Reading every historical marker on your cross-country trip
+ Pruning trees and plants
+ Getting people to laugh
+ Cataloging your music CDs and tapes
+ Figuring out a way to clean the rain gutters more efficiently

2

Decide About Money

Money is America's most powerful drug.

—Philip Slater

Money can buy almost anything we want—the problem being we tend to want only the things money can buy.

—Jacob Needleman,
Money and the Meaning of Life[1]

How much value do you put on money? Is money your primary drive or only a by-product, because you are more concerned with the game, the project, the challenge, the performance, or the service that you're providing? You may say that both the money and the content of your work are vitally important, but which drives which? Could you give up some money but never surrender the game? Or would you take less challenge but always must have the money?

Don't listen to advertisements. TV, radio, and print ads would have you believe that you need and want as much money as possible all the time, so that you can buy everything that a "successful" person is supposed to have. To advertisers, there is no choice about money—you gotta have it.

Get free of the consumerist culture for a minute. How much influence do *you* want money to have on your life and career decisions? Which priorities rank higher than money and which rank lower? Can you enact these priorities without getting seduced by the marketplace?

On your tree of life there are many parts. Does money anchor your tree, or is it just some of the leaves? Does it weigh your tree down or lift it up? Does money give your tree life, or, like a stormy wind, does it threaten to knock it down?

These are not useless philosophical questions. The role you assign to money will be present in all your career deliberations. Do you want money to be a stern taskmaster, or will it be subservient to other key players in your career drama?

What Kind of Relationship with Money Do You Want?

Money is like a passenger in your car every day you drive to work. You'd better decide how you're going to relate to this rider in the car pool, because it affects every decision you make. No two people relate to money in quite the same way. Some almost ignore it even though they don't have a lot of it. Others seem obsessed by it. Most of us fall somewhere in between.

Here are several different kinds of relationships to money, from which you can choose, or you may want to define your own:

Comfortable and Predictable. This is perhaps the most popular. In this relationship, you are saying that regularity of income is most important, that you don't want to face any great risks that your earnings will disappear anytime in the foreseeable future, as long as you do your job well. This relationship usually has less high-side potential, because you are not accepting much risk. It also has the danger of potential boredom. But many people are happy with this relationship and would not trade it for any of the others. However today, predictable, safe income is harder to find than it was even ten to fifteen years ago. Demand outweighs supply. More people want it than are going to get it.

Stormy but Exciting. Money is always a factor in this relationship, because there is continual doubt about how much you're going to make. The thrill of competition is mixed with the risk of losing. In situations like this, people are usually shooting to "make a bundle" and are willing to accept the risks, in exchange for the challenge and combativeness. People who stay with this relationship may win more often than they lose, but some even stay when the results are poor. They like the fun of the chase as much as the bottom-line earnings.

More Is Better. In this relationship, money is in the driver's seat. Usually in some form of self-employment, this person wants to see the results of his/her efforts pay off directly in terms of economic gain. The harder and better you work, the more you earn. Sounds simple, but it requires talent, perseverance, and single-mindedness. Other gains, such as job satisfaction, new learning, or work relationships, may have to take backseats. The quality of the relationship here is a dollar count, and you always know what the score is.

Unconscious. You would prefer to be completely oblivious to money. Some people manage this type of relationship well. No, they are not street bums or independently wealthy. They hold jobs or sometimes are self-employed. The key here is that they *do not think* about money. If you were such a person, you would concentrate on your work, be as good as you could be, and accept whatever earnings came to you. This is a pure state, and many are already partway there. Many readers will think it is even a little ridiculous. Often a person has some kind of professional training or marketable credential to be able to ignore money completely. However, others do it too. This relationship requires the ability to say: "If I give my best to the work that suits me, whatever money comes will be fine."

A Balanced View. You want to develop a compromise between money and creativity/satisfaction. You keep a close eye on finances, but you don't let money rule you to the extent that you would ignore expressing your creativity and seeking challenge and stimulation in your work. You're looking for the best that you can get of both worlds, even though you know you'll trade off some financial gain for satisfaction at times, and vice versa.

What Won't You Sacrifice for More Money?

It has been said that everyone has his price. This rather cynical view predicts that every man or woman will do a particular something if offered enough money. Such a dictum could also apply to a career decision. Would you do any kind of work if the money rewards were high enough? Some would answer yes.

What kind of undesirable work would you do if the pay were high enough—almost anything? You're not sure? It's a tough question. You'd like the money but don't know what you'd be willing to give up.

It is helpful to consider what you would *not* trade off in exchange for greater financial gain. Given the opportunity to earn a lot more than you are presently earning, which of the following would be unacceptable conditions?

+ I would not give up the pleasure of the kind of work I am doing
+ I would not live in an undesirable part of the country
+ I would not work for people I don't like
+ I would not take on significant risks of failure
+ I would not disrupt my relationships with my family members
+ I would not give up my relationships with colleagues/friends/etc.
+ I would not give up the recreational opportunities I have available

There are many other possible trade-offs that might modify your desire to go for the most money available. Though it sounds simple to say "I would always go for the most money I could earn," you have probably already made certain decisions about the conditions of your work and life that are not tradable. These factors are sometimes called "psychological income."

Status Rewards

Let's face it. We rate ourselves all the time. "Where do I stand compared to my friends, relatives, and coworkers?" Most people derive some of their self-respect from relative standing, or status, in the working world. How do you measure your self-esteem? If money is your primary index, then you'll want as much of it as possible.

Are there other ways you measure the status of your occupation? How about any of the following?

+ The respect that my profession/occupation has among the general public
+ The importance of the work I am doing
+ The reputation of the organization I work for
+ The academic credentials that I have earned
+ The power of my position
+ The relative excitement or allure attached to my field of work
+ The value of my work to others
+ My position of importance within my profession

Thus you can derive self-esteem from your work in many ways other than money earned. Certainly each of the above is a form of psychological income. Though you'd like to have more money, you can count your job or career success in terms of many of the above measures of status.

In some cases, the above factors will become even more important than earnings. If you were offered a different job with more money, you'd want to consider whether sufficient status would also be present. Money and other sources of self-esteem need to be weighed together in any consideration about possible change of work.

Dealing with Money: A Three-Point Plan

I would recommend that you approach the question of money in any job or career decision in terms of three steps:

1. Act As If Money Did Not Exist. Initially, go for the kind of work you like. Try your best to ignore potential earnings when you are considering various fields of work. Choose what you think will stimulate you most, and go where you believe you have the most to offer. You won't be able to block money completely out of your mind, but do your best to keep it from being a guiding factor.

There are many who believe that this approach to career choice will net you the most money in the long run. By aiming at the kinds of work that fit you best, you will make maximum use of your talents and will thus be most successful, which usually means succeeding financially too. Entrepreneurs and professionals often say they got into their work to show that a particular idea (or product) would succeed, to prove the worth of the idea. Thus it is the challenge of doing something different, making a statement, or simply offering something that people need, which draws certain individuals to their businesses or their professions.

If you're seeking a salaried job, the "don't think of money" approach can still apply. Go for the work that appeals to you, and worry about money later, when negotiating the salary. Try to find the employers who will pay you the most for doing what you like to do.

2. Settle Your Self-Esteem Contract with Yourself. Is the job you are considering good enough for you? You can't enter comfortably into a job if you don't have enough respect for it and it does not have enough respect for you. You can evaluate the self-esteem factor in any terms you want—salary, importance of the job, public visibility, contribution to others, etc.—just make sure it is there. The better you feel about yourself as you go to work each morning, the more energetic and productive your work will be.

The only reason to ignore the self-esteem contract, temporarily, is if you need money immediately and cannot avoid taking an interim job to make ends meet. In such a case, you should keep looking for the better job even harder once you have taken immediate employment. Otherwise, getting stuck in a low-status job can wear you down. Keep pursuing jobs that you believe fit your talents. Self-respect is a factor in every job. Make sure you get enough of it.

3. Resolve Your Relationship with Money. Money matters to everyone in a career, though perhaps in different ways. It's time for you to get serious about your relationship with Money, get down to the day-to-day prospects of living together. Will it be "stormy but exciting," or do you prefer "comfortable and predictable"? Perhaps you would like the "same time next year" approach— "each year Money and I will reunite to renew our acquaintance and see where things stand. In between, I don't want to bother with it."

However you want to handle the ties that bind you and Money, try to settle the matter so that you don't have to reevaluate your partnership every day. Too much thinking about money will detract from your interest in the job and may cause you to overlook other rewards you are gaining from your position.

Settling your relationship with Money is important, because it frees you from being obsessed by how others are relating to it. If you understand, for example, that "comfortable and predictable" is right for you, then you can be calm about someone else's pursuing "money at all costs" or "earn a lot, risk a lot." Every relationship is different, but yours is right for you.

Career Decisions and Money

Here are a few guidelines for evaluating how money may pertain to your choice of a job or career:

If the Pay Isn't Good Enough for You Now, Don't Expect That You Will Get Used to It. Don't take a job where you feel seriously underpaid, hoping that everything else will compensate. If you are unhappy about the pay before you even start, you're likely to feel worse about it as time goes on, and will eventually struggle to escape.

Don't Settle for Less. Even if other factors make low pay more tolerable, don't acquiesce to a situation you may regret later. Do everything you can to get paid what you think you are worth, or at least as much as the market will allow.

Potential Earnings Are at Least as Important as Present Earnings. Starting salary often does not correlate with what an experienced person earns in a given field. Be sure to weigh your future prospects against immediate pay, and decide how patient you are about letting your earning potential develop. In some fields pay is deliberately low at the start, because it is considered a probationary period during which you are evaluated for future promise. How much do people earn who have been in this field for five years? For ten years? are good questions to ask.

Check the Reality of an Occupation Before You Decide for or Against It. You may get caught in stereotypes about the earning potential in a given field. A lot of people today avoid social services because they have heard "you can't live on that income." Well, perhaps the pay is low, but there are still social workers, and somehow they survive. There are also some social workers who do better, either by working in high-paying clinics and administrative positions, or by supplementing their paychecks with part-time private practice. If you're interested in that field, talk to social-service people; ask them how they manage financially and what they earn, versus your stereotype. When talking with practitioners, be sure to sample as broadly as you can. Don't limit yourself to one or two individuals, because their situations may be unrepresentative.

Consider Both Earning Potential and Degree of Risk. A high starting salary may be less attractive if there is considerable risk that the job won't last. No job is permanent. Risk can be present in three areas: (a) The financial health of the organization you work for. If profit-making, is it doing well compared to the competition? Is there a history of laying off people? (b) The outlook for the industry. Is this organization in a field that has a good future? Check references such as the current *Occupational Outlook Handbook* to see the forecast for that particular occupation.[2] (c) You versus the competition. Are many people competing for your job? How much will you have to worry about your performance level in order to keep your job?

A degree of risk may appeal to you. In any case, risk is part of the equation in any consideration of initial earnings.

Look for Potential Secondary Sources of Income. Before accepting the job that pays the most, consider whether your job options can produce other sources of income for you, either now or in the future. The knowledge or expertise that you acquire on the job may allow you to earn a part-time income on the side. For example, working as a government lobbyist may allow you to become a consultant. Or, working as a career counselor in a college may enable you to offer your services for résumé preparation on a private basis. A speech teacher for a public school may offer seminars for business executives who desire public speaking skills. Such secondary income may even outweigh the original salary, so consider this possibility carefully when choosing a job.

On the Trail of Discretionary Income

Of course, money can be measured in different ways, but you still want to have some left in your pocket to spend after living necessities are taken care of. Economists call this "discretionary income." You want a decent starting salary, so that you will be able to negotiate your next job without having to bargain for a tremendous increase in pay.

Here's a way to deal with the importance of starting pay without letting it dominate your decision or dwarf all of the other factors that make a job offer good or bad. Develop two figures that you'll carry in your head whenever you negotiate salary for a job:

+ Minimum = The rock-bottom dollars-per-year earnings that I need to feel good about myself, and to have enough discretionary income to satisfy my minimum needs. I won't accept a job that pays less than this.

+ Maximum = The most dollars per year that I believe I could possibly be worth in this field (where I am applying) right now. This is the figure that I will ask for.

You will have to determine the minimum from personal considerations. It relates to what your friends are earning, how much money you like having in your pocket, where you perceive yourself on the status scale, and the minimum you believe you're worth.

The maximum will appear from the research you do about the field of work where you are applying. What do the best job applicants (with your level of education and experience) earn in this field, in the geographical area where you intend to locate?

There is plenty of room here for other factors (new learning, coworkers, etc.) to affect your decision. You'll try to get the maximum, but if other factors make an offer worthwhile, you won't feel bad about taking less. The minimum is always there to remind you how low (and no lower) you may go in order to reach an agreement.

3

Trust Your Intuition

The term [intuition] does not denote something contrary to reason, but something outside the province of reason.

—Carl Jung

I'm saying that we should trust our intuition. I believe that the principles of universal evolution are revealed to us through intuition.

—Jonas Salk

I have some shocking news for you about how people make good career decisions. Often a person cannot explain how or why he or she moves in a certain career direction. It just "feels right." The decision maker is using his/her intuition. Your intuition is the sum of all that you understand about yourself and what you want, but that you sometimes can't explain to others.

In case you feel awkward making decisions that way, don't worry about it. Michael Ray and Rochelle Myers, in *Creativity in Business*, tell us the biggest and most crucial business decisions are made by CEOs according to the mysterious forces of "gut," inner feeling, and intuition.

Intuition often flies in the face of "practical" reasons—money, labor market, etc. When people give you advice, they tend to focus on the "practical," often because they're trying to be cautious on your behalf. You might even say your advisers are often being "parental"—"go where the money is"; "look for the hot spots in the labor market"; "follow paths of others before you."

Those who advise you may be trying to protect you from risk. But that is impossible. "Practical" is what they might agree upon for everyone. That does not speak to what is right for *you*.

Cyndi knew she wanted to own a construction business, but all the "good reasons" seemed to point against her. Cyndi did a number of stereotypically female activities as a youngster—cheerleading and so forth—but she reserved her special energy for wood chopping, learning how to use tools, and helping her friends at the metal shop. Imagine a nineteen-year-old who could discuss the intricacies of rebar!

All this was considered a passing phase, as people waited for Cyndi to look for careers that were not so dominated by men. However, Cyndi "knew" instinctively that construction was where she belonged. She couldn't explain why, because other careers looked more promising. She took a job as a foreman's assistant on a housing construction project, learned the physical skills, learned to keep the books, talked frequently to the owner, and the rest is construction history. Today Cyndi owns a highly profitable company that constructs commercial buildings.

Cyndi trusted her intuition, even when others were advising her to take the less risky path. According to Ray and Myers, "intuition" is generally considered to be the direct knowing of something without conscious use of reason.

I think of intuition as paying attention to what is important to you, regardless of whether it makes sense to anyone else. Only you can decide what feels right, because you have access to all the factors that are uniquely important to you.

Let's say you want to be a journalist. What drives you may be many different things—you may like seeing your name in print, it may be your "excuse" for meeting anyone and everyone, or you may have a deep belief that newspapers are especially needed in the computer era. No two journalists will be drawn to their profession by exactly the same factors.

"Reason" is a small circle of what you know that you can explain. "Intuition" is a much larger circle of all the things you know about yourself that you cannot identify or explain, but that are true for you nonetheless.

When you respond to something intuitively, you're letting your unconscious inner guide take over. "Explanation" is available to you only in small pieces. Your "inner reasons" will unfold as time goes on.

How do you apply intuition to your career decisions? (1) Above all, trust your inner voice. It has access to everything within you that matters. (2) Frame every decision as a Yes or a No. That sounds overly simple, but it's fundamental. As you're deciding about how you feel about a career, consider the next step—is it a Go or a No Go? This gets you in touch with whether your energy is moving you forward or holding you back.

Ray and Myers suggest that you do a coin flip when you have a decision to make. Assign Go and No Go to each side of the coin. Flip it. As it's in the air, ask yourself: "Which side am I *hoping* it lands on?" That is your inner voice, your intuition, speaking to you.

You can develop your intuition by frequently using the coin flip to make decisions, thus getting used to accessing your inner voice.

Even though you don't have to justify your intuition to anyone, you can encourage others to give you input. You remain in charge of the process. If certain people have too much sway with you, keep their input away until you've made your Yes-No decision.

An interesting feature of intuitive choices is that no choice is either right or wrong. You decide what feels like a good fit for you, and then you work to make it right.

How Intuition Appears in Your Life

Intuition tends to appear in one of two ways, as your career decisions develop. First, there is the "all-at-once" insight, what you might call "Kaboom!": "Lightning flashed, and all of a sudden I saw what career is right for me." We all know a few people who have had these kinds of insights.

Maybe you hope to have such a flash of inspiration. It happens for a few, but for most of us it happens a second way—our intuition works through accumulation of our experiences. As you are exposed to a career possibility and various people who work in that field, you increasingly feel comfortable with it and excited by it. This happens gradually; after reflecting over a period of time, one day you might say: "Yes, I think this is right for me." But don't expect it to happen all at once. Let your intuition unfold at its own pace.

Intuition and Zen

Trusting your intuition is compatible with many principles of Zen, and the spirit of Zen teaches us to be cautious about overdependence on science and rationality. This chapter helps us to take an Eastern look at job search, so that we're not confined by a Western perspective.

Our culture is predominantly a scientific one. In our eagerness to validate the power of the scientific method, we have assumed that a career field is no different from a wheat crop, an engineering problem, or the solution to an algebraic equation: it can be observed, measured, and brought under control. We then compound the scientific arrogance by proposing that a career journey can be charted, planned, and understood in advance.

It is too easy to graft the mentality of the Western Hemisphere onto the processes of the work search. All the convenient props for rational thinking are available. A Western mind would have us think about alternatives, weigh the pros and cons, assess probabilities, and predict outcomes. In short, Western thinkers do everything possible to impose crystalline logic and rational thought on a set of decisions and processes that probably are highly illogical, unpredictable, and perhaps even impervious to rational inquiry.

Rational thinking has been so successful in solving modern-day problems—how to place human beings on the moon, how to control inventories of billions of units—that we assume such thinking can accomplish anything. We conveniently forget that rational thinking succeeds best only when the relevant variables are under our control, observable, and objective in the sense that any two observers agree about what they are seeing. We must recognize that the work search is not a highly predictable process, many of its variables are not known or observable, and certainly many of them are not subject to the individual's complete control. Hence, scientific, rational methods of inquiry may be of dubious value.

All our efforts to impose reason on the individual ignore that life choices—career, marriage, and the like—are essentially irrational, perhaps even unconscious, acts. By attempting to introduce order into a disorderly process, we disturb a highly effective but murky process by which an individual makes life decisions.

When we talk about an interpersonal process that is as highly complicated as the work search, the intellect has severe limitations. This is what the Zen master D. T. Suzuki has to say about the intellect:

> Let the intellect alone, it has usefulness in its proper sphere, but let it not interfere with the flowing of the life-stream. . . . The fact of flowing must under no circumstances be arrested or meddled with, for the moment your hands are dipped into it, its transparency is disturbed, it ceases to reflect your image which you have had from the very beginning and will continue to have to the end of time.[1]

Zen emphasizes direct experience rather than the intellect as a means for understanding oneself.

> Zen proposes its solution by directly appealing to facts of personal experience and not to book knowledge. The nature of one's own being, where apparently rages the struggle between the finite and the infinite, is to be grasped by a higher faculty than the intellect . . .
>
> By personal experience it is meant to get at the fact at first hand, and not through any intermediary, whatever this may be. Its favourite analogy is: to point at the moon, a finger is needed, but woe to those who take the finger for the moon.[2]

You are more likely to understand yourself and what you want by direct experience (and a review of your past experiences) than by making arbitrary choices based on criteria external to your own feelings.

Julie loved to dance and move from the time she was a child. But Julie did not know her career possibilities, other than dancing professionally—a difficult path indeed. Her parents were puzzled about how to advise her, her boyfriend tried to interest her in business (it was the furthest thing from her mind), and her schoolmates did not know what to say. Julie continued to dance, took lessons when she could afford them, and read books about dance in her idle hours. In her early twenties, Julie became aware of the healing aspects of movement and the many benefits she had received from dance. She began to read about psychotherapy with great enthusiasm. She formed small creative-dance classes during college. It wasn't long before Julie discovered a tiny band of people doing what they called "dance therapy," an exciting, brand-new profession. She became one of the first therapists registered with the American Dance Therapy Association. By following her best instincts, not what people advised for her, Julie found her career direction. Today Julie is the author of two major books that define the dance therapy profession, and she is an acknowledged leader in her field.

Suzuki encourages a semiconscious or unconscious flow toward those people and activities that feel comfortable for you. He encourages a "let it happen" mentality and suggests strongly that there is greater wisdom in trusting your inner instincts than in *thinking* about what you should do. "The master [Tenno Dogo] said, 'If you want to see, see right at once. When you begin to think you miss the point.'"[3]

Direction by Indirection

As nearly as I can determine from applying Zen concepts to what is essentially a Western process—the formalized search for better work—Suzuki and other Zen masters would advise us to focus our energies by not organizing them. Are these senseless riddles that only confuse you? I believe Zen ideas have some promise for us, and that they can be translated into our work-search language as follows.

1. Let go of judgments. Begin by forcing yourself not to assign external ratings to the work possibilities you explore. If a job pays $50,000 and all your friends say it is a good opportunity, forget that. Explore without making judgments or assigning ratings. Let yourself experience how you feel about the work. Tim Gallwey's brilliant book about the applications of Zen principles to teaching tennis urges a close consideration of the word *abandon:*

> "Abandon" is a good word to describe what happens to a tennis player who feels he has nothing to lose. He stops caring about the outcome and plays all out. This is the true meaning of detachment . . . It is caring, yet not caring; it is *effortless effort.* It happens when one lets go of attachment to the results of one's actions and allows the increased energy to come to bear on the action itself. In the language of karma yoga, this is called action without attachment to the fruits of

action, and ironically when this state is achieved the results are the best possible.[4]

You will note this principle of deferred judgment is echoed in the section that explains how to use creative brainstorming (see chapter 5). Alex Osborn's view that the best things happen when the mind surrenders its power to evaluate is essentially a Zen idea.

2. Try by not trying too hard. Zen assumes that the best things occur when you turn off your conscious mind and let the unconscious take over. Hard effort is usually associated with hard thought; Zen masters insist that such effort intrudes upon the life-stream and inhibits the ability to act.

> As soon as we reflect, deliberate, and conceptualize, the original unconscious is lost and a thought interferes. . . . The arrow is off the string but does not fly straight to the target, nor does the target stand where it is. Calculation, which is miscalculation, sets in.[5]

> Perhaps this is why it is said that great poetry is born in silence. Great music and art are said to arise from the quiet depths of the unconscious.[6]

All this means that your collective unconscious has stored considerable knowledge about what you want in your work, and much of your work-search effort should be arranged so that you let the unconscious have its way. Grafting mechanical procedures or formulas onto your instinctive (unconscious) pursuit of compatible work will probably disrupt the process.

> A Zen master once asked an audience of Westerners what they thought was the most important word in the English language. After giving his listeners a chance to think about such favorite words as love, faith, and so on, he said, "No, it's a three-letter word; it's the word 'let.'" Let it be. Let it happen. Though sometimes employed to mean a kind of passiveness, these phrases actually refer to a deep acceptance of the fundamental process inherent in life. . . . In the more general sense it means faith in the fundamental order and goodness of life, both human and natural. . . . [Let] problems be solved in the unconscious mind as well as by straining with conscious effort.[7]

3. Remember that insights occur at the times you least expect them. It was Pasteur who said: "Chance favors the prepared mind." The more you have been trying to decide what to do about your work, the more likely you are to

find a solution when you are least prepared for it, if you let your unconscious roam freely.

I was struggling with my preparation for a talk to a group of counselors and made little progress when I sat down to think about it. Time overcame me, and I had to depart by car for the conference site four hundred miles away. En route, I parked in New York City, had my car towed away, spent several exhausting hours tracking it down, learned that I didn't have sufficient cash to rescue the car, and had to trundle my belongings to a late-night bus bound for the conference site. By the time I plopped into a bus seat, I was physically drained and mentally exhausted as well. During the four-hour bus ride, I discovered my thoughts falling into a most coherent pattern and was prepared to talk the next morning at half past eight.

> The unconscious picks its own times and places. Some time ago a group of research chemists were asked where and how they got their scientific ideas. Here are some of their answers:

> "While dodging automobiles across Park Row and Broadway, New York."
> "Sunday in church as the preacher was announcing the text."
> "At three o'clock in the morning . . ."
> "In the morning when shaving . . ."
> "Just before and just after an attack of gout . . ."
> "Invariably at night after retiring for sleep . . ."
> "While resting and loafing on the beach . . ."
> "While sitting at my desk doing nothing, thinking about other matters . . ."
> "After a month's vacation, as I was dressing after a bath in the sea."[8]

So prepare your mind for the task at hand by reading about the skills described in this book and then let your unconscious take over; it will orchestrate the process, put the pieces together, and provide the insights you are seeking in the moments you are least prepared for them.

4. Notice clues in your tiny experiences. As you flow into your work search, assume that every event has meaning for you, perhaps especially events that seem to have no meaning at all. When you review your broad areas of experience—major field of academic study, the job you have now, the project you completed last year—you will have a marked tendency to overlook the small events, the tiny ones that contain the clues with deeper meaning.

A friend of mine spent many years after his graduation from college trying to figure out what to do with himself. He ignored his engineering major because it didn't excite him enough; he refused his father's offer to enter the family business for a similar reason; he turned down graduate school offers because he had no idea what to study. His frustration came out indirectly with his family; he fell into the habit of criticizing their speech, grammar, and spelling in fancy letters. All concerned dismissed his behavior as the angry rantings of an unemployed, unmotivated loafer, until finally it dawned on Jim that he unconsciously focused upon *words* in all his idle interactions; these tiny events in which he released frustration revealed an important clue to his future work—he became a copy editor at a publishing house and is prospering in that work today.

How to Apply Zen Principles

The foregoing discussion suggests that you cannot apply Zen ideas to your work search except by trying *not* to apply them, that you will be penalized for any conscious effort, that thinking is disqualified. Certainly Zen principles caution you to minimize the extent to which conscious thought interferes with the flow of your life-stream. However, I believe that certain conscious processes are implied and that you can reorient your mental activity to take better advantage of your unconscious knowledge of yourself in the following ways.

Think of Pictures. Instead of focusing on words (job titles, job descriptions) or numbers (salary, number of people supervised), use your imagination to envision scenes and situations where you would like to work. Pictures are more powerful than words and can tell you a great deal about what you desire. When you picture yourself at the peak of your capabilities, what do you see? Do you see yourself wandering around your room alone, thinking of solutions to difficult problems? Do you see yourself standing in front of a crowd, persuading your audience of an idea? Are you surrounded by children, teaching them, nurturing them? Are you orchestrating a process even though no one can see you?

Defer Judgment. Every authority on creative thinking (Osborn, DeBono, Crawford, and others) insists that the best ideas occur when a person is not inhibited by evaluation or judgment of goodness or badness. Thus, Zen insists that the mind roam freely, without concern about popular opinion, judgments of relatives, or the wisdom of one's meanderings. Creative ideas about work possibilities occur more frequently in an environment of *acceptance*.

Focus on the Present. Decisions made for tomorrow require that you pay close attention to how you feel today. You may think too much about the past ("What have I done before, and how should this relate to what I do next?") or the future ("If I do this, what will happen five years from now?"). Such backward and forward thinking can help you avoid pitfalls, but it can also seriously inhibit your sense of risk taking, your willingness to respond to what you feel is right for you now. Zen masters would persuade us that the present is our only reality.

Consult Your Senses. The intellect has its particular way of judging the worth of a career plan; the body and its visceral senses have other ways of viewing the situation. The next time that you explore a career possibility, ask your body whether it feels comfortable. Do you tighten up when you are at the work site? Do you feel in the hands, abdomen, and back of the neck that this place and these people are right for you? The senses have a lot of information for you, if you will allow it to be presented.

Work and Play Together. A powerful test of compatibility between you and your career is the extent to which you can view it as *both* work and play. You can view *work* as all effort that you expend toward a set of desirable outcomes, while *play* is an inherently enjoyable activity, done for its own sake, without concern about outcomes. The most intrinsically rewarding work has elements of play within it, so that you can look forward to what you are doing on a moment-to-moment basis in addition to anticipating the ultimate rewards.

What educator Bill Harper has to say about play expresses this attitude:

> Play, I think, is very close to being an innate characteristic of man, and for that reason as long as man is man, it is never going to be forgotten or abolished. But there are times when we get very grim and serious, and the whole style of society tends to make it harder for people to play. When this happens—and we are in that kind of period—people languish, become spiritually spindly as they might physically if they did not have sufficient or proper food. I think play is an essential element for spiritual well-being.[9]

Take Advantage of Your Skills

I believe there is no one principle which predominates in human nature so much in every stage of life, from cradle to the grave, in males and females, old and young, black and white, rich and poor, high and low, as this passion for superiority. Every human being compares itself in its own imagination with every other round about it, and will find some superiority over every other, real or imaginary, or it will die of grief and vexation.

—John Adams, 1777

Your ability to define and acknowledge your personal strength will contribute greatly to your career success. This bit of advice would seem self-evident, except that many people constantly underrate their skills.

We prize modesty; the individuals who are enraptured with their own accomplishments can be a pain. Yet strongly needing to present yourself as modest usually undermines your ability to acknowledge your own accomplishments. You become so worried that others may think you egocentric or pompous that you build a hedge factor into every victory or achievement so no one will accuse you of boasting. "I had a lot of help from my friends." "I couldn't have done it without old so-and-so." "It wasn't much; I certainly should have done better." "I was playing over my head, out of my tree."

You protect yourself from future criticism, but short-circuit your ability to derive praise from your achievements. Praise is the precious fuel that propels you to surpass yourself. You need not depend on the compliments of others or judge yourself by their opinions of you, but you must maintain (or regain) the capacity to congratulate yourself on a job well done. Remember—*there is no praise like self-praise.*

Here are some things to be aware of regarding your skills*:

---

*Throughout the book, I use the word *skills* to denote those competencies that are important to successful completion of a career search. In this chapter, *skills* refers to all competencies that can be used by people in the widest possible variety of work settings and tasks. Thus, identifying one's marketable skills is a skill of the career search. I trust you will understand this double use of a most valuable word.

- Once I acquire a skill, I will always have it to call upon.
- I will stockpile my skills for future use.
- I can detect one or more skills in everything I do.
- I won't be concerned about how long a task takes me.
- I will judge a skill by my own standards or satisfaction.

Skills Inventory

What is a skill? I have in mind any of the widest possible variety of attributes that represent your strengths, your key abilities, the characteristics that give you your greatest potency, the ways in which you tend to be most successful when dealing with problems, tasks, and other life experiences. There can be little doubt that you do some things better than other things. You are more comfortable in certain situations than in others. You consistently prefer particular tasks over all others. Your strengths reveal much of what makes you unique, a person who is different from any other individual alive.

Here is a sample list of skills found in a cross section of careers:

administering programs	dispensing information
advising people	displaying artistic ideas
analyzing data	distributing products
appraising services	dramatizing ideas or problems
arranging social functions	editing publications
assembling apparatus	enduring long hours
auditing financial records	entertaining people
budgeting expenses	estimating physical space
calculating numerical data	evaluating programs
checking for accuracy	exhibiting plans
classifying records	expressing feelings
coaching individuals	finding information
collecting money	handling complaints
compiling statistics	handling detail work
confronting other people	imagining new solutions
constructing buildings	initiating with strangers
coordinating events	inspecting physical objects
corresponding with others	interpreting languages
counseling people	interviewing people
creating new ideas	inventing new ideas
deciding uses of money	investigating problems
delegating responsibility	listening to others
designing data systems	locating missing information

managing an organization
measuring boundaries
mediating between people
meeting the public
monitoring progress of others
motivating others
negotiating contracts
operating equipment
organizing people and tasks
persuading others
planning agendas
planning organizational needs
politicking with others
predicting futures
preparing materials
printing by hand
processing human interactions
programming computers
promoting events
protecting property
questioning others
raising funds

reading volumes of material
recording scientific data
recruiting people for hire
rehabilitating people
remembering information
repairing mechanical devices
repeating same procedure
researching in library
running meetings
selling products
serving individuals
setting up demonstrations
sketching charts or diagrams
speaking in public
supervising others
teaching classes
tolerating interruptions
updating files
visualizing new formats
working with precision
writing clear reports
writing for publication

What Good Are Skills?

Aren't people who have been around for a while aware of their strengths and weaknesses? If a person cannot assess himself accurately by now, isn't it a little late to wake him up? The answer to these questions is a resounding no. Almost all of us are unaware of some of our key personal strengths. The Johari Window[1] (below) proposes four areas of self-knowledge; only one area is available to both self and others.

	Known to self	Not known to self
Known to others	Open	Blind
Not known to others	Hidden	Unknown

The Johari Window

I propose that a similar statement can be made about skills and, further, that the largest proportion of this Johari Window for skills is the "unknown" area, where skills exist but are known neither to the person who possesses them nor to others acquainted with him or her. Why is this so?

We Have No Vocabulary for Skills. Most people have a severely limited set of words to use when they try to describe their strengths. Thus, vocabulary must be created in order to make the task of skill naming easier. The skills inventory in this chapter serves this purpose. It is not an exhaustive list, but simply suggests skills labels to allow people to talk about their strengths with the beginnings of a common language.

Skills Are Trivialized. Have you ever done something well, but then immediately thought to yourself: "What good would that possibly do me? That talent is useless, surely not relevant to anything in a career." Everything is practical in some special context. You should learn not to trivialize your assets, but to imagine contexts in which they might be useful. If you are a whiz at sorting mail quickly, determining its contents, and filing it appropriately, imagine someplace where that skill would be useful (purchasing office of an organization? complaint department of a store? assistant to Dear Abby?).

> **Example:** Ever since I can remember, I have liked writing slaphappy, funny letters to my friends and relatives. They seem to pour out of me naturally, the more ridiculous the better. Well, it turns out that I have adapted this skill to my work as a claims representative at the insurance company, where I maintain the "personal touch" with those who file claims by writing to them in my own fashion, which they get a kick out of.

Skills Develop Late in Life. In contrast to the few highly noticeable skills that emerge early in life (musical talent, artistic talent, or mathematical facility, for instance), most skills come along much more slowly and are infinitely more difficult to recognize when they appear. Many of them relate to ways of interacting with other people (a talent for organizing other people into smoothly functioning units, a talent for persuading others to do things for you, a talent for explaining difficult concepts to others in clear, everyday language). Such talents do not ordinarily merit the status of "genius" and do not prompt standing ovations when displayed to the population at large. Nonetheless, they are strengths worth applauding because they move people and even mountains at times. Such skills may not become apparent until the age of thirty, thirty-five, or even fifty, but they can be seen as they grow gradually into potency.

We Put Ourselves Down. It is probably only a minor exaggeration to say that we live in a putdown culture, a social structure in which claiming that you possess an extraordinary talent (especially one people have difficulty labeling) is an open invitation to ridicule. It is far easier to say "Oh, I'm not really that exceptional" or "What good could that talent possibly be?" than to value a skill and talk about it easily, even among friends. However, the quieter you keep about your strengths, the more easily they tend to fade into the woodwork and become invisible even to yourself.

Put Your Worst Foot Forward

I believe everyone feels that some skills are less reputable or desirable than others. If this is true, then many of us probably suppress certain talents because we suppose that others would think less of us, or even laugh at us, if they knew we possessed these attributes. The happy message of skill identification is that any skill is worth crowing about, and the so-called status of a particular skill has little meaning when it comes to getting a job done well. For a moment, take a sneaky sideways glance at one or more of your own attributes that you believe are prominent but somehow a little less than desirable in the eyes of others. Do any of these skills belong to you?

+ *Compulsive.* I do everything in the same order, according to schedule.
+ *Confronting.* I cannot help being very direct with people, saying exactly what I feel regardless of the consequences.
+ *Talkative.* I have an overwhelming desire to talk, even though I know others would like me to shut up for a while.
+ *Nosy.* I cannot restrain myself from nosing into everyone's affairs.
+ *Persnickety about detail.* I leave no stone unturned, cannot rest unless the last crumb is picked up, the last note jotted, the last word said.
+ *Antisocial.* I prefer to do most of my work on projects that let me be by myself for long periods of time.
+ *Loud.* I can usually be heard by most of the people around me when I am talking and have a habit of speaking louder than normal conversational level, whether to an individual or in a group.
+ *Methodical.* My work has always been described as unexciting, proceeding at an even pace, so steady as to have no highs and lows at all; I purposely maintain an even pace so I will not have to deal with uncertainties.
+ *Offbeat.* I prefer to do things the wrong way, or at least the crazy cockeyed way, so I don't fall prey to dullness, so I can build some adventure into what I do. No one knows what to expect of me and it bothers them, but I don't care.

✦ *Slow.* I am slow as molasses in January in every task I undertake, but that is all right with me. I enjoy consuming a lot of time so I never need to feel pressured by a deadline.

Is there any doubt that every one of these personal styles has been denigrated, ridiculed, or sneered at by many people? If you are a closet practitioner of one or more of these traits (or skills), remember that you will benefit far more by acknowledging your particular traits, valuing them, and searching for contexts in which they are marketable than you will by trying to hide these traits.

Here are some examples of how "low-status" skills can be used successfully in job contexts:

✦ The *compulsive* person keeps perfect and orderly records of all calls, correspondence, visitors, and intrusions (birds flying in the window, etc.) in his department.

✦ The *confronting* one has an excellent record in approaching bank customers who have borrowed money and failed to make payments on their loans.

✦ The *talkative* individual is the best person we have in greeting new people in the community, making them feel wanted, engaging them in conversation when they feel shy.

✦ The *nosy* person hangs around enough coffee shops, courthouses, barbershops, and shopping malls to hear about things before they even happen; that's why we couldn't be without her as a news reporter.

✦ Mr. *Persnickety* shines all the pots himself before leaving at night, makes sure no chair is out of place, and sees that all supplies are replenished; we need him as kitchen manager, even though he drives the staff buggy at times.

✦ Ms. *Antisocial* works over there in the corner, reading stacks of old manuscripts; someone has to do it, and I'm glad she prefers this to buzzing around the library making idle conversation.

✦ *Loudmouth* can be counted on to liven up a new group of people who are having difficulty talking to each other. That is why we use him as a greeter for tours of visiting firemen; whenever he wants to announce a departure or a change in plans, he has little difficulty getting the group under control.

✦ The *methodical* one takes care of the tremendous flow of paperwork in this department by subjecting it to careful and systematic attention; we know that no important document will be missed, nor will any schedule be ignored.

✦ The *offbeat* person provides the unusual whenever we need it to promote a new idea to our membership; she is creative and knows how to catch people's attention, even if the other staff members think she's a little nutty.

✦ The *slowpoke* takes care of difficult mechanical tasks that carry risks of overload or mechanical error; he's patient enough to work a task relentlessly just so it will be done correctly.

Transferable Skills

Sidney Fine[2] has identified what is probably the single most important concept in viewing how personal skills are usable in career development. Skills that have potency in career contexts are not limited to being useful within a single kind of work, occupation, or vocational setting. On the contrary, most skills valued in work have the virtue of cutting a wide swath across many occupational boundaries. For example, the ability to write effectively and in clear language is valued highly in private industry, government agencies, educational institutions, and nonprofit organizations alike. In fact, most of the skills that are important in any responsible job have a similar virtue: they can be applied in a wide variety of work contexts to a wide variety of tasks. They are *transferable*.

Fine distinguishes among three broad categories of skills: functional, adaptive, and specific. The first two categories—functional and adaptive—contain all the transferable skills. Adaptive skills can be distinguished from functional skills because they usually refer to personality traits, characteristic ways of behaving. Adaptive skills tend to develop earlier than functional skills, yet they may not be valued or even noticed until the individual has done many years of career exploration. Adaptive skills, like functional skills, are eminently transferable.

> *Adaptive skills* refer to those competencies that enable an individual to accept and adjust to the physical, interpersonal and organizational arrangements and conditions in which a job exists. Included are punctuality, grooming, acceptance of supervision, care of property, getting along with others, and impulse control. . . .
>
> *Functional skills* refer to those competencies that enable an individual to relate to Things, Data, and People (orientation) in some combination according to their personal preferences and to some degree of complexity appropriate to their abilities (levels). . . .
>
> *Specific content skills* refer to those competencies that enable an individual to perform a specific job according to the specifications of an employer and according to the standards required to satisfy the market.[3]

Adaptive and functional skills are frequently coded in specific content language. That is, the word you use to denote a skill that seems highly specific to your job obscures the fact that the skill is eminently transferable. If you are an accountant, for instance, and regard yourself as good at being an accountant (content-specific), you may fail to recognize that you are effective working with numerical data, handling detail, or adapting to peaks of the seasonal workload.

Let's take another look at how skills are transferable. Say you aspire to be a bank officer. You list the skills you believe are most crucial to effectiveness in the role of bank officer:

Being careful with money	Working patiently
Analyzing numerical data	Making financial decisions
Dealing with the public	Reading detailed reports
Anticipating community needs	Supervising others

Of course, the above list might be different if you knew a bit more about what bank officers do. However, for the purpose of this example, ask yourself: If I were to take away the title of bank officer from this list, would the skills listed indicate clearly that it is a bank officer we are describing? The answer is a clear no. The skills noted are either functional or adaptive, and they are all transferable. They might be applied to any of numerous other occupations.

When a person asks you (or you ask yourself), "What can I do in my life that will improve my chances of advancing in the world of work?" don't concentrate entirely on the specific content skills available from formal programs of educational credentials. Talk about the transferable skills that can be acquired anywhere:

✦ *Communication skills.* Writing reports, essays, and correspondence in plain language; speaking effectively to individuals and to groups; listening carefully and empathically whenever necessary; portraying ideas clearly and imaginatively.

✦ *Thinking skills.* Defining a problem cogently; evaluating alternative courses of action critically; creating divergent solutions to a problem when more than one answer is possible; shaping new ideas in the context of old circumstances.

✦ *Human relations skills.* Interacting cooperatively with superiors, subordinates, and peers; communicating orders, instructions, and feelings with openness, genuineness, and understanding; delegating tasks in ways that show respect for the other person and receptivity to his or her ideas.

✦ *Valuing skills.* Being able to view and assess an area of work activity in terms of the effects it will have upon human welfare; making and enforcing decisions in terms that will maximize such welfare.

+ *Research skills.* Discovering and identifying people who have information that is relevant to a task or a problem; identifying resource materials necessary to the solution of that problem.

+ *Interviewing skills.* Acquiring information from people when they are reluctant to divulge it or when information is difficult to reach; generating trust in such situations, necessary for future contacts.

+ *Planning skills.* Being able to sense an idea whose time has come, to move toward work modes that capitalize on this idea, and to sell the idea to appropriate people.

You Can Acquire New Skills

Even though we have focused skill identification on what you have done before, new experiences will occur that will add to your stockpile of skills. Furthermore, you can be deliberate about choosing future activities that will nurture *new* skills. It is a big mistake to assume that your skills are fixed, that you are unable to acquire new talents. Most skills people bring to the work marketplace are ones they have nurtured and practiced in their informal, nonpaid lifetime of experience. Many of the most powerful skills are developed by accident, in the name of just plain fun, for purposes other than their current use or perhaps even for opposite purposes (as when former criminals bring marketable skills to their work as law enforcers).

Here are a few hypothetical and whimsical examples of people whose job-related skills were cultivated in contexts far removed from the marketplace:

> *Examples:* Organized Orville is chief steward at the Roney Plaza Hotel, which serves a thousand people nightly. He stocks the entire place every week by keeping track of drinks served, glasses washed, dollars spent, table napkins needed, etc. Orville's talent for detail is compulsive. He used to inventory his father's toolshed, his mother's cupboard, his uncle's auto-parts store, and anything else in sight, just to keep himself amused when he got home from school.
>
> Oratorical Olive is chief spokesperson for the United Fund of Bigtown. She promotes social services everywhere, raises funds with in-person appearances, and speaks to community groups at the drop of a hat. Olive grew up making speeches at the dinner table, imitating the politicians while they droned away on TV. Olive was applauded by the family, encouraged to speak out no matter what people thought. She ran for school offices just to get the chance to make more speeches.
>
> Dignified Dan is maître d' at the Sans Souci Restaurant. His cultivated speech, attention to formality, and sensitivity to the subtle needs

of his guests make Dan a natural for this position. Where did he acquire this skill? Dan's years on the stage in comedies of manners were not wasted, nor were his trips to Buckingham Palace with an uncle of royal lineage.

Persuasive Paula is a lobbyist in state government. She twists tails of tigers, bends ears of elephants, and tweaks legislators' noses when necessary to get their attention. Paula learned on her block as a six-year-old that bargaining is done best by tone of voice, persistence, and attention to the individual ego. She learned long ago that peanut butter and jelly can be traded for roast beef if the proper words are applied to the bargain.

Six Cardinal Rules of Skills Identification

As you become accustomed to identifying your skills in your daily routine, keep in mind these six rules.

Compare Only with Yourself. Avoid at all costs having to compare your level of talent with others'. Your only consideration is that your skill rates highly within your own private system. Which activities do you perform better than other things? The only relevant comparison is internal.

Be Sure the Skill Is Fun. A skill is really not worth calling attention to if you hate doing it. Only those activities you both enjoy and do well matter for future reference to your work. Count only those skills that wear comfortably on you when you are using them, ones you smile about when you anticipate doing them.

Look for Evidence. Make sure you are talking about actual life experiences, not just something you wish had happened. The only credible validation of a skill lies in a real experience; something you did cannot be taken away from you. If you have evidence of a skill, you cannot be argued into denying it by superficial criteria such as test scores, interest inventories, or other externally generated data.

The Function, Not the Title. Make sure you are talking about what you actually did, rather than any title you may have carried. Titles and labels of positions often do not reveal functions especially well. Camp counselors do not always do a lot of "counseling," for example.

Label It Yourself. Even though you will get some help with the vocabulary of skills by referring to the skills inventory on preceding pages, you should ultimately call the skill by its rightful name. Your own descriptors are more accurate than any label I have suggested. Since you are in the best position to describe the function as it really was performed, don't hesitate to use the words you feel best reflect exactly what you did.

Focus on Irrelevant Experiences. This rule may startle you a bit; however, I suspect you will instinctively look for those life experiences that seem somehow more important to you and will ignore those that seem irrelevant. Hardly any life experience can be called irrelevant. I insist that some of your most special and powerful skills can be found in the life experiences you would dismiss out of hand.

Five Ways of Identifying Skills

There are several different ways you can tap into your particular skills.

From Personal Achievements. Describe an experience that made you feel good about what you did and satisfied with your behavior by your own standards, not anyone else's. Is it difficult for you to imagine you have done anything well? Then try something really tiny, a skill you bet is no good to anyone.

> ***Example:*** I wrote a short verse for my daughter on her sixteenth birthday, making fun of her talents, yet extolling them, to the tune of "We're Off to See the Wizard." (This skill with words and music and sensitivity to an individual's traits bodes well for your ability to express yourself creatively.)

A Happy Role You've Occupied. If you still have difficulty thinking of things you did that were successful, try remembering any position or role you held that made you feel reasonably satisfied with yourself. Boy Scout or Girl Scout leader, organizer of the kitchen on camping trips, keeper of the keys, editor of the social section of your school paper, the one who restores order when things get out of hand—any role has its attendant skills that enable you to perform the role successfully.

> ***Example:*** I was always the one who kept the group calm when something went wrong, by telling stories, creating a little foolishness, and

generally getting people's minds off the trial of the moment. (Interpersonal skill, timing as a skill, perception of tension, and so forth.)

A Peak Experience. You cannot think of anything you would call a peak experience? You say just getting out of bed each morning is the peak for you, and everything else is anticlimax? A peak experience need not refer to a high-level accomplishment. When was the last time you laughed really hard? Which single moment of the past week would you most like to repeat? Whom did you meet recently who sticks in your memory?

> *Example:* I heard this fellow talking at the grocery store about his life at home in Maine. I'll never forget his regional accent and way of expressing himself. I guess I just have an ear for speech, a fascination with it, and some talent for imitating it.

Skills Inventory. Use the skills inventory (pages 50–51) to help you recall experiences from your memory bank. As you spot a skill you have used before, you should be able to remember when you used it. Run through the inventory, checking off skills as you go, and let your memory make the connections.

Ask Your Friends. Your family, friends, and acquaintances see attributes in you that you may overlook yourself. They may even be more likely to notice the skills that are subtle but nonetheless marketable. Others will probably tune in to many of your adaptive as well as functional skills, because they are receivers of your personal traits every day.

> *Example:* You are really good at getting out of doing things. You have a talent for making other people smile. You are a champ at nagging people to get things done.

The Curse of the Single Outstanding Talent

People born with a great talent, and many of those who depend on a single prominent skill, often get themselves into trouble. They depend heavily on the single great ability to surmount any crisis and gain approval from others, and in general they expect the talent to compensate for any other shortcomings they possess. In fact, highly talented people are so hugely rewarded for their abilities that it becomes all too easy to rely on the talent and neglect everything else.

Some of the most difficult cases in career planning are professional athletes whose talents have dwindled with the years, college professors who have been denied tenure, dancers who've suffered injuries, artists who haven't found an immediate market, and others who have depended on a single talent for many years. Their problem can be stated simply: It is not necessary for them to build other skills as long as the one big talent is working for them, drawing acclaim and winning temporary rewards, so by the time the one big talent fades, a vocational rigor mortis, known as learned helplessness, has set in. The talented one has been fussed over, catered to, and provided for. The whole idea of struggling along like us working stiffs has been anathema. Bill Bradley writes in *Life on the Run* that the end of an athlete's playing career is a death in every sense but the physical. We no-talent folk look for a skill to perfect that will answer all our prayers, solve all our career worries, and be always in demand. If you get too good too quickly with a particular skill, beware of the same perversity that afflicts the one-talent person who suffers decline after a brief period in the sun.

* A supersalesman who ignores management skills suffers when the time comes to direct the efforts of others.
* A whiz accountant who handles the numbers like a Ouija board finds his numerical skill small comfort when he learns that interpersonal skill is necessary to deal warmly and effectively with clients.
* A dean of students who can establish friendships on a personal basis with everyone finds to his dismay that planning skills have eluded him because he was too busy making friends.

To become very effective with a single skill is to become drunk with power. For a time, this skill seems to work in every circumstance, people reward you for it, and there seems little need to waste time with other matters. Read on, however.

The Hidden Charms of Multipotentiality

Artur Rubinstein was known as the King of the Wrong-Note Pianists. There are probably many more technically competent than he, but he brings an extra dimension to the stage, a sensitivity of interpretation and a personality that sparkles and breathes life into his music. People prefer him to the pianistically perfect drone who lacks the twinkle and personal magnetism. Rubinstein can also talk with the best of them, charming folks away from the keyboard; people appreciate this dimension of his talent and reward him for it.

It would be extremely difficult to find a career that depends entirely on a single talent. One might think of artists first, but Rubinstein and others dispel this notion. The blessing of calling upon a cluster of abilities instead of just one is that almost every career imaginable demands a cluster of different skills. Being a social worker, for example, involves helping others personally, researching sources of community information, writing reports to public agencies, and recruiting unpaid volunteers. A carpenter must be able to handle materials, measure with precision, visualize space requirements, and deal with homeowners' personalities. A store manager has to relate effectively to customers, organize the ordering of merchandise, and create effective visual displays. A secretary prepares written materials neatly, deals with the public, and develops a careful filing system.

The curse of multiple demands is also its blessing, because you are never required to be flawless in a single category of skill. It is the cluster that counts, not the single outstanding strength.

> *Example:* John was a young man whose transferable skills included the ability to supervise other people, the ability to mix social life with promoting ideas easily, the ability to manage money, and a good sense of what kinds of leisure activities people enjoy. He had studied biology in college and had cultivated an interest in scuba diving. It occurred to him that the scuba background should not go to waste and that he might train a group of people to provide weekend lessons to vacationers. "Rather than get a real job, I decided to fool around in the sun for a while and see if anyone would pay me and my friends to teach them scuba." So he flew to the Bahama Islands without delay, rented quarters, and started the first of weekend excursions for scuba devotees. John's Underwater Explorer Society is a prosperous business today.

The contest between multiple talents and a single outstanding talent is a modern-day version of the tortoise-versus-hare contest. The single-talent person gets off to a blazing start, then is outdone by the industrious but non-flamboyant person who parlays many marketable skills into a winning combination. You need not regret your lack of a single prominent skill; your future success hinges upon your unique cluster of abilities that, when combined, are highly marketable.

Use Your Career Imagination

Most failures of careers are failures of imagination.
—Leona Tyler

All your carefully collected values and skills are destined to be lost, scattered like the pieces in a jigsaw puzzle, if you cannot put them together in creative and imaginative ways. Isolated attributes make little sense if they float in space by themselves, not hinged to any coherent whole. The ability to be creative with yourself allows you to infuse any job with a style of your own, allows you to take a seemingly unrelated collection of traits and attributes and weave them into a coherent pattern.

> *Some say the very purpose of human existence is to get acquainted with your own essential qualities and express them in your daily activities.*
> —Michael Ray and Rochelle Myers, *Creativity in Business*[1]

What Is Creativity?

Ellen wanted all her life to be involved with cycling in some way, but recreation jobs seemed few and far between. So she poked around looking for work in state or local government, hoping someone might sponsor bike trail legislation that would trigger some new employment. She canvassed every bicycle club, volunteered her time to map new trails, and started a part-time repair shop on her own. One day a state legislator brought his children's bikes for fixing; Ellen rattled on about her plans for the future and the legislator told her she should bring her ideas to the Community Service Department. Ellen discovered that, lo and behold, this department wanted a combined researcher/promoter for bicycle resources and two weeks later found herself writing grant proposals to the federal government to acquire funds for her favorite community service.

Brian was a college minister who, weary of the campus routine, decided to resign and take a long trip. He toured forty-two states, exploring every new lifestyle he could discover. His travels led him to the Personal Growth Center in Arizona, where he took a job as a dishwasher. He used his mechanical skills to fix the dishwashing equipment when necessary and his ministerial skills to develop relationships with the people in permanent or temporary residence at the growth center. This center had not thought of assigning itself a ministerial role, but Brian created it, relating to life crises as they occurred, providing gentle counsel to all members of the group—and supervising the dishwashing after every meal.

Creativity is really several different animals called by the same name. It is, first of all, combining diverse elements, pulling together values, skills, and traits that seem unrelated. What do you do with mechanical ability, a love of the outdoors, a desire to work with numbers, and a passion for furniture? Perhaps you investigate forests for future timber crops, count the trees, set up an inventory system for manufacture of furniture.

Creativity also means changing horses in midstream. The metaphor is a caution against giving up one work style for another, but when you think about the process—getting off one horse and mounting another in the middle of the water—it sounds like a lot of fun. Creativity is a way of periodically wiping the slate clean. Whoever invented the ballpoint pen had watched too many fountain pens spill too many times on too many pairs of pants. Imaginative people never want to do the same job the same way twice and are willing to risk falling off a horse or two in the process of figuring out a better way to negotiate the stream.

Creativity also involves taking new skills off the old shelf. Since the person is always larger than the job, we can assume you are forgoing the use of certain skills because the job does not seem to call for them. But wherever there is a job that might be done better, there is an opportunity for a new skill to be introduced. Which of your favorite talents have you not used for a while but would like to send into the game? Writing is fun for you? You like to build things? You really get a kick out of interviewing people? Assume that you have the power to rewrite your job description, because you do.

We have become accustomed to thinking that creativity refers exclusively to the fine or performing arts. In the context of the work search, however, I call *creativity* all forms of thought that focus on the production of ideas rather than on the solution to problems. Creativity here means *divergent* rather than *convergent* thinking. You should assume there is always more than one solution to any career problem and expend your energy toward developing new ideas before becoming concerned about the direction you will take.

Stimulate Creativity Through Wrongheaded Thinking

The more we submit career decisions to logical, analytical thought processes, the more such decisions seem to elude us. Hence, our solutions may lie in thinking *illogically*, so that we do not expect answers to flow in an orderly way from the gathering of data about the self.

Wrongheaded thinking encourages a plentiful stream of ideas, images, possibilities, and random meanderings. If we can accept that career development is more a creative than a scientific process, we must be most concerned about teaching you to think freely and imaginatively, like an artist, rather than strictly and deductively, like a scientist seeking a natural law.

What I call imaginative or nonscientific thinking will be recognized by scientists as the hypothesis-generating stage of scientific discovery or problem solving. Fresh, original ideas always precede scientific rigor. It is these that are most lacking in career awareness. The individual who cannot decide what to do gropes for the nearest alternative, not yet having learned ways to generate many career hypotheses.

Wrongheaded thinking suspends judgment and thus frees you from limiting your possibilities. An example of limiting oneself would be: "I have good mechanical ability, therefore I must study architecture or become an automotive designer." The career options that seem connected to your key abilities often will not be the ones you want to pursue.

Several key propositions are central to your having the power to roam freely in designing possible career futures. I urge you to accept and practice all these propositions in order to accumulate a rich collection of ideas that you can sort, compare, and explore.

The Rigidity of Words. The words we assign to career matters—occupational titles, names of skills, and so on—may do more to bind and hinder our thinking than to assist it. Words are symbols that denote classification, and any classification restricts thinking. If we call a person an accountant, does that mean all he or she does is "account"? Of course not. An accountant manages, counsels, analyzes, writes, and performs a hundred other functions. Does your title adequately represent what you do? Do other people who have the same title as you perform the same functions or carry out their responsibilities in the same style as you? I doubt it. You must begin with a healthy measure of caution about what words mean when you are selecting a career direction.

Thinking Visually. Richer and more descriptive insights will occur as you begin to use pictures and symbols instead of words to describe your career hypotheses. Is your career a cyclone? A treasure hunt? A comedy of manners? A Noah's ark? I have often thought of my own career of counseling psychologist and business owner as a pinball machine, in which I bounce crazily from one standard activity to another, never settling into just one place. The pinball describes the process of my career; a kitchen blender characterizes the content of my work, a bubbling mixture of psychology, education, marketing, and applied mathematics. Visual imagery allows you greater use of fantasy and far greater latitude in portraying your own set of objectives and the environment in which you desire yourself to be. If you can picture your career—where you are, what you are doing, by whom you are surrounded, and other details—you will have a fuller version of what you hope for yourself than you can attain simply by attaching your wishes to one or two sterile words that carry nothing more than abstract meaning.

Irrelevant Data. If it is true that the obvious things we know about ourselves may be misleading (Should I be a politician just because I have a gift for giving speeches?), then perhaps the missing pieces of our career puzzle lie in the darker corners where we would not immediately look. The seemingly irrelevant things we know about ourselves may provide the best clues. If, for example, you are a social worker by training and inclination, but spend your spare moments in political campaigns and reading about new legislation, perhaps you belong in politics more than the person who has oratorical skills. If you devour stock market data when you are supposed to be preparing lesson plans, this may be a clue for your future involvement. Any activity that commands your attention is relevant, no matter how separated it seems from your professional training or visible career history. Stamp collecting or an abiding interest in flood control, dams, and levees—anything may be a missing piece in your career puzzle.

Lateral Thinking. Edward DeBono, in *Lateral Thinking*, characterizes vertical thinking as digging in the same hole deeper and lateral thinking as digging the hole in a different place. "Lateral thinking . . . has to do with new ways of looking at things and new ideas of every sort."[2] Lateral thinking raises questions without immediate answers and freely permits the individual to be as *wrong* as he or she wants to be. Lateral thinking allows rich interpretation of one's work. A waitress in Studs Terkel's *Working* likens herself to Carmen, who dances fluently while her audience throws coins. Vertical thinking encourages objectivity, an agreement among observers about what is being observed. (It is nearly impossible to have such objectivity in your perception of your career; hence, lateral thinking is more suited to your interpretation of the work you choose for yourself.)

Reversals. You will increase your creative insights about your career by often doing what is not expected, by doing the opposite of what seems most obvious to do. Reversal thinking encourages you to turn a situation around or inside out in order to gain a completely new perspective. For example, to reveal what is most salient about your work, take a close look at your play. To discover your areas of strength, examine your most extreme weaknesses. To isolate what you really like best, identify the things you dislike the most. A clever reversal uncovers a new reservoir of data. Reversals can also be used in different ways. Suppose you took an obvious function, such as counseling, and asked: "How might a counselor do the work by being the object of counseling rather than the provider of it?" The answer might be a counselor who devises a new therapeutic process enabling people to counsel each other. Reversals are necessary to counter habitual thinking. Whether a reversal yields right or wrong answers is beside the point; what are needed are new viewpoints and ideas.

The Arrogance of the Dreamer. Perhaps the more outlandish a goal, the more power it has to propel you. An unusual goal provides direction for you and establishes incentive; an ordinary goal probably bores you. If you are not daring enough to suggest a goal that others will view with skepticism, then your goal is probably not imaginative enough. Unless your goal jars some people, you have probably not succeeded in departing enough from what is already known.

In *Your Creative Power*, Osborn[3] tells us three characteristics to develop in divergent, or creative, thinking: (1) strive for quantity of ideas, (2) defer your judgment—when being creative, do not be concerned about quality, and (3) make sure your ideas are as wild as possible. Any and every idea is okay in the brainstorming stage; judgments of quality and worth are postponed until a later time. In the words of the poet William Blake: "The road of excess leads to the palace of wisdom. . . . You never know what is enough unless you know what is more than enough." George Bernard Shaw used to look at the title of a book and then write a full outline for the book before opening it up to read. He didn't want the book to disturb his creative powers for imagining what might happen in the volume.

Nine Creative Processes

It may help you to know there are ways of thinking creatively—not formulas designed to reduce the creative process to a technocrat's delight, but nine excitingly different ways of shaking up your thinking, looking at an old situation in a new way.

Here is a summary of some of the questions to ask about a situation in order to stimulate ideas, as described in Alex Osborn's book *Applied Imagination*:

Put to other uses? New ways to use as is? Other uses if modified?

Adapt? What else is like this? What other ideas does this suggest? Does past offer parallel? What could I copy? Whom could I emulate?

Modify? New twist? Change meaning, color, motion, sound, odor, form, shape? Other changes?

Magnify? What to add? More time? Greater frequency? Stronger? Higher? Longer? Thicker? Extra value? Plus ingredient? Duplicate? Multiply? Exaggerate?

Minify? What to subtract? Smaller? Condensed? Miniature? Lower? Shorter? Lighter? Omit? Streamline? Split up? Understate?

Substitute? Who else instead? What else instead? Other ingredient? Other material? Other process? Other place? Other approach? Other tone of voice? Other power?

Rearrange? Interchange components? Other pattern? Other layout? Other sequence? Transpose cause and effect? Change pace? Change schedule?

Reverse? Transpose positive and negative? How about opposites? Turn it backward? Turn it upside down? Reverse roles? Change shoes? Turn tables? Turn other cheek?

Combine? How about a blend, an alloy, an assortment, an ensemble? Combine units? Combine purposes? Combine appeals? Combine ideas?[4]

Let's take an example and show how each of these creative processes would operate. Let's assume you have a job that doesn't seem creative at all. You're a claims examiner for an insurance firm. Here is an example of how each creative process could enliven the job.

◆ *Put to other uses.* Can I arrange the claims files for other purposes? By last name, by type of accident, by geographical location, by year of policy, and so on?

◆ *Adapt.* How can I adapt my work as a claims examiner to another position within the insurance company? My skills in dealing with the public, corresponding, handling detail, and organizing files are transferable to other contexts.

◆ *Modify.* How can I take an essential procedure and modify it to work better? I have to file the claims in order of their occurrence, but will change the system to record also the dates the claims were filed, so that we can correlate type of claim with length of delay in reporting.

✦ *Magnify.* How can I magnify my passion for working with statistical computation to make it a larger part of the job? I can figure out how many claims were handled for how many dollars in each of the categories, or tabulate the environmental conditions that precipitated each accident, or figure the number of miles between home and accident for the actuaries.

✦ *Minify.* What detail in my work might be reduced to the smallest possible importance? If I can reduce the exchanges of correspondence until I have thoroughly researched each claim, I will save both myself and the claimant a lot of needless communication.

✦ *Substitute.* If I wanted to substitute a special skill in my daily routine, how would I do this? I can substitute my conversational ability for the painstaking correspondence I labor through by talking with claimants before writing to them, so they can understand what we are doing without my having to write it in great detail.

✦ *Rearrange.* Is there some way I can rearrange the sequence of contacts between myself and the claimant so that there are fewer steps each of us has to complete?

✦ *Reverse.* Is there some aspect of my work that is so boring or distasteful that I would like to reverse it? I have always hated answering the phone, so I will try calling the claim filers before they interrupt me, so I can answer their questions and then get on to my other paperwork.

✦ *Combine.* Which of my responsibilities can I combine without sacrificing effectiveness? I have papers to process, reports to write, and people to notify. I will design a form that can be used both to notify the claimant and to serve as entry into the monthly report, so that one need not necessarily duplicate the other.

Creativity-Stimulating Exercises

Here are a few mental devices that will stimulate your creative, lateral, or divergent thought processes and enable you to postpone vertical thinking, or problem solving, until you have generated a large number of possible alternatives.[5]

✦ *Exercise One*

1. *Challenge assumptions.* Identify a key assumption in your present idea and test whether the assumption can be violated, eliminated, or otherwise altered.

> *Example:* Must all accountants work with numerical data? Is it possible they might work instead with pictures (of financial records) or computer languages that would eliminate the need for numbers?

Must all counselors counsel? Is it possible that counseling service can be provided *indirectly* through the management of resources, training others to do direct service, creation of self-help materials?

2. *Fractionate.* Break your work idea into parts, examine each part, and discover which you like best. Or fractionate a nonwork experience to look for new data.

> *Example:* What parts of being in a fraternity/sorority did you like when you were in college? The socializing, the philosophical bull sessions, living in a group situation, the group tasks, the identity, the adventures?

3. *Analogy.* The analogy or picture or metaphor can help you envision what you are trying to accomplish. Use words to create a picture of your situation.

> *Example:* I have often thought of an individual's career as "stable as a hog on ice." I also like to picture self-assessment as "sorting out the pieces in a jigsaw puzzle."

4. *Random stimulation.* In this variant of creative thinking, one uses an artificial device to prod and jiggle the collective memory bank. DeBono suggests looking up words randomly in the dictionary or wandering around a room or open space to experience a variety of stimuli without looking for anything in particular.

> *Example:* I tried the random-word approach and came up with the words "orchestra" and "lobby," and wondered if I could write government grants within the career-development profession for using music in the counseling process or in career workshops.

5. *Force relations.* Osborn suggests that you take highly dissimilar concepts and try to force them into some sensible connection or find a common ground between them.

> *Example:* What do an engineer and a seamstress have in common? (Work with precision.) What do an oil rigger and an antiques dealer have in common? (Patience.) What do a plumber and a police officer

have in common? (Keeping situations from becoming harmful, working under pressure.)

6. *Deliberate exaggerations.* Take a normal, common work situation and stretch it to an unusual degree. See what ideas occur.

Example: Sell insurance to dogs, cats? (Pet insurance.) Education as total deprivation? (Wilderness experiences such as Outward Bound.) A camera as big as all outdoors? (Radar.)

7. *Alphabet system.* Use the alphabet to generate ideas by hooking your problem to each letter in turn, and see what results.

Example: What kinds of employers might want a person with numerical skill?
Actuary, accountant, bookkeeper, computer programmer, credit manager, and so on.

8. *Attribute listing.* Brainstorm as many attributes as possible about a given occupation (the same procedure can be used to describe a person) in order to generate data relevant to the decisions you might make about this occupation.

Example: Attributes of the work of an insurance salesperson: social, financial, personal, abstract-intangible, future-oriented, risk-related, numerical.

✦ *Exercise Two*
Find a relationship between a past experience and a future aspiration by using one of the nine creative processes.

Example:
1. Rita is a program director for the local YMCA. She would like to get involved in the retailing business.
Creative process: adapt. Rita can adapt her experience in promoting programs and services to the task of learning how to promote merchandise to customers.
2. David has done a newsletter for his Hebrew school synagogue group. He would like to do personnel work with college students.

Creative process: magnify. David can attempt to magnify his writing and data-gathering skills into a research and program development position with a large university student personnel staff.

3. Phil has done numerous bake sales in his neighborhood. He would like to become involved with a community arts program.

Creative process: substitute. Phil can substitute a different artistic skill—such as handicrafts—and apply his manual and creative skills to developing new programs.

6

Reality-Test Your Ideas

One thorn of experience is worth a whole wilderness of warning.
—David Campbell,
If You Don't Know Where You're Going,
You'll Probably End Up Somewhere Else

Most people look for new employment as though they were walking the plank—blindfolded, hands bound, last rites on their lips, hoping everything will work out okay. You are leaping into the dark unknown if you choose to enter and make a commitment to a field of work you have never even sampled. Here are some things that people say about their chosen profession: "Oh, I just fell into it, gave it a try, and it worked out okay"; "I heard what my neighbor said about it, and it sounded good, so I signed up"; "Nothing better came along, so I figured what else could I do?"

Reality testing is any method of personal research in which you can gather data and be involved in the actual work activities at the same time. By both doing and observing, you can look upon the work as insider and outsider at the same time, to sample the wine before opening the bottle.

Probably the most common mistake people make in job hunting is to disqualify themselves before the horse race even starts. Perhaps the universal fear of failing or discovering the limitations of one's abilities leads people to say: "Oh, I could never succeed in that field." "There's just too much competition there." "They'd never want a person like me."

Better not to know your limitations than come face-to-face with them. Maybe it all goes back to our fear of speaking in school classrooms, lest we look foolish or say something wrong. Whatever the reason, it doesn't take much to throw a job hunter off the track. Other people are quite willing to add to the chorus that says: "Be careful before you enter the field of work."

"Be realistic," they say, which usually means, "Be practical, be safe, choose a job or career that you are sure of doing okay in." How can anyone be *sure* of what will happen in a job? Outsiders don't bother to answer that one.

Reality is in the eye of the beholder. One person's minefield is another's career adventure. Sometimes the cautions of others are translated to mean: "Do what I think you ought to do." The problem with "reality" is that others are always defining it for you. Their information can be helpful, but it can also contain bias. You must take care not to make their opinions your own.

Don't Suffer Paralysis Through Analysis

You may have a tendency to overanalyze your career decision. A lot of people do. "If I just think hard enough, I just know the answer will come to me." "I just need a list of pros and cons, an assessment of all the relevant factors." People talk like this and then they get twisted in their own data, as though enmeshed in a ball of yarn.

Analysis goes only so far, because you may be operating in a vacuum. What you need are experiences that help you discover what factors are most important to you.

Firsthand Experiences Rather than Secondhand Opinions

Do you let anyone else pick your social companions, your friends, your automobile, or your spouse for you? I didn't think so. A job or career is equally a personal decision, where personal taste must rule.

If anyone else talks you out of a job or career, you will never know if they were right or wrong. Others' viewpoints are no substitute for your firsthand experience. The person who says "Museum work is a tight field. I would avoid it if I were you" may be right about its competitiveness, but may not know that (a) You have talents uniquely suited to that field; (b) You have a special area of knowledge (e.g., your archaeology background) that would be attractive to museums; (c) You have enough desire that you are willing to work for low pay to acquire experience. Furthermore, they may be turned off by their own failed attempts to get museum work, or they may know people in that field they do not like. Other people's biases can come from a hundred different directions, and seldom should they influence you.

You might say: "Of course I will make my own decisions. What made you think that I would not?" Forgive me for underestimating you. My concern is that you gather as much information as you can firsthand, from experience, from talking with people in the field, from personal observations of the work you are considering. Because all this takes time, you may be tempted to skip it and rely on an "expert" to tell you the best field for you. There are plenty of such experts around who are only too willing to tell you what they think the

Truth is—psychological testers (the Truth about you), labor market forecasters (the Truth about where the jobs will be), futurists (the Truth about where the world is going), etc. Such experts have seldom been accurate over the years, and there is little reason you should rely on them to help you make a career decision.

Why Reality Testing Is Good for Your Health

It Keeps You from Making Premature Decisions. Everyone is pushing you to make up your mind. It seems like you're the only one left who is still debating with yourself about what to do. As you tell people "I don't know yet," the pressure builds. Reality testing allows you to keep people at bay, giving you time to think things over. Reality testing also makes sense to other people. They may even wish they could be as careful and forward-thinking as you.

It Keeps You from Being Eaten Alive by a Career Stereotype. Stereotypes are voracious. They chew up individual differences and spit them out. They are ruthless; they allow no room for individual deviations. A career stereotype insists that you see a job and its inhabitants in a certain way—an engineer as a thing-oriented noncommunicator, a public relations person as a glad-handing fast talker, or a social worker as a weepy do-gooder.

Without reality testing to save you, you may be trapped in the jaws of a career stereotype and not get away. Let's suppose you want to be a news reporter, but you imagine they all are hyperenergetic and aggressive, and you don't want to be like that. Thanks to reality testing (talking with some of these characters), you find out pretty quickly there are plenty of reporters who do not fit the stereotype. Thus, you can see there is ample room for you.

An Ounce of Reality Can Equal a Pound of Self-Assessment. Just when you have done a lot of self-assessment, and think you have yourself all figured out, you can do a couple of reality checks and find out:

I can understand those stock market terms and work with those numbers better than I thought; they're not so hard, and I'll get even better with practice.
I don't really like the pace and lifestyle of advertising people; it's even worse than everyone told me.
I thought I would like people well enough to run a restaurant, but now that I see what you have to put up with from the public, I'm not so keen on it.
Now that I see what a technical writer does, I realize I could do that without much trouble, even though I don't have an engineering background.

It is easy to underestimate ourselves. It's better for you to find out now what your possibilities are than to say years later, with perhaps an ocean of regret, "I could have been a good ———."

Reality Testing Is Not for Everyone or for All Situations

"If I had known what this job was like before getting into it, I never would have done it."

How many times have you heard someone say that? And they have a good point. The reality of a field of work—its many problems and complexities and difficult people—might scare a person away if he/she looked too closely before deciding to enter. Sometimes it is better *not* to know everything when you are ready to take a big step.

Is it all right to take a risk when you know little about the field and are not willing to investigate it? Well, only so long as you can handle the consequences of whatever happens and can learn to "fail forward."

Judy had wanted for years to quit her job as a bank examiner and become an independent financial consultant, but said: "Every time I look at what becoming a consultant would be like, I see too much—my husband's modest income, the competition I would face, my two growing children and their needs. I think I am going to have to hold my nose, shut my eyes, and jump."

Jumping can be a lot better than standing over the water, trying to decide what it will feel like, or the discomfort of getting yourself wet one body part at a time.

There is also a limit to how much can be known about a work situation before you actually enter it.

✦ How can Emil know the future of rowing and boating in Austin, Texas, when he builds his boathouse? He makes an educated guess, but only the future will tell whether regattas become a tradition and participants flock to the sport of crew.

✦ How will Margie, who has been in the private sector for several years, know the politics of working in state government before she takes the job as a coordinator of training? She has some idea of the problems, but will only know the full story once she is there.

Using the reality-testing guidelines below, you can cut down the number of surprises waiting for you when you change careers, but much will not be as you expected and you will decide then how long you want to stay. "Ya pays yer money and ya takes yer chances."

Reality-testing a career is easy and it is fun. There is no reason why you cannot gather data firsthand about any job or career. Undoubtedly, you are already doing some of this on your own. Perhaps reading this section will enable you to say: "Ahh, I have been doing this right all along." If so, keep up the good work. Here are some key guidelines for reality-testing job or career ideas most effectively.

1. Allow the Career Idea to Get Born Before Evaluating It

While you are cooking up a great idea for a career, do not allow reality to intrude. Let your imagination have its full play. Cultivate the idea of "what I most want to do" in your mind's eye. Get a clear picture of your possible future. Follow yourself around. What tasks are you performing in the course of a working day? What people are you interacting with? What are your best moments?

Does all this sound too fanciful? Creating images is nice but perhaps a little ridiculous? Are you worried that this is just a fun exercise that will shatter when it sees the light of day?

That sort of fear and wariness is exactly what keeps people from having good ideas in the first place. That is *why* career ideas must get born before reality-testing them. So what if the thing doesn't fly when you let it out the door? That's something you can find out later, without serious consequences. A career idea needs room to breathe. Don't suffocate it by judging the outcomes before it even has a chance.

2. Any Career Idea, No Matter How Far-fetched, Competitive, or "Unrealistic," Can Be Tested—by You

Reality testing focuses on two key questions:

1. Can I become good enough to make it in this field, and how much do I want to?
2. Is this field what I think it is—will I like it well enough?

Here are the key ways you can reality-test yourself to answer these questions. Use all of these if possible. These reality tests are listed according to the easiest first, so you may want to start at the top and work down.

Observe the Work Being Done. Follow the person around. Watch the person at work. Ask yourself: Could I do that, with sufficient training and experience? Be careful in evaluating yourself here, because you could be intimidated by watching people who are very good at their work. You could be overwhelmed by their seeming expertise. They could even be showing off for you, letting you see their best side, not showing you the situations where they perform less well. In general, though, firsthand observation will give you some idea of the ability required. Don't render a final judgment on yourself yet. Move on to other reality tests.

Simulate the Experience. Often you can reality-test yourself for a particular field of work without actually entering that field. This may be necessary for careers where you cannot get immediate experience. For example, you cannot get part-time or volunteer experience as a company executive, practicing physician, or courtroom lawyer.

A simulated experience is one in which you test the skills and temperaments needed in the real career. For example, you can test your verbal skills (lawyer) by pursuing activities in which you speak a lot and argue for your point of view. You can test your leadership skills (company executive) by getting involved in the management of a community program or campus organization. You can test your physical and analytical skills (doctor) by working in science courses and giving personal attention to your own body. The examples are numerous: future psychologists and counselors are usually tested in simulated experiences such as camp counseling or informal conversations with friends; would-be architects try their hand at building things or designing rooms in their own living quarters.

Read About It. An easy way to reality-test a job or career you know little about is to read about it in one of the many career reference books that exist or to research it on the Internet. The *Occupational Outlook Handbook* (*OOH*) and many other career references provide concise information about a particular field—nature of the work, methods of entry, types of qualifications required, job outlook, and places of employment. Your local colleges or universities will be likely to have these references, and will usually let you read them even if you are not a student there. Libraries also have many of these career books, and a reference librarian can help you find them. As you read about a field, if you find your enthusiasm growing, you can move on to the next reality test.

The Internet is a handy place to get general information about a career field. You can tap the *OOH* online and conveniently access many other sources that describe occupations. This is one of the best uses of the Internet for job hunters, because the information does not go out of date too quickly and it allows you to "shop" for careers whenever you choose.

Talk to People in the Field. We tend to stereotype fields of work. All lawyers are regarded as highly vocal and argumentative. All accountants are perceived as reclusive, numbers-oriented people who seldom interact with others. All musicians are perceived as wild and disorganized characters who live by their feelings. Such stereotypes may not fit how you perceive yourself, and may discourage you from considering a field of work. Talk to a wide sample of people in this field before you make your judgments. Check out if you like them, and see whether your own personality could fit in that environment.

Even more important, talking to people in the field will enable you to reality-test whether the challenges and problems of that field appeal to you enough to weather the preparation you must go through. People who work in a career can tell you things that you will not find in career books and references, which tend to either glamorize a field or talk about it in emotionally neutral terms. People can tell you both the joys and frustrations of that kind of work from their own experiences. Be careful to sample broadly, because everyone is biased by her particular job, personality, or life situation. Talk to both successful and unsuccessful people. Ask them about the good points and the bad points. "What keeps you in this field?" "What are the most exciting challenges in this field?" "If you were ever to leave, what would drive you away?" are good questions to ask.

Firsthand Experience. Firsthand experience will be the best reality test for finding out whether you like a field enough to make a commitment to it. A job or career can look good on paper and as described by its practitioners, but until you try doing it, you really do not know if you will be enthusiastic about it.

An all-or-nothing mentality often keeps people from using experience as a reality test. They believe mistakenly that if they try out a new kind of work they are making a commitment to it. On the contrary, you can experiment as much as you want with new fields of work, particularly if you do it on a volunteer or part-time basis. It can be as simple as helping a friend with his/her work, or volunteering to work on a political campaign, or helping out at a florist shop at night to see if you like the work routine.

The value of doing volunteer work is a well-kept secret. Often you cannot get a paying job in order to reality-test a field of work. Does it make sense to work for free? In many cases, yes, because the experience may be more important than the loss of income. If you need badly to test a career before committing yourself to it, then be willing to make whatever temporary financial concessions are necessary.

Unpaid work is a useful bridge between careers, but many people do not take it seriously. It's a secret that you can learn without earning. Take advantage of it, and understand that you are being paid in ways other than money.

You will usually arrange volunteer work on an informal basis rather than applying for a volunteer job. You can approach someone and say: "I'd like to get some experience working here, and am willing to offer my time and energy without pay. Could we talk about working something out?" As in life, almost anything is negotiable.

3. Evaluate Each Reality Test Yourself

Be your own judge of what each reality test means to your career decision. Sometimes the people you talk with will want to offer judgments for you, such as: "Don't go into this field, it's too crowded . . . too discouraging . . . too demanding," etc. Or their opinions may be overly positive: "It's a great field. You can't miss . . . plenty of opportunity."

Practitioners are no better forecasters about their own fields than the labor market experts are. Your decision should depend not on what they believe the future of the field to be (though this is good information to have), but on whether you are sufficiently attracted to it and believe you have the ability to perform reasonably well. In other words, after adding up all your reality tests, if you still feel good about the field and think you might be a pretty good fit, then give it a shot.

> *Example:* Al was a social worker who wanted to switch to being a carpenter. In his first reality-test experience, he tried building a doghouse and made a mess of it. Others laughed and said that was proof he should stick to social work, but Al decided he would keep after it until he got it right. Al tried another doghouse, did a better job, moved up to building outdoor decking, did a few chairs, built a staircase, and eventually learned cabinetmaking from an experienced craftsman. He knew he had done bad work initially, but held on to his belief that he could become competent. His initial failures were temporary. When people began paying him well for a few side jobs, Al decided it was time to change careers.

4. You Don't Have to Be Better Than Everyone Else

"If I can't be the best, I don't wanna do it." Nonsense! If you are good enough to earn a living at it, and people respect you for it, then you'll be all right in that kind of work. We compare ourselves to others too much. Give yourself credit for jobs well done.

5. It May Not Be the Right Time, but You Can Try It Later

Sometimes you do your reality testing when conditions are not quite right. Your family is having problems that require your attention . . . or your confidence is not quite where it should be . . . or you have some physical ailment that is slowing you down. Perhaps you should come back at a later time and reality-test again, when other problems have faded. I am not trying to give you excuses for giving up (it *is* important to persist, and to overcome frustrations if you feel you're on the right track), but am simply acknowledging that timing can be important, and you can repeat reality tests later, whenever you would like.

6. Make a Career Move About One Week
Before You Are Completely Ready

Why? Because you will seldom feel completely ready, that everything is right and the stars are all in their right places. If you feel you're within one week of having All Systems Go, then go ahead and do it. You have probably done enough reality testing and are simply sitting around gathering up your courage. Yes, there is a risk, and you're not sure what's going to happen, but do it anyway. If you find out you were wrong, you will still be right, because the experience of trying a new field will teach you something about yourself you did not know, and you will use that experience to move on to something else. But let's not talk about failure. You've researched this thing intensely by now. Do it. It's going to work.

How Reality Testing Helps the Career Search

Businesspeople use the phrase *caveat emptor* ("let the buyer beware"). In "buying" new work, there is even more to worry about than the quality of the merchandise—the personalities of the coworkers, their lifestyles, the demands of superiors, and numerous other factors. Shoes, refrigerators, and automobiles can be tested in a relatively simple manner before they are bought. *Consumer Reports* has no laboratories for work environments.

Reality testing often paves the way for actual job offers because it gives people a chance to see what you can do. In such situations, your exposure to the employer accumulates and you develop close relationships with the people who may one day employ you. Two examples illustrate this point.

> *Example:* Mo was a young man who had a lot of sensitivity to the drug- and alcohol-abuse problems of college-age people. He spent most of his time during college and summers between terms getting to know drug users and the ways they think, the attitudes they hold toward their lives. During college, he spearheaded the creation of a study group and informal counseling service that would reach out to his friends and provide information, counsel, crisis support, and a place to ventilate feelings. He obtained a federal grant for the purpose and grew closely acquainted with community leaders in his efforts to build town support. When Mo graduated with major fields of study in philosophy and English, he wanted to continue this work. He discovered that a suburb heavily populated by adolescents wanted to begin a community-based counseling and referral service for drug and alcohol abusers. Many trained scholars of pharmacology, psychology, mental health, and other disciplines applied, but Mo was hired to direct the

center because he had experienced the problems of drug abuse and the difficulties of extending this service to adolescents. The selection committee felt that the youth population would trust Mo more easily and would respond to his experience.

Example: Sara worked in an office of local government but longed to play a role in encouraging the growth of performing arts in her city. She attended theater, concerts, dance programs, music recitals, and every artistic event that appeared within a hundred miles. One day she heard from a neighbor that a few people in town were trying to create a summer arts program for high school students. She decided this was her opportunity to learn about arts administration firsthand, so she volunteered to help in every phase of the project. She raised funds, wrote publicity brochures, interviewed prospective students, surveyed the schools, talked with potential faculty, and helped develop budgets. The summer program eventually came into being, and two months later Sara was hired by the executive director to return with her to a nearby town and become assistant arts administrator for the county.

Reality testing becomes most important for you when you practice the more intense levels, such as volunteer work and part-time work. The employer who may one day seek a new assistant or other staff member, and wonders how to decipher the quality of candidates' abilities from résumés will likely be glad to accelerate the selection process and hire the familiar volunteer or part-timer—*you.*

How to Obtain This Skill

How do you become a skillful reality tester? First, be curious. Cultivate a higher level of curiosity than you have ever had before. Snoop around as though you were a detective. It's great fun to pay attention to details ordinary mortals would not notice, pick up a few pieces of information that are hidden from public view, and push your limits of visual observation.

Second, practice taking the person-on-the-street role. This you can do in many ways: you might want to buy a new suit, seek information from a government agency, or inquire about child-abuse services from your local courthouse.

Third, play dumb. Except when you are asking someone to hire you, it ordinarily helps to approach a work site as though you know nothing. Take little for granted; ask questions about even the things you think you understand. People will be more willing to explain what you see if you approach them as though you are the novice and they are the advice givers, which is the truth. Let every informant tell you his or her own version of why things look that way, so you can collect and merge these data and opinions into a consensus view.

Finally, be willing to risk. Every instance of reality testing means doing or seeing something new to you. If your tolerance for change and variety hovers near the zero line, take some small risks first. Be prepared to try a new environment, knowing you can return to the old fireplace anytime you choose.

7

Don't Worry About What Everyone Else Thinks

Sammy walked into his living room and all he got was grief—at his own party.

"You should be a management consultant; you always think you know everything anyway."

"You're crazy to give up the accounting field."

"Insurance, estate planning, financial counseling—that's the ticket. Go for the money."

"Potatoes?? Unbelievable! You're going to jump into a pile of potatoes . . . in Idaho??"

Sammy had just decided to leave his comfortable job at the Big Six accounting firm, move to Boise, Idaho, and join a company that farms and distributes potatoes.

"We understand it's a lifestyle decision, but potatoes? . . . give me a break."

You don't often get a standing ovation when you make a career choice. Sometimes it's even a chorus of boos.

The picture of your career is forming in your mind and heart. You're getting excited. It's looking good enough that you're starting to talk about it. What do your friends and family say? Some like it, others are not so sure. You don't care what they think, but you do care too.

This is not a contest to see how much applause you can get for your career choice. No group of friends and family will ever agree on what they think of your career goal. You're going to have some doubters. So what? What do they know?

If others question the direction you have chosen, it may be because they don't fully understand what motivates you. They bring their own motives and biased perspectives to whatever they "see."

Careers of every shape and magnitude got funny looks when they started, and they just rumbled on. Who but you knows where this train is going?

> *The only "D" I got in college was in dance class. I deserved an F . . . when the football team heard there was going to be another De Mille dance fantasy at the awards rally, they said they'd rather not get their letters.*
>
> —Agnes De Mille, choreographer

> *My interest in planetary astronomy was outré in the fifties. Since the moon was the paradigm of the unattainable, I didn't know if my career was possible; girlfriends felt awkward about my aspirations. [The University of] Chicago gave me no active discouragement, it was just that hardly anybody shared my interest at school.*
>
> —Dr. Carl Sagan, astronomer

> *My ego was so damaged by high school, which was big and judgmental, that I graduated in the bottom tenth of my class. I didn't fit into any of the groups in high school, and American University was the only college that would take me.*
>
> —Ann Beattie, novelist

It's nice to have support from others, but don't count on it. Creative thinking is often misunderstood. People who care about you the most will often support whatever you do, no matter what they think of the idea. Others will not support you. Take it in stride. Cheerfully accept all input. You're in charge, so they can say what they want to.

Judy wanted to start a pet-sitting business. After completing a bachelor's degree at Smith College, this was not what her parents had in mind. Maybe management consulting in Washington, D.C., or Boston, or perhaps investment banking in New York. But . . . pet-sitting? Judy absorbed the resistance and moved ahead. She started small with a few kitty clients in Haverhill, Massachusetts, built her resources, and now has a staff of ten in the Boston area and high-profile clients who count on her to take care of their pets during their numerous trips each year. Judy is an entrepreneur, and her laid-off friends wish they had income as reliable and growing as she does.

If you're too eager to gather support from everyone, you may be more interested in receiving approval than focusing on what you want to do. Approval feels good. But a slavish pursuit of it may lead you away from your innermost goals.

Lots of people have career conflicts with important people in their lives. You may want to be an entertainer, but family members would be happier if you sought a corporate job. You may want to be a newspaper reporter, but those close to you would cheer more loudly if you kept going toward the Ph.D. in chemistry that you had once talked about. Approval is a tempting lure. Family reunions and gatherings with friends are scenes where you're bombarded with "What are you doing?" and where all the family career preferences come out into the open.

When you try to "explain" the heart of your career goal to people who don't fully understand it, their eyes glaze over and you feel misunderstood. That's part of the game. You don't understand their careers either.

Sometimes your friends and family try to protect you. Their approach is "parental." They take a conservative stance and recommend against careers that might not work out. They try to nudge you toward what appears to be as close to a "sure thing" as possible. There are no sure things, and if you were to pursue them, you would be losing sight of your motivations.

Most any career worth pursuing has an element of risk in it, because the world of work is inherently risky. Chaos is normal for the marketplace. No one can predict consumer behavior, nonprofit budgets are subject to change, etc. It's far better for you to accept the risks and adapt to them than to try futilely to chase a "sure thing."

If all people important to you are applauding in unison your choice of career direction, ask yourself: "Was approval my top priority?" If you're too concerned about receiving approval from people you value, you may lose sight of your own priorities.

Your top priority should be to follow your own muse, your inner creative genius that says: "THIS is what I must do." Your career direction emerges from the center of your being, a powerful mixture of motivations, conscious and unconscious.

People give you flak about your job or career choice, others misunderstand, others ask why. Roll with it. Take your support where you can get it. You know what you're doing. If you follow your right path, they'll catch up to you later.

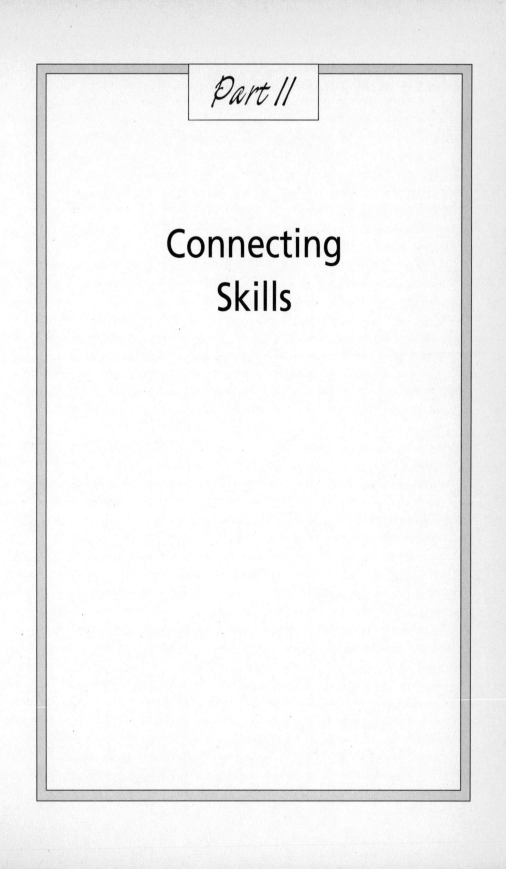

Part II

Connecting Skills

8

Jobs Are Everywhere

The first fundamental truth about the job hunt—There are always jobs (vacancies) out there, waiting to be filled.
—Richard N. Bolles
1999 What Color Is Your Parachute?[1]

Why Any Job, Anywhere, Is Potentially Available to You

"Where are the jobs?" is a dominant question among job seekers. The quest for openings is like a treasure hunt, but a frustrating one since, as many authors have said, much of the job market is hidden and therefore difficult to uncover. Yet we persist in trying to keep track of this ever-shifting thing called the labor market. An army of Geiger counters called "employment agencies" attests to people's desire to have someone keep sweeping the landscape, looking for the openings. It also attests to the individuals' belief that they cannot find the openings themselves.

Employment agencies, job banks, and other such enterprises are hitting certain pockets of employment, but missing large numbers of others. The job market moves too fast and is too diverse to be tracked with any thoroughness. A little like catching raindrops—the more you try, the more you become aware of the larger task before you.

The Hidden Job Market

In many cases the employers are trying hard *not* to make the opening widely known. Employers would prefer to broadcast their vacancies only to the people best known to them (informal sources), in order to get applicants they know the most about. Hence, much of the job market is "hidden."

The oft-used term "hidden job market" refers to the vast proportion of jobs (estimated to be 80 percent of all jobs) that are relatively unpublicized, because employers prefer to attract and contact job candidates through informal sources. Many have deemed this unfair; but it is natural for employers to seek candidates through their most trusted sources, and it will probably always be this way.

So, what are you to do about all this? You still want to know where the jobs are, and feel that somebody ought to be able to tell you. You don't want to waste your time looking down blind alleys or canvassing everyone you see, or calling at random in the Yellow Pages.

Don't despair. You can do an effective job of uncovering potential jobs through the principles of Targeting.

Jobs are everywhere. Remember, there is continual turnover in job markets. It's been estimated that one of every ten employed people changes jobs every year. Because there are so many of these jobs that are "hidden," there are hundreds of openings right under your nose if you will investigate them.

Targeting Jobs, and the Elegant Logic That Lies Behind It

Targeting is two things:

1. *Targeting Content.* Identifying the specific kinds of work that you want to do and concentrating your energies on these areas of the labor market.

2. *Targeting Geographically.* Identifying the specific towns, cities, or regional areas where you would like to live and find employment.

The basic principle of Targeting is that any job can be uncovered, no matter how "hidden" the job market may be. The accessibility of occupations can be explained in a three-step logic that opens up the entire world of work to you. Never mind "Where are the job openings?" Pay attention only to "Where are the organizations that employ people?" and "Where can I find them?"

◆ *Principle 1: If a job can be imagined, there are people who are doing it.*
Fortunately, there is enough diversity of employment in our economy that, no matter how specific, detailed, or far-out your desired job may be, there are (with rare exceptions) already people doing it. Never mind whether they are leaving these jobs, or whether you can compete successfully for them. Because the labor market is continually in a state of turnover, one or more of the people who occupy these jobs may leave sooner or later. Furthermore, there are strategies you can use to qualify or prepare yourself for such openings. For now, be happy in knowing that the jobs you want already exist—somewhere. And, since they exist, you can get access to them.

In those unusual cases where no one is doing the kinds of work you would like to do, consider two possibilities: (1) There are people who are doing work that is similar; (2) There are organizations that have a need for that kind of work, and may create jobs in the future to take advantage of it.

✦ *Principle 2: Since there are people already doing the kind(s) of work that you want, you can find them.*

You can locate and walk right up to meet people who are doing the jobs that you might like to have one day. For the most part, people in their jobs do not hide, nor could they hide if they wanted to. There are a few exceptions to that, but mostly people at work are aboveground, not covered by burlap bags, and generally accessible. Sometimes it takes a little travel money and time and persistence to find them, but they are there. And since your target people exist and can be found, they may have some information about when and where future job vacancies are likely to exist. Or, even if they don't, they can give you some clues about how people move in this field and how you might find a way in. So, your second task is to *get there*, find the people who're doing your target jobs. Once you have found them, you're two-thirds of the way through successful Targeting.

For example, when I lived in Austin, Texas, I wanted to learn if technical companies hired liberal arts graduates and why. I called and visited with a lot of people and discovered that they hire liberal arts grads for their writing skills, analytical skills, speaking skills, and leadership potential. I "uncovered" many "hidden" job openings that the graduates did not know were there.

✦ *Principle 3: Since any job can be imagined, and people can be found who are doing it, you have some opportunity to get experience that will qualify you for doing that kind of work.*

Having found the people who are doing your target jobs, looked them in the eye, and made their acquaintance, you are already ahead of many others who are still trying to figure out "Where are the jobs?" Now, let's assume there are no openings, the field is competitive, and you're wondering why you're wasting all this time.

Don't back off now, just when you're at the front gate. Direct contact with target people usually gives you some opportunity to ask: "How might I gain experience in this kind of work, so that I can make myself qualified when openings become available?" Good job hunters are thinking a step ahead. Does the target person know where you might get part-time work, an internship, volunteer experience, or perhaps enter a training program? Well, maybe not, but it's all right for you to ask, and sometimes they can recommend avenues for you. "How did you get into this field?" or "How did the most recent people hired here get into this field?" are good questions to ask.

Do not complain that there are no jobs. There are plenty of jobs, you're just not in them. The name of this game is early access. Get there before someone else does. Identify what you want, find the people who are doing it, and figure out a way to do some work with them. People are better than paper. Paper methods—job listings, job banks, classified ads—leave you on the outside unable to look in. People methods give you access to the possibility of any job in the world. When you arrive on their doorstep it may be just the day they decided to move on.

Easy for me to say. To take advantage of targeting, it sounds as though you would have to quit your present job, or drop out of school, and roam the countryside looking for target people, all the while going into debt and wishing there were a way to give up this search and let someone else do it for you. Is targeting nice in theory but impossible in practice? Certainly there are difficulties in the logistics of getting in touch with targets, and problems in making yourself available for the experiences they may recommend. You must work within your limitations of time, energy, and money.

But remember this: If you want something enough, you ought to be willing to investigate it. The people who can help you best are the people who are doing the work you want.

In addition to the many jobs available through the hidden job market, new jobs are created to meet existing needs. A job may be created as a result of your initiative. Stranger things have happened. Your presence, your ability to describe your skills and experiences, and the employer's needs could come together in a chemical reaction that results in their offering you a job.

Example: Ron went to Washington looking for a job as a junior lobbyist. Armed with his English degree from Dickinson College, he checked with one agency after another. He got nowhere for several weeks. Since he had done some theater in college, he decided he might as well try the National Endowment for the Arts. The dance department had no jobs but needed someone to deliver sets and other materials to the public schools within a fifty-mile area, and help them set up their programs. They were having a hard time finding someone who would not mind driving a truck, loading and unloading it, and working odd hours. When Ron said he would do it, through the magic of government, they created a new job and started Ron in his career of public service. Today, six years later, he is a key administrator and lobbyist with the National Endowment for the Arts.

Maps of the Labor Market

The job marketplace seems like too vast a territory to be covered. People and their jobs are everywhere at once, and there is no central clearinghouse or grand map that shows you who is doing what exactly where. Hidden job possibilities are out there, but how can you efficiently tap this large number of opportunities?

1. Keep an Open Mind. Assume that ANY employer in your targeted field *might possibly* have an opportunity for you. This optimistic assumption will yield you more results in the long haul than saying: "Oh, they probably don't have anything." Because of continual turnover, and the reality that new jobs are created every day, job possibilities may exist where there appear to be none. The day you show up may be the day that Marv Ziltz decided to move to Sheboygan, or Sadie Corbisher got it together to start her own beach-blanket business and now can leave the company for good.

2. Use Directories. While there is no single map that tells where all jobs are and who is leaving them, there are a large number of published directories that you can use to "map" your target areas of work. In fact, these maps are so useful and available that you can find hundreds of organizations that employ people whose jobs you would like to have—simply by making an easy trip to your local library.

Why settle for a few job vacancy listings (from job banks or employment agencies) when you can scan the entire landscape that you want and select many different places to contact? The directories listed here are widely available, in either public libraries, the reference sections of college and university libraries, or the career planning and placement centers of your local colleges and universities. You can use these "maps" at your leisure and identify many potential employment targets. Of course, many of these same directories are available on the Internet.

This is a small sample of directories that are widely available. References to many of these books are available on the Internet:

A Sampling of Available Directories

1999 Artist's and Graphic Designer's Market, edited by Mary Cox, Writer's Digest Books, Cincinnati.

The Biotechnology Directory, 1999, edited by J. Coombs and Y. R. Alston, Grove's Dictionaries, New York, 1998.

The Book of U.S. Government Jobs, 6th edition, 1996, Dennis Damp, Bookhaven Press, Moon Township, PA.

Career Opportunities in the Music Industry, 3rd edition, Shelly Field, Facts on File, New York, 1995.

Careers in International Affairs, 6th edition, edited by Maria Pinto Carland and Michael Trucano, Georgetown University Press, Washington, D.C., 1997.

1999 Conservation Directory, edited by Rue E. Gordon, National Wildlife Federation, Vienna, VA.

Directory of American Firms Operating in Foreign Countries, 15th edition, 1999, edited by Barbara Fiorito, Uniworld Business Publications, New York.

Directory of Federal Jobs and Employers, Krannich and Krannich, Impact Publications, Manassas Park, VA, 1996.

Directory of Foreign Firms Operating in the United States, 9th edition, 1999, edited by Barbara Fiorito, Uniworld Business Publications, New York.

Dun and Bradstreet Million Dollar Directory, 1999, Dun and Bradstreet, Bethlehem, PA.

Editor and Publisher International Yearbook, 79th edition, Editor and Publisher, New York, 1999.

Good Works—A Guide to Careers in Social Change, 5th edition, edited by Donna Colvin, Barricade Books, New York, 1994.

Government Job Finder, 3rd edition, Daniel Lauber, Planning/Communications, River Forest, IL, 1997.

Green at Work—Finding a Business Career that Works for the Environment, Susan Cohn, Island Press, Washington, D.C., 1995.

International Directory of Little Magazines and Small Presses, 1998–1999, 34th edition, edited by Len Fulton, Dustbooks, Paradise, CA, 1998.

The ISS Directory if Overseas Schools, 1998–1999, International Schools Services, Princeton, NJ.

The Job Bank Guide to Health Care Companies, 1998, Adams Media Corp., Holbrook, MA.

Jobs and Careers with Non-Profit Organizations, Ronald and Caryl Rae Krannich, Impact Publications, Manassas Park, VA, 1996.

LMP (Literary Market Place) 1999, R.R. Bowker, New Providence, NJ.

Non-Profits and Education Job Finder, Daniel Lauber, Planning/Communications, River Forest, IL, 1997.

Peterson's Job Opportunities for Engineering and Computer Science Majors, 1999, Peterson's, Princeton, NJ.

Peterson's Job Opportunities for Health Science Majors, 1999, Peterson's, Princeton, NJ.

Peterson's Job Opportunities in Health Care, Peterson's, Princeton, NJ, 1997.

Plunkett's Infotech Industry Almanac, 1999–2000, Jack W. Plunkett, Plunkett Research, Houston, 1998.

Principal International Businesses, 1998–1999, Dun and Bradstreet, Bethlehem, PA, 1998.

The Sports Business Directory, 4th edition, edited by Michael Patino, E. J. Krause and Associates, Bethesda, MD, 1998.

1999 Working Press of the Nation, volume 1, *Newspapers Directory,* R.R. Bowker, New Providence, NJ.

1999 Working Press of the Nation, volume 2, *Magazines and Internal Publications Directory,* R.R. Bowker, New Providence, NJ.

1999 Working Press of the Nation, volume 3, *TV & Radio Directory,* R.R. Bowker, New Providence, NJ.

Ulrich's International Periodicals Directory, 1999, 37th edition, R.R. Bowker, New Providence, NJ.

> *Example:* If you were targeting social change careers, you would consult *Good Works* and *Careers in International Affairs,* because both have extensive listings and descriptions of organizations that employ people for such work. Representative social change employers include the American Friends Service Committee, the Peace Corps, Amnesty International, and Common Cause.

> *Example:* If you were targeting medium- to large-size businesses in a particular geographic area, you would consult *Dun and Bradstreet's Million Dollar Directory.*

> *Example:* If you were targeting agencies of the federal government's executive branch, you would consult the *Directory of Federal Jobs and Employers,* which lists and describes every federal agency.

There are no tour guides you can hire to lead you through the swamps. There are no other ways to find employers conveniently listed and organized for you, by geography and types of work. Make it easy on yourself. Consult a map at your local library or career library, or on the Internet, and travel on.

3. *Find Key People.* Make a list of your target employers, show it to people you know, and ask each of them:

1. Do you know anyone who works at these organizations?

2. Do you know any people who work at similar organizations?

3. May I call or visit these people and say that you referred me?

4. *Meet Face-to-Face.* Call to make an appointment with any of the people you are referred to, regardless of their level of importance in the organization. If you're contacting them on your own, and do not know names of key people, call and ask: "Who is head of that department?" or "Who works for him/her?" Then do your best to meet with one or more of these people.

Presto! You have discovered maps of the labor market. These directories give you a way to organize your detective work, and a strategy for tapping into the hidden job market.

Maps Are Never Complete

Don't count on the maps to tell you everything. They will inevitably miss many of your prospective employers. Be aware of these limitations:

+ Directories cannot keep pace with changes of organizations, new ones being created, or others going out of existence. If you have a current directory of a given field, it will probably cover 70 to 90 percent of the existing large and medium-size organizations. That is a lot better than you can do on your own.

+ Small organizations are often missed by national directories such as those listed here. Don't overlook the small ones in your job search. Many of them will be known to your contacts, and some will be listed in local directories, which are often available through local chambers of commerce. Smaller organizations are "sleepers." They do not have glamorous names, but some of them will grow into leadership roles and therefore offer more exciting potential for growth than the larger, better-known companies, whose growth may be leveling off. It has been well documented that small firms create more new jobs.

+ Certain fields of work do not have any directories at all. In such cases, try the Chamber of Commerce or United Way of your town or city, because these organizations have overall directories of profit and nonprofit organizations, respectively.

+ Try the *Encyclopedia of Associations.* Every field of work is represented by one or more professional associations. This is available in print in the reference section of any library, and it also can be tapped on the Internet. Look them up using the Key Word Index in the *Encyclopedia.* Then write or call the association and ask if they know of a directory that will help you. If not, they usually have a directory of members and can tell you where to find one in your local area. They also usually have journals that tell about the field, and about national and regional meetings, and they will usually send you free or inexpensive literature describing careers in that field.

Example: By looking up the American Psychological Association in the *Encyclopedia*, you would learn that they produce several journals, hold many regional meetings, and have headquarters in Washington, D.C., where you could write for further information. Your letter could request *Careers in Psychology* and other related career materials (which are free). APA would also tell you about their member directory, and if any directories exist for mental health centers, mental hospitals, and community guidance clinics.

Often a contact with a professional association will put you on the trail of what you need. It is best to call the association and ask to speak with the executive director, his/her assistant, or the head of the resource library, if the association has a large staff (the *Encyclopedia* tells you the size of the staff).

Finding Jobs in Small Organizations
In sum, you can tap the small companies and other small organizations missed by directories and the Internet in these ways:

+ Use the resources of "umbrella" organizations such as the chambers of commerce in your target area and the United Way.
+ Use the *Encyclopedia of Associations* to lead you to local chapters of professional associations in your target field.
+ When you're stuck, keep asking your friends and acquaintances about people they know who are in the ballpark of what you're looking for.

Detective Skills

The image of the sleuth or detective is a good one for characterizing the career search, because it merges the elements of excitement and anticipation with judiciousness, the awareness that your quest for information will always bend to intellect and persistence. Just as a good detective knows the puzzle can be solved, the necessary information is at hand, and what may be invisible to the eye is deducible by the inquiring mind, so the work detective can say with assurance: "The work I want is out there; all I must do is find it."

The best work is awarded to those who are most diligent at finding it, at putting themselves in the *right place at the right time*. Since most job contacts have an element of luck in them, it follows that a good detective takes advantage of every ounce of luck available. An employer will have no particular compulsion to conduct a cross-country search for the best candidate. He or

she will assume you are the best that could be found, because the others simply
have not appeared.

The Work Detective Has It Easier

When you consider that the crime detective and the work detective function
according to similar principles, you realize that as a work detective you enjoy
the advantages of the trade without the disadvantages of having criminals,
paranoids, and competing sleuths attempting to hide information from you.
Everything you are looking for is open to public view. If I want to learn more
about what a carpenter does, I don't have to sneak around corners and bribe
people to give me hot information. The information you want does not hide
under rocks.

A friend of mine wondered where in the world she would learn about the
banking field and get the contacts she so desperately needed. Meanwhile, she
sat beside a bank teller on the bus to work, tripped over a bank vice-president
on her way into the building, had lunch with a friend who lived next door to a
big money man in the financial district, and went bowling that night with a
city manager who was about to close a deal with his local bank for downtown
redevelopment. The best sources are walking past you, if you have the presence of mind to tap them on the shoulder.

How to Get Started with Detective Work

As you set forth in search of people or information about your intended career,
the questions to ask yourself routinely are: Who would know? Who would
know anyone else who knows? Where would they meet? Do they have any
formal association or affiliation group?

Any good detective looks in the places that have the greatest promise. Don't
wait on park benches for the clues to sit in your lap. Let's say you want to make
contacts in the field of recreation.

+ *Who would know?* Town recreation boards, youth groups, anyone engaged
in athletics, and people who teach recreation at the state university.

+ *Who would know anyone else who knows?* People who participate in recreation a lot, such as parents, older people, church leaders; and people whose
business it is to know what is happening in recreation—retailers of recreational equipment, keepers of parks, and so forth.

+ *Would they have an association?* Of course. Don't any groups that share
common interests, problems, and needs for enrichment find a way to get
together? Ask any active recreational specialist where colleagues meet when
they want to share new ideas or have a good time together.

You can make useful connections through seemingly unlikely sources. Butchers know bankers, and street cleaners have made the acquaintance of government officials. I know a college professor who knows Mideast high potentates. It is within your grasp to start a chain from potentates to that special camel dealer you've been wanting to meet all these years.

> *Example:* Steve always wanted to meet an alligator wrestler. He really half-suspected there were no such people. He tried the local zoo, and they laughed at him. Undaunted, he slipped into the town's luggage shop on a lark and asked where the alligator suitcases came from. "I just get them from my wholesaler, Mac," replied the store owner. Thus began a trail from the owner to the wholesaler to the manufacturer to the alligator trappers in the bayous of Louisiana. A few letters and a phone call later, Steve was invited to an open market for trappers and traders. This led to a very interesting part-time job.

Seeing It from the Employer's Perspective

Consider who is really the helpless one in this job-search process. It is the poor employer who must discover you from among thousands of potential applicants. The employer has precious few resources to find you easily and no systematic method for even detecting your existence. You at least have the advantage of knowing what you want and being able to find the employer, who is listed in the telephone book or some other convenient directory. By contrast, you are nearly invisible to the employer who seeks you.

The Employer Doesn't Even Know You Exist. Directories are little more than organized frustration for the employer who wonders: "Who would want this job? What is this person doing now that is relevant to our situation? How do I find this person without having to interview everyone at the national convention?" It is far easier for you to know that the employer exists.

The Employer Is Usually Under Great Time Pressure. When an employer has a job vacancy, it must be filled in a specified period of time. How many hires are made because the employer simply got tired of the hiring procedures and took whoever was handy at the time?

The Employer Must Depend on the Least Reliable Data. Anyone who has ever stared at a pile of a hundred résumés, trying to decide which of them reveals the right person to hire, will understand that a stack of résumés can be characterized as a parade of wooden soldiers. Any relationship between résumé data and what the person is capable of doing is often purely coincidental. Following the résumé-screening process is the thirty-minute canned interview, in which the interviewer asks questions hoping to elicit the essential qualities an individual has cultivated during twenty-one or more years of living. Small wonder that a blind interview, based on a résumé that has been carefully manufactured to present a selective truth, often results in a process resembling a Martian talking to a person from the moon.

The moral of this story is: *If you don't find the employer, the employer will not find you.* Hence, the employer will be forced to hire the cluck instead of you, and you will become some other employer's cluck because you too have managed to find the wrong job for your particular talents.

It is much easier for you to find the right employer among thousands than for the employer to discover you among millions.

In Sum

Jobs are available in many, many places, so many that you couldn't possibly investigate them all. You will find many of these jobs if you're willing to initiate contact with people. As you gather data regarding what they're looking for when they hire, you'll be in an excellent position to present yourself as a marketable candidate when the right time comes.

Build a Network of Relationships

Whatever you do in life, somebody helps you.

—Althea Gibson

Everybody wants "contacts" in job hunting. The oft-stated "it's who you know" has a ring of truth about it. People sometimes say this resentfully, as though having contacts were unfair. Contacts are how the job world works. Those who hire always prefer to have job candidates referred by someone they know.

Still, "getting contacts" sometimes has the flavor of power-hungry yuppies who try to manipulate their way into job opportunities. There *are* ways to misuse contacts, and being manipulative is the worst of them. Power-oriented individuals may get away with their slickness for a while, but eventually they trip over their own superficiality, because having contacts is not about brief introductions. It's about building a trusted network of relationships.

As you read about "contacts" in this chapter, consider each initial meeting as the beginning of an ongoing connection. You'll see many of these people in other contexts. Some will become friends; others will be mentors. Each meeting has the potential to grow into something more than an exchange of information. Treat every individual as though you expect to see them again and again.

The "I'm a Nobody, I Don't Know Anyone Important" Blues

"You need to know people in high places to get ahead." "Only people with connections get anywhere." How many varieties of this tale of woe have you heard or said to yourself lately? I do not claim that all people have equal footing as they begin the work search; some folks *do* have contacts that are more influential than others. However, this complaint is still a weak excuse for not mobilizing yourself and taking advantage of the contacts you do possess.

No matter how lowly you believe your station in life to be, or how private a person you think yourself, you still have valuable contacts. This chapter discusses the wealth of possible contacts within your comfortable grasp. No, contacts will not necessarily obtain a job for you; nonetheless, they provide a vital link between you and the people you are trying to meet.

People more often find their work through direct referral by other people—usually friends or acquaintances—than in any other way. Crystal and Bolles, in *Where Do I Go from Here with My Life?*, call this *organizing your luck:*

> There is always an element of "luck," "the fortuitous crossing of paths," or "serendipity" that is beyond your control. But the question is: "How can you best organize your luck, so the factors that *are* within your control are working for you?"[1]

Many people who call themselves lucky are ones who have unconsciously refined their ability to learn about things as quickly as they happen and have developed the habit of putting themselves in touch with the right ears. If questioned, these talented people may not be aware of how they do it.

> *Example:* Jane asked the local automobile dealer to tell her about antique cars, where they are located, how they are acquired, and all that. She was just curious, you understand. The dealer invited Jane and her grandmother to an automobile show where antique cars were on display, and there Jane met another dealer who was looking for a young person to get into the business. Thus did Jane have the "lucky" break of meeting her future business partner in the trade that is her heart's desire.

Every planned contact can lead to unexpected ones. Expect the unexpected breaks and ask for them if they are not immediately proffered. Every time you make contact with a person who is in direct line with your career interest, you set up the possibility that he or she will lead you to more people of similar persuasion.

> *Empirical sociological studies continually demonstrate the crucial importance of informal interaction . . . the heavy dependence of individuals on their personal contacts for information about job-change opportunities.*
>
> —Mark Granovetter, *Getting a Job*[2]

It's Truly a Small, Small World

"But I don't know anyone in that field at all," you protest. "That's like trying to meet the Prince of Wales." The intermediate contact, the person who knows both you and the Prince of Wales, is the person for whom you are looking.

The skill of expanding a personal referral network is the skill of connecting people, the skill of stringing together enough intermediate contacts so that you can reach anyone. Anyone. Acquiring employment is a *social* process. People are connected to one another by a nearly infinite number of pathways. Many of these pathways are available to you, but you must activate the circuits to make them work to your advantage.

An illuminating research study known as the "Small-World Problem"[3] reveals the extraordinary power of having and using your own personal contacts. Stanley Milgram estimated that any person of adult age has accumulated between 500 and 1,000 personal contacts, and he reasoned that each link between two individuals generates a total pool of contacts numbering between 250,000 (500 × 500) and 1,000,000 (1,000 × 1,000). Three links in a referral chain permit an astronomical number of contact possibilities. Therefore, he reasoned, anyone ought to be able to reach anyone else in a populated country simply by putting a few links of the referral chain into operation. He tested this empirically by asking a sample of people in Massachusetts to use their personal contacts to reach a randomly selected group in Lincoln, Nebraska, whom they did not know at all. Results showed that the Massachusetts people reached the town in Nebraska typically within two links ("I know a plumber here who has a brother in Nebraska who has a friend in the target town"). The implications of this research for job seekers are little short of staggering. It means that you have the power to reach almost anyone if you simply use your existing contacts.

There is no such thing as a person who cannot be contacted, reached, tapped, or otherwise made a friend. Everyone has a friend who also has a friend. Somewhere in that chain of friends you are standing with your arms at your sides and your eyes closed. Now if you carefully open your eyes, reach out to the two friends waiting on either side, and grasp their hands firmly, you will feel the electricity of a personal contact network begin to course through your body. It will be stimulating, but not shocking. You will feel alive with the circuit of energy that comes from plugging in to people networks. However, be aware that anytime you drop your hands and close your eyes again, you have broken the connection. The life of the circuit depends on your ability to keep the switches open. I don't know how to help people who are asleep at the switch.

People like to make their contacts known to you. It takes a lot of restraint *not* to tell another person about your contacts. Try it sometime. Most people's natural egotism takes over. "Why, of course, I know Dradnatz. Been a good friend of mine for years." Once you subtract a constant for puffery, you have a good measure of a person's contact potential. By telling you the people I know, I accomplish two things: (1) I reaffirm my membership in the human race and show that I have some history of having kept my relationships over a period of time—no small matter; and (2) I can be helpful to you in a way that requires little effort, yet does you some definite good.

To take the fullest advantage of natural contact networks:

♦ Never underestimate the value of any person you know. The milkman, the druggist, the country butcher, or the sandwichboard man (now, there's a person who meets and greets a lot of people) can all be helpful to you. You-never-know-who-you're-talking-with incidents happen every day. The street-sign painter on your block this summer may be the daughter of the local bank president.

♦ Keep your mouth open at all times. Get in the habit of asking anyone and everyone what they do, whom they know, where they have been lately. Curiosity opens the most unexpected doors, I once asked a woman at the dry cleaner's where she got the Maine sticker on her car and discovered she had taught at a camp in that state where I had been trying to establish a contact for several months.

♦ Keep your ears open at all times. Listen more closely than you usually do to what people say about themselves, where they have been, who they have met along the way. Be curious about everyone's travels and meanderings.

How to Acquire a Personal Referral Network

There are three basic principles for networking:

1. The Best Time to Look for Contacts Is When You Are Not Looking for Contacts. When you are in a desperate hurry to find the right contact, you will probably turn this person off with your impatience. You will also probably fail to relax enough to ask the best questions, wait patiently for the answers, and allow the person the freedom to reflect. You will be focused less on the person and more on your own private anxieties, and this will transform him into a functionary for you, which he will not like at all.

The less pressure you feel to ask the person for direct job information, the more likely you are to develop a comfortable rapport, talk easily about your mutual enthusiasms, and give the other the space in which to offer personal referrals without feeling compelled to do so.

2. You Never Really Know Whom You Are Talking To. Take, for instance, the man who went to a magazine office one day to get some back issues, fell into conversation with the receptionist, asked her a few questions about her work, got interested a little in her as a person, and, lo and behold, discovered she was the niece of the magazine publisher, just working there for the summer. She introduced him to her uncle, who led him to the newspaper editor he had been wanting to meet. There is nothing at all mysterious about the skill of generating personal referrals. To some extent, you may have been doing it naturally all your life.

3. Always, Always Ask for the Names of Other Contacts. You can then say: "So-and-so suggested I call you." Always make sure you have the person's permission to use his or her name in this way. These linkages between colleagues, friends, or associates in the same line of work are your magical door openers. If you fail to take advantage of these connections, your work search will bog down.

People Who Should Become Your Friends

Regardless of where you are searching for better work or what kind of work you desire, when you arrive in your chosen location, there are certain categories of people who are always in a position to be helpful to you. They are special people because they have more knowledge of the citizenry than almost anyone else in town. They are not officially designated as job-information experts. They would not think of themselves as such, but they are, nevertheless.

Police Officers. Probably no individuals see more of what occurs in a town or make it their business to know more occupations and what they are doing than police officers. They know where the bank presidents are, where the dope pushers hang out, and where the politicians can be found when the legislature is not in session. They have to know these things because they depend on these people for information when they need it.

Barbers and Beauticians. These folks may well see a steadier stream of people on an individual basis than anyone else. For this reason, they know not only who does what kinds of work, but how they feel about it, the organizations they work for, and probably who's going where, how it all happens, and when the openings will occur. No one ever accused a beautician or barber of being 100 percent accurate about his or her information, but you are less concerned with total accuracy than with getting leads and gathering data.

Other People Supplying Personal Services. This category includes manicurists, masseurs, masseuses, house cleaners, and a variety of others with whom you come in personal contact. Many of these people acquire a great deal of information from the people they routinely see, their regular customers or occasional contacts. They usually enjoy sharing this information. It is part of the reward of *their* work. Make them happy; encourage them to talk.

Retailers. Anyone who operates a retail establishment of any kind—grocery, clothing shop, toy store, sporting goods store—sees a lot of customers and tries to know them as well as possible.

Secretaries/Receptionists. These people are gatekeepers; they have the keys to the executive chambers and the knowledge of everyone's comings and goings. They have to know the people they serve in order to survive the daily blizzard of inquiries. They are your experts in discovering where the target people can be found, who is grumpy to talk with at what time of day, and how the information you need can be obtained without violating anyone's privacy, sanity, or company regulations. They can lead you to your destiny or frustrate you at every turn, depending on how well or how poorly you have persuaded them that you are worth helping.

Librarians. These almost forgotten people would probably escape your attention in any work search where you are walking streets, taking buses, and focusing on office buildings. However, librarians know more than most of us about almost everything because they are surrounded by so many resources. Even if they don't have the exact sources directly at hand, librarians are some of the few people who see it as their professional *obligation* to help you find what you want. Librarians are detectives by another name.

Socializing Can Be Good for You

You can meet contacts when you're out having fun. Sometimes you seek them as contacts by design and other times it just happens unexpectedly. Many good contacts are made through parties or other social occasions, but do not be too quick to assume that this is where most of your networking opportunities are. Some people just don't socialize, and others are resistant to being networked when they are away from work. Take what comes and don't present yourself as hustling or trying hard to meet people who can help you, because the results will be counterproductive.

What they *can* do for you: (a) Give you names of people to talk with; (b) Refer you as a person they find "likable" and "worth talking to"; (c) Occasionally give brief on-the-spot information interviews.

What they *cannot* do for you: (a) Comment about the quality of your work; (b) Sometimes they cannot do what they say they can. Name-dropping at parties is common. Sometimes you will get a referral and find out the person who gave it hardly knows the contact at all.

The main message is this: Do not expect or demand too much from any individual. A contact is a favor granted. There are usually limits to what a person can or will do for you. Be grateful for what you do get, and try to get referrals when you can.

The World Runs on Personal Referral Networks

Remember that over 80 percent of the people in the nation work for companies that employ sixty or fewer people. These small employers depend upon networking, on referrals, and on front-door traffic.
　　　　　—Kirby Stanat,
　　　　　　　in *Careers Without Reschooling*[4]

Referrals are important for the employer as well as for you. Both small and large employers take advantage of them. It may sometimes seem unfair that people get jobs through contacts, but it is not. Most of the best hiring decisions will always be made this way, because employers prefer sources of information they can trust. Thus, you owe it to yourself to use the power of personal referral. If you have good contacts, use them. If you lack contacts, use the principles in this chapter to build networks in fields where you need them.

Contacts Should Lead to Ongoing Connections

A contact is not meant to be a superficial, one-time deal. The best contacts are people with whom you have an ongoing relationship. Stay in touch with many (*all* would be impossible) of the people you meet. Let them know how and what you're doing. Help them out in some ways, whenever you can.

Don't look at initial contacts simply as people who lead you to someone else. Be interested in their work lives. Some of these people will welcome maintaining contact with you.

The real value of networking accrues as you build continuing bonds with numerous people in your field of work. Mutual trust develops, because you get to know each other and find ways to be supportive. Your initial "contacts" become your lasting friends, and you help each other in many ways over time. As you change companies, change geography, and change careers, these ongoing work-related friendships are vital anchors for you, and for them.

Information Interviewing

The most dependable and up-to-date information on jobs and careers is found by talking to people . . . if you want to find out if this new job or career fits you, you must go talk to people actually doing the work that interests you.

—Richard N. Bolles,
1999 What Color Is Your Parachute?[1]

There is something elegantly simple about the information interview. You *talk* to people and, as long as you do it properly, good things tend to happen. Why has it been necessary to tell people that they need to talk with each other? In other spheres of life, checking with other people is natural. You wouldn't buy a car without asking around, getting opinions, and building a mental file of information, would you? Even your decision whether to see a movie often depends on what others say about it. So, why do we have to be coached to track down information about jobs and careers that we are thinking of making our own?

The answer is that people have treated the job world as if it were an impenetrable fortress, where you have to find crowbars to break in and see what is going on there. The emergence of personnel hiring procedures has contributed to this perception. Human resources offices exist as much to keep people out as to let people in.

While the information interview may not free you entirely from the shackles of HR hiring systems, it certainly gives you a superior method for getting information about fields of work and jobs that you cannot obtain from books or formal job descriptions. For example, you can seek answers to questions such as:

What kinds of educational and experience backgrounds do the other workers in this department have?
What is the pace of work here—frenetic, relaxed, off and on, high volume?
What are the ways in which this field is changing?

Information interviewing exists to answer the questions that *cannot* be answered by anything in print that describes the field, the industry, the organization, or the job that interests you. Sure, you could get some of those questions answered in formal interviews. But why wait until then? You may find out things about the job that dissuade you from applying, and therefore save yourself a lot of trouble. Or you may learn things that fire you up and make you a much more enthusiastic job candidate.

Many have known about and used the information interview for a long time—rich folks and their clubby interconnections, people in small towns or small companies where insights about jobs travel like brush fires, and people in tightly organized professions where practitioners often visit each other's offices or talk on the phone and share information, opinions, and the latest revelations.

But you may not have any of these advantages. Either your field of work is too big to know many people in it, or your city is too large to have natural connections, or you're changing from one career to another, or you are a long distance from the job markets that you want.

In these cases, the formal methods of information gathering (job announcements, company literature) are weak, so you must rediscover your talking muscles and put them to use. Once you have exhausted everything available in print (which often is not very much), you must move to the telephone and the in-person contact. In most any job search, they're the best games in town.

Information interviewing has become a centerpiece in the practice of job hunting. It's a household phrase for everyone engaged in the job search and is an indispensable tool. Unfortunately, job hunters sometimes attach exaggerated expectations to their use of information interviews.

- Job seekers expect that doors will fly open and job openings will materialize soon after they utter the magic words: "I want to ask for your advice about entering your field of work."
- Many job hunters use the method amateurishly. They exaggerate the extent to which a person will enjoy talking about his/her work, bumble in without much preparation, and often overstay their welcome, thus negating any positive impression they might have created otherwise.
- Job hunters often overdo it, operating on the theory that a hundred information interviews are ten times better than ten of them. Just like mailing a carload of résumés and waiting for the job offers to pile in, they push for safety in numbers and thereby treat each individual interview hurriedly and perhaps carelessly. Information interviewing is not a numbers game. It's about getting the information you need most from credible people.

✦ Even people who are not job hunting at all make the mistake of calling hardworking professionals out of the blue, interrupting their workdays, and launching into a series of difficult questions ("What are the main trends in your field?" "What do you think is the best approach for a person with my background?" "How do I deal with the credential problem in your field?") that put the respondents on the spot and ensure that all they will do is try to get off the phone as fast as possible.

✦ Worst of all, job searchers often crudely attempt to use the information interview to set up job interviews, even though they have been cautioned to resist that temptation. When you treat the respondents in the information interview this way, they will carry a negative impression of you.

While many people avoid these errors and use the information interview process well, large numbers of others do not. The sheer number of career changers has created a flood of information seekers in the offices of working people. Predictably, employers and professionals have caught on to this trend and have dug in their heels, learning ways to resist the advances of newly coached "information interviewers."

The concept of information interviewing is still quite sound: (1) You should seek as much information as you can, because you need it to actively *choose* the job or career that suits you best; (2) People may help you greatly, in ways that printed materials and secondhand informants cannot.

You cannot afford to conduct your job search without information interviewing. But you had better do it right, or the potential gains will turn to losses. If you are well organized, do research in advance, ask answerable questions, moderate your expectations, and show sensitivity to the person and the situation, you will probably get good advice and perhaps some referrals to others. If you misuse your opportunity, you'll get very little and may even produce irritation.

Three keys to successful information interviews are:

1. *Information.* (a) Reading in advance about the field, the organization, and even the person, so that you can ask informed questions; and (b) Having a clear idea of the information that you most need to know.

2. *Introduction.* If possible, get yourself introduced to the target person by someone you know, or at least be able to say "———— suggested that I call to ask if you might meet with me." Make sure you have permission to use the referring person's name.

3. *Integrity.* Make the purposes of your interview very plain on the phone, respect the limits of what a person can do for you, and then don't fudge at all about your stated objectives.

How to Get an Information Interview

Normally you will call on the telephone. Occasionally, you'll run across an opportunity for an information interview in person.

Try, if at all possible, to have a referral, using your network of relationships, described earlier (chapter 9).

Here is what you might say:

> "My name is ———. I was referred by ———, who suggested you might be agreeable to talking with me about your work. I'm new to this field and I'm seeking information about what this field is like. I'd be interested in talking with you briefly, no more than twenty to thirty minutes. Could we arrange a time that is agreeable to you?"

Keep your request brief. Be prepared to repeat it three or four times—to a receptionist, to a staff person, to a secretary, and others who may pick up the phone before you reach your target person.

Don't be shy about asking. The worst they can do is say no.

Levels of the Information Interview

Information interviews can have different purposes. You should be aware of them, use them all, and state your purpose clearly when you request a meeting with someone. The purpose of your interview will vary according to the amount of information you already have. You will probably do Level 1 interviews before you move on to Level 2, etc. However, it is not necessary to reach Level 5 in order to begin having job interviews. You may reach Level 2, 3, or 4 and feel you are ready. Use these various levels as they suit your particular situation.

✦ Level 1: Background Research on a Field of Work

This type of information interview is used when you know very little about a field or an industry and are deciding if you want to get serious about pursuing this kind of work. Use it to learn about work responsibilities, lifestyles, work conditions, and so on; to learn as much as possible while accumulating acquaintances from people in that field. Interviews for this purpose should be started many months before you intend actively to pursue a change of employment. You will have many of these interviews across a long period of time.

Certain behaviors are permissible in this type of interview that are ordinarily not desirable in a formal job interview. You may make an appointment on the spot, without the benefit of a previous phone call or contact, if you desire this approach and if the respondent is willing to see you. You may also bring a notepad with you and take notes occasionally, being careful not to let note taking detract from the attention you give the other person.

Typically, you should ask for about twenty to thirty minutes of the person's time. You may well end up with more time than this, if you ask interesting questions and succeed in getting the other person to talk about herself (not hard to accomplish), but you should not make a point of asking for a long meeting.

When you make your initial approach, smile warmly at the receptionist, secretary, or target person. People like friendliness, especially from strangers; it makes the day a little brighter. A good initial approach to the secretary is to say something like, "I need to know more about the organization and its purposes." Act as though you know why you are there, because you do. Do not be timid about your request. If you are confident you know what you want, others will feel comfortable with you; if you are unsure of yourself, they will not be sure why they should want to see you. Let the other person talk as much as possible. Don't try to control the conversation any more than you must in order to ask the questions you desire. Be genuinely interested. Remember that you are talking to a human being who has strong feelings about that work; you must *really want* to hear those feelings. If you are just going through the motions in order to get to someone higher up, the person you are interviewing will sense your insincerity.

When you complete a meeting, always ask the interviewee to refer you to someone else in the field of work, if you are still interested in it.

✦ Level 2: Researching a Type of Organization

The purpose of this method is to investigate a specific type of employer within a field of work. For example, you may want to know about organizations offering services for the mentally retarded, now that a Level 1 interview helped you to become interested in social science. Level 2 interviews are extremely useful. You should do much of your information interviewing at this level, because you can focus on the type of employer you want, without zeroing in on a potential job.

The character of the Level 2 interview is similar to that of Level 1. You are exploring, becoming familiar with the type of organization, and asking the questions that will help you decide where you want to focus your job-search energies:

Does your organization prefer to stay medium sized? If so, why?
How do you locate the students who want internships?
How is your store competing with the larger clothing chains?

Is funding for the agency holding up these days? Where are you seeking sup-
plemental support?

Does an editor's job usually involve acquiring new books as well as editing
them?

✦ Level 3: Finding Out Where the Jobs Might Be

Let's face it. By talking to people, sometimes we're hoping to tap the hidden job
market, find out about those positions that are not advertised but are becoming
available. It is necessary to look for these possibilities because the hidden job
market is a continuing fact of life. Many jobs are publicized only on a limited
basis or not at all. So why don't you just come right out and ask about them?

People do not want to be job exchange bureaus. Remember, in any meeting
you are building a relationship and forming an impression. If I am the person
you're talking to, and I happen to know about some job openings, I may not
want to tell you about them unless I have enough confidence in you that I want
to refer you. The openings I know about are probably connected with friends
of mine. I don't want to waste their time (and perhaps hurt my credibility in
the process) by sending them people of uncertain quality. So, you have to earn
your referral from me, and not ask for it prematurely.

What should you do about all this? First, hope that the person brings it up
himself. If the person likes you, and is impressed by how you have conducted
the interview, he may want to be helpful, and would have every reason to tell
you about places where jobs may be. Often people will be thinking about these
openings when they are talking with you. Even if they don't know about real
live openings, they may suggest places where they judge there are possibilities.
Let them do the suggesting. Don't push it.

Second, if you can't restrain yourself—and sometimes your instincts will
tell you it is all right to ask—wait until the end of your interview and say: "I am
very interested in this field, and think I may look for jobs in it. Could you suggest any places where I might apply?" Once again, don't push this very hard. A
simple prompt may be enough to get a lead or two, if the person knows of any
and wants to give them to you.

✦ Level 4: Exploring a Particular Organization

Usually, once you have done many Level 2 interviews, you will be focusing on
a certain department within an organization because you know the kind of
work you want, and you want to talk with people who do it. At this level, you
usually know a job opening exists or that there is a strong likelihood of one.

You have some interest in applying to this organization, but you would like
to know more about it. You're not sure what the job responsibilities are and

need some insights about how the department functions. Be sure to indicate that you are considering applying for the job, so that you are honest about your purposes. You might ask questions such as:

How does this job fit with the purposes of your department?
What do you hope the person in this job will accomplish?
Which people in your department and organization does this job relate to most often?

You can have a Level 4 interview with any member of the department, not just the person who makes the final decisions. Regardless of whom you talk with, remember that any conversation you have at this level, no matter how informal, will contribute to the impression you make as a prospective job candidate. If an employer agrees to see you for a Level 4 interview, she probably considers it an informal job interview, even though neither of you may refer to it as such.

Level 4 information interviews are often arranged through your friends, professional colleagues, or people who know you well. Typically, it might go this way: You ask around if anyone knows someone who works in the target organization/department. Hopefully, you find a friend who says: "Call ——— over there and ask her if she'd be willing to talk with you. I have known her for years and I think she can give you a few ideas about that department. I'll call her too and let her know she'll be hearing from you." Things won't always work out this well, but you should always be alert for the possibility.

In the absence of such contacts, it is more difficult to get Level 4 interviews. But, if you need more information before you go to the trouble of submitting formal applications, go ahead and request them on your own. One good Level 4 interview can save you a lot of time and make you a better job candidate.

✦ Level 5: Talking with Decision Makers

This level of information interview has been widely recommended as a means for getting the closest possible look at a job, prior to a job interview. At Level 5, you seek a meeting with the person who has the power to hire and ask him questions about the job. It can be valuable to have such Level 5 interviews, and often it is possible to arrange them. However, employers are increasingly resistant to them, because they cannot accommodate the large numbers of information interviewers, and because often they would prefer to do their evaluating during the selection process. Sometimes they even regard such requests as an intrusion, so you have to be careful whom you approach and how at Level 5. Here are the main cautions:

1. If you are considering applying for the job, be sure to say so.

2. Once again, working through friends is the preferred method. You're more likely to get a Level 5 interview if you call and say: "———— suggested I contact you . . ."

3. If you don't have any connection to the decision maker, just tell her: "I have done a lot of research on your department and the specific job, but I still have some questions I have not been able to answer and thought you could help me." Be prepared to explain what research you have done, if you are asked.

Most people who make hiring decisions are aware that a Level 5 interview closely resembles a job interview, even though you do not call it by that name. When you ask to meet with them informally, if they accept, they will regard it as a chance to get acquainted with you. That's fine, but you should proceed with your agenda for an information interview. Of course, if you are asked questions about yourself, be ready to answer them. If the decision maker decides to make it an informal job interview, that is her choice, and you must be ready to flow with it.

An interview at this level may be a way to stand out from the pack. If you can get in to see the decision maker—and otherwise you would have been just a name on a piece of paper—then anything you accomplish here might give you an edge over the other applicants. So, in a competitive situation, it is worth the effort. In many cases, the decision maker will appreciate your self-initiating and will judge that as a measure of your motivation. Level 5 interviews don't always happen, but you should definitely try to arrange them.

Guidelines for Using the Information Interview to Your Best Advantage

We are not dealing with a new concept anymore, one that other job seekers will be unaware of. The word is out, and everyone is using this method to get an edge. Hence, you must extract the best results from the information interview and take care to avoid its pitfalls. You can stay well ahead of the competition if you use it wisely, because so many people abuse the concept and make bad impressions when they are trying to gain an advantage.

Here are seven key guidelines for before, during, and after the information interview, which will enable you to develop a valuable pool of information and obtain a lot of personal support along the way:

1. *Don't be overly assertive.* Tact and diplomacy go a long way. You are asking for a person's valuable work time. Don't regard getting in as the main goal. You may get in the door through manipulating a secretary or catching a person

at a weak moment, but if you are too insistent about it, the person you interview will undoubtedly remember to forget you.

2. *Be interested in the person you're talking with.* There is a tendency among information interviewers to regard the person they're talking with as "one more name and face to connect with, so I can move on toward my goal." People you interview may feel you are using them to get to someone else. Each individual wants to be valued for him/herself, not just be another connection in a string of electric lights leading to your job interview. Genuineness goes a long way in this game, and rushing through an interview to get a connection or a key fact will not make a good impression for you. Don't follow the example of one job seeker I know who said to a person at a conference cocktail party: "It's been nice getting a few names from you but excuse me, I've got to keep networking now."

3. *Be open about everything you are doing.* Don't mislead anyone about what you are up to. If you want to know who the decision maker is in a particular department, because you plan to call there, then say so. If you have already applied for a particular job, but are still seeking information about it (which is legitimate), then tell the person you are a candidate. If you withhold some information or lie about something, it will probably come back to haunt you. Any hint of sneakiness in the job-search process will undo much of the progress you are making because an employer will regard you as untrustworthy.

4. *Be willing to talk with someone else, when you cannot see the person you asked for.* Often you will ask to interview a person who is not available. In most cases, there are other people in that department or organization who can be helpful to you. If you do not know their names, say: "I would like to know more about the ———— functions in this department. Is anyone available who could talk with me?" Any interview that you have is valuable. Especially at Levels 1 and 2, it is not crucial that you talk with particular people to get general information about a field or an organization. Even at Levels 3, 4, and 5, if the target person cannot be seen (as is often the case), then talk with anyone who can give you some time. Pleasant surprises happen this way. You meet someone who works closely with the target person, and you may accomplish as much as if you had met with your original target.

5. *Tell the person how he/she has helped you.* Anyone you interview may want to keep track of how your job search is going. We're all curious to see how the story turns out. As you proceed in your search, call back the people you interviewed and tell them how it is going, and what they told you that was especially useful. You can also offer such feedback during the information interview itself: "What you have told me about the company structure, and the way you handle multiple orders, is very revealing. It helped me to see that . . ."

People like to know that their words have been heard and have had an effect. Don't assume they know this. Tell them. Often this can be accomplished with a personal thank-you note, but you can also telephone a person to express your thanks or even stop by to see them if the organization is a more informal one.

6. *Use the telephone when they cannot see you in person.* A telephone interview is not a waste of time. A few questions on the phone can save you and them a lot of time. Once again, it helps to have a referral: "——— recommended that I call you." Be sensitive to the person's telephone availability: "Is this a good time to ask you just two questions, or would you rather I call later?"

7. *Sample widely.* Every time you interview individuals about their work, you run the risk that what they tell you will be biased, colored by the particular lenses through which they see the situation. Therefore, you must sample as widely as possible among people who work in your field of interest. Take special care to include some of each of the following:

+ Happy workers—people who are pleased with what they are doing
+ Unhappy workers—people who are dissatisfied with the nature of the work itself
+ People who have different frames of reference toward their work, perhaps because of their previous work history

11

Don't Make the Five Most Common Networking Mistakes

Like any good idea, the personal referral network—often called networking or making contacts—has been overused, overdone, overbaked, and its users often complain it is underproductive. "I have loads of contacts, but they don't seem to lead anywhere." "I network all the time, but I am just not meeting the right people."

Contacts are necessary to any effective job search, but you cannot build an entire strategy around them. People will not hire you just because you know them or happen to have wangled an interview with them. The misuse of networking is evident in these problems:

+ People try to make networking a substitute for competence.
+ Networking has the potential of becoming a king-sized nuisance, and the people who overuse it are quickly labeled pests.
+ We have taken innocent human interchange and raised it to the level of a high art, thereby destroying its spontaneity and making it more difficult for everyone. People who become contacts now wonder: "Who is this person talking to me and for what reasons?"

Networking functions best when it is part of a daily routine, not when it is used all at once and must carry the burden of a hurry-up job search. Too much reliance upon contacts can become offensive to those who are being tapped. A personal referral network should occur naturally, not by brute force.

Some job hunters follow the motto "Take the contact and run" in their rush to keep moving toward their goals. They get referrals but they do not produce results. Why not? Because often they have "turned off" the contact by their methods.

The key here is credibility. If I do not know enough about you, or you don't stop long enough to tell me, or you ask me for more than is appropriate for a relative stranger, I will give you a referral with little enthusiasm, or give you a contact of little value, or give you nothing at all. Why would I act this way? Because I do not want to lose credibility among *my* contacts. I have more at stake with these contacts than you do. I want to refer only those people who will present themselves well.

Unfortunately, networking has been unfairly lumped with a lot of greed-is-good behaviors exhibited by job seekers in the eighties and nineties. No matter how it is misused by self-centered job hunters, networking is still a vital part of the job search and is quite enjoyable when done right. The following guidelines will enable you to maximize your gains from networking and avoid the ways it has been done selfishly and superficially.

Here are the five most common networking mistakes, and what you can do about them:

1. Networking on the Fly

Job hunters make the same mistake with networking that they do with résumés—they go for volume, assuming that more is better. They try to rack up as many contacts as possible, figuring that it improves their odds. They rush from one information interview to another. This approach is almost guaranteed to alienate people. When you're in a hurry, your respondents know it, and they feel "used." More is less and less is more. Aim for fewer contacts of greater quality. Try to get as much time with a person as you can, without overstaying your welcome. Do your homework before arriving. Know as much as you can about the person and the company.

An initial contact is the potential beginning of an ongoing connection, not a race to see how fast you can get to the next referral. Sure, time is precious and you are eager to find out how to qualify for your target career, but you'll only get that information when some rapport and trust develop between you and the other person.

2. Expecting Too Much Too Soon

Nobody's going to tell you everything you want to know just because you dress right, smile, and are eager. They're looking you over, even though it's an informal conversation. They're trying to gauge the depth of your motivation, find evidence that you're really serious, signs that you're working on some of the skills you'll need in this field.

In preliminary information interviews, you can be fairly naive, because you're just getting started. But once you've been out there a while, each contact is deciding just how much attention to give you. Here's how to get considerable attention without overstepping: (a) Ask questions that you're pretty sure the person can answer; (b) Indicate how the information will be helpful to you; (c) Ask open-ended questions such as:

+ "What do you think I ought to know at this point?"
+ "How would you suggest I best prepare myself for entry into this field?"
+ "Based on what we've talked about so far, what do you think my next steps should be?"

In other words, you're letting the "contact" decide what she wants to tell you.

People can give you a lot of information about succeeding in their fields, but they won't give it all at once, because they don't know you well enough and it takes more time than they have in one meeting. As you and your "contact" have more than one meeting, trust develops between you and the advice becomes more detailed and complete. Without this relationship-building over time, contacts can often be superficial.

3. Job Seeking Masquerading as Information Interviewing

This is the most common blunder. Job searchers hope that their contacts will reveal job vacancies. They're impatient with "merely" gathering information; they want to fast-forward their job hunts by leaping into available positions.

Why this is a bad approach: (a) It is dishonest. If you misrepresent yourself, the respondent will resist considering you for any job. If you mislead a "contact" into thinking you want only information, when you're really salivating about possible job openings, how can they trust you? (b) You short-circuit your ability to find out if *you* want that kind of work; you need that information before you decide where you want to use your talents; (c) The "contact" feels pressured to give you something she probably cannot provide. That ruins the atmosphere of mutual exchange.

I know what you're thinking. Real, "live" jobs are sometimes revealed during information interviews. It happens, so why shouldn't you hope for it, long for it? Yes, you may hear about jobs "by surprise," especially if you're developing a comfortable connection with the person. I would recommend that you respond this way:

"I appreciate knowing you have a job opportunity, but I'm still in the information-gathering stage. How may I contact you if I determine that this work would fit my goals?"

You could rush to judgment, and say instead: "Sounds great to me. When do I start?" But you'll be making your choice prematurely and are likely to make a mistake. The purpose of networking is for you to make the best choice possible, not grab the first thing that comes along.

4. Not Enough Attention to Learning Objectives

Naive networkers make the mistake of forgetting about their learning objectives. Networking helps to inform you about the skills you need to acquire and improve in order to be successful in a target career. This may be the most important reason to do information interviewing. You should ask the "contact":

"What skills are most important to being effective in this field?"

Her answers will give you important guidelines about where to put your energy for future development.

You may believe that you already have the skills you need for a given job, but don't be so sure until you've asked the above question to a number of experienced people. By asking "What do I need to work on to be really good in this field?" you demonstrate a certain humility, and that's not a bad thing. Even if you already are chock-full of skills, admitting room for improvement is an attitude that wears well.

5. Ignoring the "Give-back" Dimension

By the time you start job hunting, you're already in a hurry and wanting to make something happen—fast. This means you're probably highly focused on your favorite subject—yourself. You may tend to believe that the total focus of the job search is you. It's so obvious, why do I need to say it? Because the self-centered approach is misguided.

Once again, be careful of leaving a person feeling "used." The person you're interviewing did not wake up in the morning saying: "My number one goal today is to see what I can do for the person who will be information interviewing me." No, he had a few other things on his mind. You can't solve his problems, but you *can* ask yourself:

"I wonder what I can do for him while I'm asking him to be helpful to me."

Helping is usually best when it's a mutual exchange. Here are some ways that you might be useful to the person whom you're asking for information: (a) Tell them your impressions of other companies or employers you've visited; (b) Give them information about articles you've read that might be of interest; (c) Suggest courses you're taking that might be of value to their employees; (d) Offer to work as a volunteer, for whatever time each week or month you may have available; volunteer to help on a particular project or work team.

It's a give-back world out there. Why would someone want to grant one information interview after another and get nothing in return? After a while, the interview-giver feels drained. People notice genuine acts of giving that have substance. Not pandering or superficial gestures, but giving value—ideas, information, or resources. View networking as a chain of opportunities for people to help each other—the proverbial two-way street.

In Conclusion

Avoid the five most common networking mistakes:

1. *Networking on the fly.* Don't do superficial networking; it will be quickly detected and will work against you.

2. *Expecting too much too soon.* Don't ask for more than is willingly given; pushiness can quickly turn a positive interview into a negative one.

3. *Job seeking masquerading as information interviewing.* If you're saying one thing and doing another, it will quickly turn against you.

4. *Not enough attention to learning objectives.* Networking should be focused on what you need to learn to enter and succeed in a given career field.

5. *Ignoring the give-back dimension.* If you view giving as a two-way street, you'll be alert for opportunities to be helpful to people who are helping you in your networking.

12

Use the Walk-In Method

The Walk-In Method involves seeking interviews by approaching a place of business without an appointment. This would seem to be contrary to all the "rules" of workplace protocol. Why, then, would I recommend it? Because of directness and the advantages of face-to-face contact. It increases the chances that you will be "in the right place at the right time."

Hiring has a lot of bureaucratic procedures, because employers don't know very much about their job candidates. Most often the hiring process involves strangers hiring strangers. You can help make a bureaucratic experience into a more human and personal one by seeking to meet people on a walk-in basis.

One More Arrow in Your Quiver

Walking in gives you a different way to access employers. In cases where your efforts on the telephone or by other methods are being thwarted, you may appreciate this untraditional approach.

Walking in will not always get you in to see people. But if you present yourself well (using the suggestions in this chapter), someone will very often talk with you. And you won't be handcuffed to the telephone all day. If a walk-in gets you in to see someone four times out of ten, who cares about the other six?

Let's look at each argument against walking in, and then propose a counter-argument:

✦ "Business people expect to have appointments. If you arrive without an appointment, you're intruding on their busy time."

You may not be asking to see a specific person. You will talk to anyone in the department. Even in a busy office, there may be someone who will talk with you. Don't go to the Human Resources Department, because they will route you into the bureaucratic mill. Instead, go to the department where you want to work.

+ "You may be wasting your time if everyone is occupied."

Even if you "only" talk to the receptionist, you have not wasted your time. She is a gatekeeper who can help you to see someone the next time you call or come in person.

+ "You are breaking the rules of acceptable job hunting."

Not everyone plays by the same rules. The smaller, more informal employers are more open to drop-ins. Some businesses are accustomed to a lot of traffic. They talk to anyone who is there.

+ "Even if you get someone's time, it will only be a few minutes."

Maybe, maybe not. A new face is often interesting in a day of the same old faces. Sometimes a few minutes can turn into an hour. Regardless of the time, you have made an impression, and when you call that person on the phone, they will remember you.

+ "You really should do it the right way (by phoning for an appointment), or else they won't respect you."

Some employers respect the person who is assertive, even bold in her approach. If you want a job, show it by showing up.

Walking in is especially useful if you have been frustrated by the telephone approach. On the phone you're a disembodied voice they've never heard before. It's easy for them to regard you as a nonperson. You may suffer through endless phone menus and voice mail. Even when you reach a real person, they pass you off like a football to someone else. You're just another "job applicant," not a face or a whole person. Another name to be filed away. Maybe they'll return your call and maybe they won't.

When the phone wastes half your day, don't turn to the letter-writing option. Put on your suit, gather up your courage, and go for the walk-in.

You'll learn how to approach people. They don't bite. They usually don't even scratch. Try three days of job hunting going cold turkey regarding the telephone or any other technology, and instead do just walk-ins.

Renfru wanted a job in a magic shop in the worst way. But he didn't know any magic. And he didn't know how to get started. Worst of all, Renfru was stymied by the telephone. He hated trying to explain himself without looking at someone. People sounded so official and imposing on the phone; they intimidated him. If only they'd give him a chance.

Desperate times breed desperate behavior. So Renfru decided to use the head-on approach. "What do I have to lose?" Renfru lived in Harrisburg, Pennsylvania, but went to nearby Reading, where he didn't know anyone. "At least I won't run into someone I know," he thought. He walked into and out of five magic shops until he got the courage to approach the owner of the sixth one: "I'd like to work here. I don't know anything about magic, but I've worked in stores before." The shop had an opening for a stock boy, but they had not advertised because they wanted to see who would show up.

Walking in may seem bold, but it can be done with low-key approaches that suggest natural curiosity rather than audacity:

"I'm new in town and your company's advertisements intrigued me. What kinds of people do you hire?"

"I'm looking for a beginning job at a radio station where I can apply my research skills. What are your needs for research?"

Helen wanted a job at Massive Insurance Company, but she had not obtained any interviews by telephone. The marbled, twenty-foot-high front of the building scared her. "No more funds in my bank account. The biggest employer in town. I have one interview suit and no interviews. They can't reject me any more than they already have. What do I have to lose?" Helen got on the elevator as though she were employed there, and approached four different receptionists at four different departments. The last one gave her a tumble.

HELEN: "I'd like to talk with someone about a clerical job. Hire me for a day. I can show you how well I work."

RECEPTIONIST: "Who would you like to talk with?"

HELEN: "Anyone who needs clerical help."

RECEPTIONIST: "We just lost two staff people and they're giving *me* all the paperwork. I'm going to get you in to see someone. . . . Do you want to talk with Mr. Inkblot?"

HELEN: "I'd be happy to."

In general, I recommend walking in as an alternative to telephoning, for these five reasons:

1. Sometimes your efforts to make appointments by phone will yield minimal results. If you have sent your résumé and it looks different than what they think they're looking for, you may be dismissed or disregarded.

2. A face-to-face contact with anyone in the office is a chance to begin a personal connection. You're a person, you have a smile, you look enthusiastic, and you're willing to put yourself forward. These are qualities of good employees, and you can demonstrate them on the spot.

3. YOU'RE THERE. If the employer has any need at all to see job candidates (maybe somebody just resigned ten minutes ago; this morning; yesterday), you've already bypassed the usual procedures, you're available, and you can talk to them right now, thus saving them the time of advertising and all the other recruitment procedures.

4. Many people are better in person than on the telephone. You may be one of them. It gives you a chance to show your more complete self. By engaging them in conversation, they get a feeling for what you would be like as part of the office team.

5. Another benefit of walking in is that job hunters find their confidence and strength growing by repeatedly approaching people and getting past their fears about being intimidated.

Walking in will work better with some employers than with others. The smaller and more informal a company, the more likely someone may talk with you. Nonetheless, you should not rule out any large employer, even those with imperious-looking receptionists, huge wooden doors, and decor like that of the Taj Mahal. People are people. If they like you, they can invite you to talk with them.

It is hard to predict exactly where the Walk-In Method will work best, because there is a lot of chance involved. Be willing to accept some risk. If people are not available or even occasionally are rude, just roll with it. That's the price of admission.

Walking in is especially good for jobs that have a lot of public contact. By being present, you pass the first hurdle right there, which puts you ahead of those who are calling on the phone. Your initial contact is thus the beginning of a job interview.

Avoiding or Minimizing Negative Consequences

There will be those who say walking in leads to bad outcomes. You may be considered "rude." You may be turned away and feel even more rejected than if you had telephoned.

Try out your walk-in skills first on some low-threat employers whom you really don't care about. Dress appropriately. Make your "bad impressions" on some practice employers. Each time you do it, you'll be more comfortable, more authentic, and more coherent.

You'll often get some initial resistance. Flow with it. They don't yet know you're for real and sincere. If they act as though you're being intrusive, say:

"I'm so interested in your company that I wanted to see it firsthand. I also know it's hard to get an appointment, so I thought the direct approach would be better. I did not intend to be rude."

There will be people who say that walking in may do more harm than good. I doubt that. Consider this rationale:

They're not calling you back for interviews. If you think you're getting the runaround on the phone, you may be. Perhaps your past experience is not getting their attention, because it's different from the requirements for the job for which you're applying. "On paper" you don't look like the person they want, but you think you can sell yourself if given a chance.

You can't afford to let them screen you out before they've met you. In person, say to the receptionist:

"I know I can do this job. Can you help me to see Ms. Winspiggle for just ten minutes? I can explain how my background will help your company." (Later, in chapters 25–29, you'll learn how to do this; right now you're just getting in the door.)

Face-to-face contact allows opportunities for "personal chemistry" to take place. There is always some chance that when you walk in, you may have a "lucky" encounter with the manager or someone else of importance in the company. Careers have started with conversations like this. It may be better than the grinding experience of submitting paperwork and trying to pass screening criteria.

At the very least, many face-to-face contacts will probably improve your chances of getting an interview later on the telephone, because you can ask for the receptionist or person whom you met in person. You've jumped from non-person to real person just by having been there.

Here's How to Use the Walk-In Method

1. Identify a company that interests you and have an approximate idea of the jobs that interest you.

2. Reconnaissance: If possible, go there and look around before you request any in-person meetings. Get a feeling for the atmosphere of the workplace, observe the expressions on people's faces, look for symbols of what's important there (signs, structures, etc.).

3. Dress up: Wear a good suit, even if they dress casually at the workplace. Dressing up communicates that you're serious. People always notice this and will treat you with respect.

4. Introduce yourself to the receptionist or anyone you first encounter. If you want an information interview, say:

> "My name is Melvin Dradnatz. I'm interested in the kinds of work people do at this company. May I speak with anyone who can tell me what you look for in job candidates?"

> "Hello, my name is Samantha Speezle. I'm looking into this field and your company has been well recommended. May I talk with someone about the nature of your public-contact jobs?"

5. If you're seeking job interviews, you might say something like this:

> "I believe I have computational and research skills that would fit some jobs here at Indefatigable Exercise Equipment Company. To whom might I talk about my qualifications?"

> "I have worked in recreation before, and I'd like to apply for a job in the Roman Coliseum Rancho Cucamunga Hotel. Maybe my circus background might help. Whom could I talk to?"

In Conclusion

Walking in is not the method you should use exclusively, but it has its merits. At the very least, use it in combination with the more customary telephone approaches. In the broadest sense, walking in allows you to begin practicing your interview skills.

Even if you find walking in scary at first, after you do it a while, you'll look forward to it. You'll gain much confidence from enlarging the circle of people who know you, and you'll be more at ease when you introduce yourself to people in other offices.

13

Take Advantage of Interim Jobs

An *interim job* can be defined as work that provides you with regular income at a level that permits financial survival. You accept this job as a stopgap, not intending to stay in this line of work on a permanent basis.

Let's suppose you're doing your networking, doing your research, working diligently to move ever closer to your job goal, but it takes time. You trudge home every night and nobody's hired you yet. It's this day-to-day scenario that drains the energy from job hunters and leaves them wondering, "When will it happen?" In the meantime, the best thing you can do is latch on to interim jobs.

An interim is time between something you're leaving and something you're moving toward. Shouldn't this period be hastened through as quickly as possible? Not necessarily.

Interim jobs are natural parts of any job or career search. You'll do much better by having them than not having them, because they are transition zones while you maneuver from one sphere of the world of work to another.

What are some immediate reasons for having interim jobs? The most obvious reason is to earn money. Debt puts on pressure, and more pressure is *not* what you need. But interim jobs are more useful than that. Don't knock them. They give you breathing room while you're in pursuit of your career, time to carefully explore and consider what you want your career to be, and time to find the people and organizations who want you.

Careers May Happen While You're Making Other Plans

Let's look at a few examples. Arthur Conan Doyle wanted all his life to be a great playwright. He began writing Sherlock Holmes stories to earn money while he nurtured his more serious literary ambitions. Holmes became so popular that the adoring public wouldn't let Conan Doyle stop writing the Holmes mysteries. He tried to end the series by killing Holmes at Reichenbach Falls, but the public's clamor convinced Conan Doyle to bring Holmes back to life.

Rod Serling also wanted to be a great playwright. He began writing *The Twilight Zone* as an income-earning way station. It became so popular that it provided him an abundance of income, recognition, and popularity (in TV reruns) that is living well beyond his untimely death in 1975.

Dineh Mohajer was a student at UCLA and decided to mix up a few batches of nail polish to match her dress. She soon was selling the polish at tony L.A. boutiques. Her "interim" source of income soon took on a life of its own, and today Hard Candy is a very profitable company and Mohajer's earlier career as a biochemistry major has been shelved.

Have you ever had a job—summer, part-time, volunteer, or otherwise—that turned out to be much more than you expected? You clicked with the people and the tasks were more intriguing than you ever imagined they would be? Is it sheer luck that such a thing happens? Often it's more than luck. Perhaps you're drawn to this endeavor unconsciously. Or it gives you the opportunity to try new skills that you didn't think you could develop.

Sometimes we don't find jobs. They find us. If a job possibility crosses your path, or someone is trying to talk you into something, or you just "happen to" hear about a job that sounds, well, interrresting, pay attention to these things. The universe may be sending you a message, and perhaps you would do well to listen.

When successful and satisfied people are asked "How did you get into your line of work?" a very common answer is: "I just fell into it." In many cases, these people were attracted unconsciously to their fields of work and they chose not to resist. Wise choices.

Seven Guidelines for Interim Jobs

1. *Don't hide in your room.* Don't go into hibernation waiting for your dream job to appear. Staying hidden will probably lead you to be depressed and lose confidence. You need contact with people, and the handiest way to get it is by working. Closet walls don't carry on a good conversation; you need human contact like your body needs water.

2. *What skills might you learn in an interim job that you can use later?* Look for interim jobs that call on you to develop and improve important skills, especially those you may need in your long-range career. Selling, public relations, research, writing, interpreting statistics, and public speaking are just a few of the "transferable skills" that you can use to promote yourself for future jobs.

3. *Imagine how the job you're doing might metamorphose into a "surprise" career opportunity.* Suppose you're feeding the animals at the zoo. Might they have an intern program for future zoo administrators? Suppose you're a bank teller. Is there a financial management role in your future? Are you working in the college bookstore and you're visited by book publisher representatives? Might you want to be one of those "college travelers" yourself?

4. *Don't limit your interim jobs to those that are related to your intended career field.* In fact, deliberately look outside of your field. Let your intuition lead you to places you would not otherwise "think" of going. Be quietly curious. Consider a job just because it "feels" interesting.

5. *Treat any interim job as though it were your sixth-grade report card.* Use the job to get a reading on yourself. If you were your teacher, how would you grade yourself? What comments would you make? "Listens well"? . . . "Talks too much"? . . . "Shows leadership . . . shows creativity . . . mixes well with others"? . . . "Learns new tasks easily"? . . . "Does more than asked for"?

6. *Don't be embarrassed.* By doing interim jobs, you are being more constructive than many job hunters, who hang up the phone, curse at the mailbox, and bemoan the unfairness of it all. Some work is better than no work. You're in the ballpark. You're using what's presently available to grow into future opportunities.

7. *Maybe you'll gain another glowing recommendation.* It may not be the job you want long range, but the interim job gives you an opportunity to be praised for your work habits, your "teamwork" skills, and your dedication to the job. Sometimes a recommendation like this can make a big difference, because employers are always looking for evidence of your recent work history.

One Person's Siberia Is Another Person's Interim Job

His friends all called him Igloo, but his real name was Milton Pearl. Ice fishing he would go, mother told him No, he moved to North Dakota where he could roll around in snow. Igloo wanted to work in the Arctic Circle, but he couldn't find any jobs there. What to do in the meantime? He started a towing business for stalled motorists on the North Dakota highways. Subzero all the time! Eventually, Igloo met some members of an Arctic research team. He had no trouble convincing them he could withstand the hardships of the weather.

Everything you do is an "interim job." Every job leads to the next one. And each job has seeds that are planted in the one that follows. Even jobs you hate have skills that are useful to you. Maybe especially the jobs you hate, because you developed certain skills in self-defense to survive in that job.

You didn't like that job at the bank because there were so many regulations and you were always getting tangled in them. But you learned how to cope smoothly in a bureaucracy and how to get yourself out of trouble by being patient and respectful to everyone else caught in the same web. You may not take a job in a bank again, but you'll know how to deal with banks when your company does business with them.

Interim Jobs Unrelated to Career Goals

If your immediate income needs are not large, there are many interim jobs you can consider that provide relatively easy entry, moderate work demands, and exposure to a wide variety of people. While you are not likely to consider many of these jobs as serious career options, you should examine them first because they make minimum demands upon you other than your devoting the requisite number of hours. They therefore provide the best conditions in which you can save energy for the continuation of your serious career exploration. The jobs listed below[1] also offer you relatively good access to large numbers of people in a variety of work situations.

+ *Census taker.* Collecting information most people consider nonthreatening gives you the opportunity to talk with many people about their work.

+ *Opinion poll interviewer.* Same as above, with even more opportunity because polls are growing in use and acceptance.

+ *Commuter train conductor.* Plenty of opportunity to talk with commuters about their jobs as they ride to and from work.

+ *Retail store clerk.* Especially in a bookstore, cigar store, clothing store, or drugstore, people often have time to chat and provide insights into the work they do.

+ *Cabdriver.* Repeated chances to pick up valuable clues about various professions; businesspeople often chat with cabdrivers.

+ *Marketing research interviewer.* Obtain product preference information and, in the process, ask people about their work situation.

+ *Bartender.* Perhaps the ideal opportunity to listen to people when they are relaxed.

+ *Museum guard.* Chance to observe and talk to a variety of people.

+ *Security guard.* If you can overcome the barrier of the uniform, there are plenty of people to talk with.

+ *Golf caddy.* People who have the time and inclination to play this game usually have rather interesting professions and often depend on you for conversation.

+ *Short-order cook.* People are more agreeable when they are being fed, and you would probably serve them at lunchtime, between halves of their working day.

+ *Comparison shopper.* You get exposure to a lot of people by visiting a number of stores each day.

+ *Receptionist.* You are the first person to meet people who visit the organization. Choose an organization inhabited by employees or customers you would like to meet.

+ *Employment agency interviewer.* A good way to learn about job availability from an insider's vantage point.

+ *Travel agent.* Everyone travels at one time or another, often for the purpose of looking for a new job.

+ *Advertising space salesperson.* Sell space in newspapers, on radio, in trade magazines, on TV to a wide range of organizations.

+ *Mail carrier.* A vital service and an opportunity to visit homes, businesses, stores, government offices, churches, hospitals.

+ *Handyman.* Offer a maintenance or repair service for homeowners and you will have a chance to visit with many people about their jobs.

Temporary Work

Temp work is now a full-fledged industry. There are many opportunities for you within the temp work field to have interim jobs. This is an all-purpose interim job most widely available in metropolitan areas, but also in areas of smaller population. Temp work may be the all-time champ for giving you a chance to sample a variety of work situations, because you can work for a few days or weeks for various employers in different settings.

Temp work is a fine way to sample the work environment of several different companies and industries. Temporary work is available for a wide range of positions today, including many professional positions (law, accounting, health professionals, etc.).

The Texas Two-Step

The two-step approach to job hunting means looking for one job to set up another, especially when the desired job is blocked for the time being. Dancing across the job landscape, you may find that two steps are better than one. In some cases, an interim job can be used as a bridge toward your target job.

Being in the right place at the right time is often a matter of *putting* yourself in the right places—

* allowing others to see the work you can do;
* working for people who know people in your target organizations;
* being there to hear about emerging opportunities.

The interim job can allow you to position yourself:

> *Example:* Angela has her sights set on being head trainer for the Women's Athletics Department. She takes a part-time job as staff writer, research assistant, and general helper for the department, gets to know the staff, and volunteers to be there at ball games to help with equipment. One thing leads to another, and guess who hears about an opening for assistant athletic trainer when it occurs?

An Interim Job Is Not a Comedown

After years of successful and responsible work as a ———, you may be embarrassed to say you're now doing work that has less of everything. Or after years of expensive and ambitious schooling, you don't want to admit that you've taken a low-level job. It looks to all the world as though you have settled for less.

But what do they know? The truth is you have made a smart move. By taking the interim job, you're giving your career more time to develop at its own speed. You're moving to the place you want instead of moaning and dying on the vine back there in East Overburn. You're moving into scoring position.

Instead of waiting to be discovered, you're making a daring chess move, one step closer to your goal. Seeing the job market as a board game, you look for an opening that will position you to create an even bigger opening in the future. Sound clever? Well, it is.

> *Example:* Ann took a job as a desk clerk at Hotels International when she could not get hired as an assistant manager. The pay was awful, the clientele overbearing, and the sight of her friends registering at the hotel was almost more than she could stand. But a manager noticed her efforts on behalf of important guests, and she became first in line for the management training program. During the interim, Ann had also taken computer skills courses and public speaking courses to sharpen her qualifications for the opportunity she knew would develop eventually. Without the interim job she would have been a less qualified candidate.

Interim jobs thus serve both short-term economic needs and long-term career development needs. For people who are making any significant change of career direction, or shift of location, or movement from school to the marketplace, an interim job is a good strategy, not simply for its immediate benefits but also for the positioning and personal growth that it makes possible. Instead of rushing headlong toward your new goal, and perhaps stumbling along the way, taking an interim job may be a sensible and productive first step that becomes a bridge to your longer-range objective.

14

Use the Library and the Internet

Job seeking can be a war of paper airplanes. Your paper credentials—résumés and the like—are pitted against the employer's paper job requirements. Read what the organizations have to say about themselves and turn their words to your advantage. You can demonstrate your devotion and good intentions with substantive knowledge instead of repeating a tired litany: "I wanna work here; I wanna work here."

The knowledge you get from printed materials enables you to do a crucial thing: to act like a professional. When you are seeking entry to a profession, it helps to adopt the attitude that you already *are* in that profession; to regard yourself not as an outsider, but as a person who has decided this field is the right one. Your research is the first step in establishing your right to be regarded as a respected member of the group. Though you may not yet have the credentials, degrees, or other imprimatur for that profession, you can behave as though you *will* be so accredited one day; it's just a matter of time. Your attitude will influence others' behavior toward you and the seriousness with which they respond to your requests. Therefore, the research skill is important because it is an opportunity to demonstrate that you are so serious about your future work that you will devote time to becoming better informed.

How to Research an Occupational Field

Any one or more of these sources is handy for researching an occupational field:

Professional Organizations. See the *Encyclopedia of Associations* for whichever group pertains to your interest. Write to this group and ask for printed literature. It will be pleased to honor your request, because it exists for the purpose of promoting its profession to you and others.

Local Societies. Many areas of work have their local societies as well as their national groups. Ask anyone in town who does this kind of work where the local group keeps its library materials.

Book References. Books in Print is available in any library or bookstore. It lists all the books written lately, organized by subject, author, and title. You can find in it a listing of books on the occupational topic you seek to research.

Periodical References. The *Reader's Guide to Periodical Literature*, the *New York Times Index*, and the *Wall Street Journal Index* are three standard reference works available in any library. They allow you to research magazine and newspaper articles pertaining to your subject area. If you are focusing on pharmaceutical companies, for example, use the *Reader's Guide* or the *New York Times Index* to tell you all the articles that have been written lately about drugs, drug abuse, pharmacology, and so on.

Join the Professional Group. Perhaps the best way to act like a professional is to join the professional society itself, so that you can attend conferences, correspond with members, receive journals, and be eligible for in-service training workshops.

If you seek employment in private industry, cultivate the habit of reading one or more of these publications: the *Wall Street Journal, U.S. News & World Report, Fortune* magazine, *Business Week*, and *Money* magazine. All these journals and others are directly involved in telling you about *change*, the shifts in human behavior and attitude that have implications for the marketplace. If you come across an article titled "Population Shifts to the Sunbelt Region," for instance, you can conclude that more jobs will be available in the southeastern and southwestern states. "Physical Fitness Activity Upsurge" may indicate that leisure industries that market fitness equipment can expect to prosper. "Water Problems in the Nation's Rivers" implies that scientists will be needed to improve water testing and control indiscriminate use.

How to Research a Specific Organization

To research a specific employer, these sources of published information are most readily available:

Annual Reports. The first source you should seek is the annual report of the company or organization, because it offers a summary of all the operations for the year, products involved, highlight events, and names of key personnel, plus budgetary data you may want to see.

Organization Chart. This chart shows all the departments and how they report and relate to each other. If it does not appear in the annual report or any of the other company publications, call the public relations office of the company and ask if one is available. If not, ask one of your personal referrals to see whether he or she can get you a copy.

Stock Reports. This is a more unbiased source of information and is available at any stockbroker's office for an organization that is publicly owned. Several research services provide the brokers with data that can help you analyze the company's potential for growth, stability, and other relevant factors.

Library References. The *Reader's Guide*, the *New York Times Index*, and the *Wall Street Journal Index* can help you locate quickly and easily stories that have been written about an individual company, government agency, or other employer, provided the employer is prominent enough to rate news space.

House Publications. While you are asking for annual reports and the like, request a copy of the organization's in-house newspaper or magazine, which gives inside stories about company operations that are more up to date than what appears in an annual report.

Public Relations Office. Ask this office for any other printed materials that can help you. The staff will know about company reports you cannot identify by name, company magazines they would like to send you, and so on.

Local Newspapers. Get in the habit of reading the local paper each day to see whether your prospective employer is mentioned. Perhaps an expansion or maybe a citation by the mayor will appear.

Historical Society. If you are dying to know more about how this organization got started and the library fails you, try whatever historical group there is in town. Such groups sometimes keep documents no one else cares about.

How to Find Out About Specific People

To obtain vital background data on individuals who are employed at your target organizations, especially those who will eventually make the hiring decisions, research these people in any of the following publications: *Who's Who in America; Who's Who in the East, Who's Who in the West,* and so on; *American Men and Women of Science; Directory of American Scholars;* and the professional directories of national professional organizations. The directory of the American Psychological Association, for instance, provides a one-paragraph work history and statement of special interest pertaining to every member of the APA.

Research Is Easy

Why is this skill easy to acquire? Every source mentioned in the previous section—the local library, the stockbroker's office, the public relations office of the company—is easy to find and is staffed by people who usually have a high degree of interest in fulfilling your request. All can be reached by telephone or in person, without a complicated series of maneuvers. In most cases, the data for which you are asking is absolutely free. Most of these places are happy to give their information away, because they often feel it promotes their interests to the public, which is none other than you. And you will find that this is an infectious method, because the more you know about a target employer, the more your appetite will be whetted for additional data.

Looking for Jobs on the Internet

Much of the above research can be done on the Internet. You should use both printed materials and Internet sources, because each has its advantages.

You can use the Internet constructively in these ways: (1) Look at the kinds of jobs in a given industry; obtain information about what the industry is doing, as background for your information interviews. (2) Research a specific employer, what has been written about this company in the commercial press. (3) Research a specific occupation or career; get information about job responsibilities in this career, pay range, training requirements, etc. The latter is available from *The Occupational Outlook Handbook* online.

However, many job hunters have been hoping the Internet would provide lots of job openings online. While job posting sites (among them JobBank USA, America's Job Bank, Career Mosaic, Career Path, CareerNet, JOBTRAK, the Monster Board, and the Online Career Center) can be useful in alerting you to job possibilities, you should not expect too much from them. You should use the many Internet job posting sites and you may find job opportunities online, but you must still practice the principles of in-person "networking" as much as ever. Note the following:

+ When jobs are listed online, thousands of people see them at the same time you do. Therefore, you have a lot of competition.

+ Most employers deliberately do *not* list their job openings on the Internet because they would prefer not to advertise their positions to the whole world.

Dick Bolles, author of the best-selling *1999 What Color Is Your Parachute?*, has written a guide to using the Internet in job hunting for the *Career Planning and Adult Development Network Newsletter* (San Jose, CA). In this guide, Bolles says:

> There are hundreds if not thousands of places that post job vacancies. What you will not believe, until it happens to you, is that it is possible to hunt through all these listings and still not find one job that interests you.[1]
> ("The Internet and the Job Hunt," Part II, p. 6)
> People hoped the Internet would revolutionize the job hunt, and set up one unified job market, one central place, at which we might find a list of all the jobs that are available anywhere in the country. That was the hope.
>
> The reality is that allegedly we now have 11,000 sites on the Internet dealing with jobs or careers. Thus, the Internet has become an electronic version of the scattered, duplicatory, unorganized, Neanderthal job hunting system that we have come to know and love so well. . . .
>
> The more significant problem with job postings on the Internet is how many employers are you getting access to? . . . Well, in one sense it seems like an impressive number—in the thousands or hundreds of thousands currently. But, on the other hand, these represent only a small fraction of the more than 15 million employers out there, in the U.S. alone.
>
> Consequently, you're back to the fact that (as the experts have been saying for decades) 80% of all the jobs available are not on the Internet or anywhere else. They are never advertised.[2]
> ("The Internet and the Job Hunt," Part III, p. 2)

And, I might add, often the 20 percent of jobs advertised are among the less desirable ones because the employers may have exhausted the informal ("hidden") channels where they usually find good applicants.

Sorry to disappoint you, but it's better that you know now and maintain the active (in-person) pursuit of jobs that you're learning in this book.

Computer-related jobs are an exception to all this, because the Internet is the world in which computer people function. But ask your noncomputer friends how many found their jobs online, and you'll see what I mean.

If you expect the Internet to magically produce job openings for you, you will be succumbing to a very passive form of job hunting. As this entire book emphasizes, job hunting is most successful when you seek face-to-face contact to uncover the "hidden job market" and present yourself on the most personal basis possible. The more you unwittingly depend on the impersonal forms of job hunting—sending résumés, using the Internet, and using job listings elsewhere—the less you will devote your active energy to getting out and meeting people, which is where all the action is.

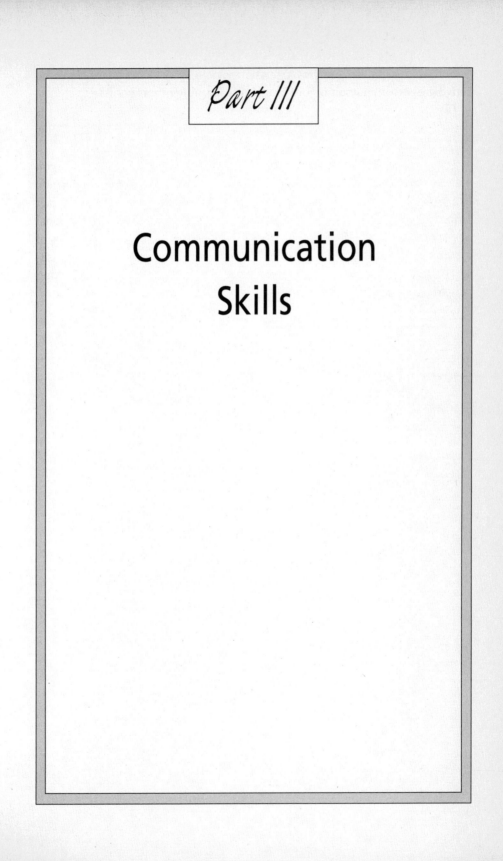

Part III

Communication
Skills

Listen Before You Talk

Then there was the story about the host at a party who greeted his guest at the door. The guest wished to discern how closely the host would listen to her, so she said: "I'm sorry to be so late, but I just murdered my husband, and it took me a while to stuff him into the trunk of the car." The host, ever conscious of his role as gracious innkeeper, replied: "Well, it's great to see you; I just hope your husband can make it next time."

Total listening is the fine art of holding your own self in suspended animation while you tune in to all the signals you are receiving from the other person. Listening, in its purest state, is the ability to restrain all your inner thoughts, to keep from rehearsing what you are going to say next, to stifle all connections you may feel between what the other person is saying and your own experience, and finally, to reject the notion that "I've heard that before."

A great listener would wait in stunned silence after the other person had finished talking in order to collect his or her thoughts for a response, not having done this while absorbed in listening. An effective listener would not only absorb all that is being said, but would also be able to report to the other person such a clear understanding of the content and feeling of the speaker's message that the speaker could recognize his or her own messages, stated perhaps even more clearly than they were originally given.

A good listener would make the speaker feel that everything said or about to be said is of great interest, that the next part will be even more worth hearing than what's already been said, and that nothing less than the whole story will be acceptable.

Does this sound like any conversation you have ever had? Has anyone ever listened to your words in a state so enraptured? Of course not. We settle for a lot less than perfection from the people who listen to us because we are happy that anyone listens at all.

All of which explains why an effective listener has a great advantage in a work search. Effective listening is the key to trust in a talking relationship.

Other people are more interested in themselves than in you. This is a cardinal rule, and you must remember it. People who feel you have come to deliver a soliloquy, give a prepared talk, or otherwise monopolize a conversation quickly lose interest in you. What you have to say has little power unless others are interested in hearing it. Their willingness to listen is a direct function of your willingness to show interest in them.

Given half a chance, many interviewers would prefer to talk about themselves, their own problems, anxieties, and ambitions, rather than listen to you. Of course, they are probably expected to listen to you as well, but your ability to allow for their needs in your conversation will influence their attitude toward you.

Furthermore, your ability to hear what they are saying gives you important clues about which of your skills or attributes is most likely to attract their attention. You will not have time to talk about everything you have ever done or are capable of doing; hence, it pays to be selective. Without knowing what the employer wants, you can only guess which parts of your experience or which items on your skills list are most relevant.

Here is an example of a young man who used his listening skills to explore a prospective career and prepare himself for entry into it.

> ***Example:*** Dan visited Mr. Zimmerman at his camera shop every Saturday, asking questions about the merchandise, what the customers buy, and how Mr. Z. deals with suppliers. In return for his curiosity, he received numerous pointers about developing strong customer relationships. One day it occurred to Dan that he would like to try this kind of work and have direct contact with customers himself. He proposed a part-time job in which he would field customer questions and complaints. Today he is happily immersed in being the owner of the most successful family-owned photography store in the eastern United States, Dan's Camera City (Allentown, Pennsylvania).

Fake Listening

I think you will agree that it is hard to talk about the art of listening because listening—like walking, eating, sleeping—is a thing we do all the time and believe we must be pretty good at by virtue of all the practice we have had. We resist with great passion the very idea that we might have to be taught such a thing. Any fool ought to know how to listen!

The problem is that we have learned pretty well how to *appear* to be listening, how to convince (we think) other people that we are in touch with them and taking it all in. We use certain cues to let others believe we are in touch—looking them in the eye, offering head nods of understanding, uttering uh-huh at appropriate intervals, delivering a knowing smile at just the right time, all this punctuated by "I know just how you feel."

But how many people really see you when they look at you? How often does a series of head nods occur *before* you have completed your thought or even before the sentence has begun? How many yeses, smiles, and other surface gestures are delivered with little connection to what you are saying outside and feeling inside? Is the person *with* you or just creating that appearance by catching enough snatches of conversation to keep the spark of interaction alive long enough to get a chance to talk next?

We have learned the skill of facilitating a conversation smoothly, at the expense of hearing a person fully. We become so preoccupied with keeping the train moving ("What will I do if the other person stops talking and I have nothing to say at that moment?") that we have trouble giving significant attention to what there is to see and hear during the ride. We figure that a conversation ends successfully if both parties were allowed to say something, there was a lot of smiling all around, and neither person made any grave errors or insulted the other too badly. We have learned to settle for less because we do not expect more.

What Is Real Listening?

You should not confuse listening to a person with listening to a train whistle, a phonograph record, or even a screeching cat. These simpler acts of listening require no particular interpretation, raise no concern about hidden motivations, and place no requirement on you to prepare a response. It is too easy to imagine that listening to a person is equally simple, just preparation of your sense receptors for some sounds that will be immediately understood.

Theodore Reik has referred to listening to human beings as "listening with the third ear."[1] This means that we can hear more than what the words are saying. What is this *more*? Don't people say what they mean?

> *Example:* Marcia talked to her husband many times about her work. She complained of the long hours, the constant squabbling with legislators (she was a lobbyist), the intricate nature of written legislation, the necessity of making deals with everyone in sight. Her husband heard all this, but watched her feelings as she talked. He said to her:

"Yes, there are a lot of frustrations about this work, but you seem to get a kick out of the whole struggle." Marcia nodded her agreement after some thought and thanked her husband for listening.

The husband had listened closely with the third ear to what his wife was saying and had "heard" her feeling for the work.

> At first glance the term "listening" implies a passive act of taking in the content of the [person's] communication, but actually it involves a very active process of responding to total messages. It includes not only listening with the ears to his/her words and with the eyes to his/her body language, but a total kind of perceptiveness. . . . It means also that we are silent much of the time. . . . When the [listener] can answer in considerable detail the question, "What is going on in this person right now in his/her life space?" s/he is listening with all his/her perceptual capacity.[2]

Levels of Listening Behavior

Seldom is effective listening as simple as the previous example suggests. The example illustrates how accurate a listener can be when tuning in to the other person on all wavelengths. Listening begins with wanting to hear what another person has to tell you.

In terms of the previous example, let's take a look inside the husband's mind to see what he was attending to as his wife spoke about her work.

+ *Identity.* This is my wife talking; I'm interested in listening to her because her work is important and I want to help her reflect on what it is doing to and for her.

+ *Voice.* Her voice is sometimes tense as she talks, though almost always excited as well. She talks hurriedly, trying to get everything in, but always volunteers more than I ask for, gets carried away, voice goes to a high pitch. Her voice is strong and confident as she talks about this.

+ *Body.* She is physically animated as she talks, yet does not seem unusually tense. Her body expresses involvement with the topic, and willingness to continue because she faces me, leans forward, and talks in a relaxed way.

+ *Words.* She is describing problems, struggles, conflicts, but they usually seem to resolve themselves in ways that give her satisfaction. If I connect all the words over several conversations, I get the picture that she has this job under control and needs to ventilate its frustrations.

+ *Feelings.* Some feelings escape her words, but are there in her attitude toward what she is saying. In keeping with her voice, she feels excited by what she is talking about, shows this in her general state of body excitement, and seldom seems discouraged or beaten by the conflicts she is describing.

+ *Values.* I suspect she feels very deeply about what she is doing, that the involvement in this political process would keep her motivated despite a steady stream of frustrations. She renews herself for this work without prodding from me or anyone else; must be something inside that keeps her going.

I have been focusing on listening as psychological attending thus far. Such mental attentiveness must always be accompanied by physical attending that enhances the overall message: "I am in touch with you, am tuning in to what you are saying." Gerard Egan, in *The Skilled Helper*,[3] writes that effective physical attending includes the following characteristics: (1) facing the other person squarely, (2) maintaining good eye contact without staring unnecessarily, (3) using a posture that is open to the other person, (4) leaning toward the other person as a sign of involvement, (5) being physically relaxed during the conversation.

Nonverbal Communication

Much of what you are seeking in effective listening will come to you through nonverbal channels. Here are a few cues that suggest what you can look for:

+ Is he giving cues that he wants to end the conversation?
+ Does she watch me closely?
+ Is his body posture relaxed and facing me?
+ Are her hands wringing while I talk?
+ Is he fidgeting?
+ Does she have a sad look?

Nonverbal signals can be the individual's unconscious effort to tell you what cannot be put into words or is difficult to describe in rational terms (because, perhaps, it does not feel reasonable). Such signals far more frequently refer to feelings than to ideas and as such tell you more about the person's inner experience than what is being put into words. Eyes, hands, feet, and other body parts are all mirrors of the soul; words are sounds we sometimes use to fog that mirror so that you are not sure what you are seeing.

Though your concentration in any conversation should be focused on the person talking, you must also be alert for cues within yourself, both when you are listening and when you are talking. Listening to yourself with the third ear means attending to your own nonverbal cues:

+ Why do I feel relaxed with her?
+ Am I getting sleepy?
+ He raises my energy level.
+ She makes me edgy when I listen to her.
+ My voice is less confident.
+ I avoid looking at him.

How to Become an Effective Listener

Your total effectiveness as a listener depends on what you see, what you say, and how well you integrate the two. The seven key elements of effective listening are described below. Before you focus on them, however, you should recognize that your personal *attitude* must be the foundation upon which your listening behavior rests. The attitude with which you must begin any communication is that you care to hear everything the other person is saying, knowing that he will say more to you than words, and that you must concentrate to hear his messages at all levels.

1. Distinguish Content from Feeling. You must learn to distinguish between what the other person tells you has happened and how he feels about it, the emotions he attaches to the events. As noted before, much of the feeling that lies underneath the events is carried by the speaker's nonverbal behavior. Does he fidget when talking about that job? Do her eyes widen with joy when describing a project she did last week?

2. Listen to the Voice. In *The Voice of Neurosis*, Paul J. Moses claims that the voice is a highly reliable index of a person's emotional state.[4] The voice is much more difficult to control than the words it is uttering, and you should look closely for clues regarding the person's inner emotional state. Hitches in speech, tiny stutters, voice cracking, the high pitch of tension, the rich sound of excitement and confidence—all these tell you feelings you'll want to know.

3. Notice Body Movements. Though we cannot claim hand, facial, and body gestures can be read for total accuracy, you should recognize that these communicators are powerful and that people tell you many things from their gestures that their words do not reveal. A shrug of the shoulder, a wink, a posture of utter dejection, or a wild gesticulation of excitement—such gestures constitute a universal language and must not be taken lightly, especially in view of how effectively people use words to mask their inner attitudes.

4. Give Encouragement. The easiest signals you can give to indicate you are a willing listener are those that urge the speaker to continue. These can be nonverbal signals or brief spoken cues, such as "tell me more about that" or "go ahead." Without these simple cues, the person speaking will take the more cautious view that perhaps you really don't want to hear more. With them, you can trigger the speaker to continue.

5. Allow Silence. Little empty spaces between bursts of talking are the all-purpose oil that lubricates any conversation. Your careful silence following the other person's talk tells him you are not sure he is finished, that you want to be sure he's completed the thought. Since most of us think and speak in fragments anyway (we do not speak in paragraphs), silence from the listener allows us to piece these fragments together. Silence tells the speaker you were actually listening, not mentally rehearsing yourself to speak once his lips have stopped moving.

6. Paraphrase. While silence and verbal encouragements facilitate the flow of the person's conversation, they do nothing to demonstrate that you have actually heard what the person told you. You must use your own words to give evidence of what your facial expression, body posture, eye contact, and other nonverbal clues have said—that you were really listening. A paraphrasing response attempts to capture the person's basic message in a much smaller number of words. ("You mean that you really like dealing with the customers.") A simple paraphrasing response usually expresses feeling as well as content in its attempt to hear the person as fully as possible.

7. Check for Meaning. The most powerful form of listening behavior you can employ is asking whether your summary of what you have heard is correct. It is your way of saying: "I want to be really sure I am with you, so I will check my perception to see if I am on the right track." This response, which can also be called "clarifying" in nature, is more complicated than the paraphrase in that it seeks not simply to repeat, but to capture an essence that may not be explicitly verbalized.

> ***Example:*** It sounds to me as though you would like to move away from the profession you are in. Is that right?

I wonder whether you feel torn in several directions by your various interests. Is that true in what you're saying?

Listening is a skill you have countless opportunities to practice, in terms of both the listening you do in the presence of others and the quality of listening people exhibit when you are talking. There are as many opportunities for practice as you are willing to seek.

Finally, you will find many opportunities to sharpen your listening skills because most people prefer to be listened to, will regard your attention as a compliment, and will probably reward you with more conversation.

How to Ask Questions

RED QUEEN: *Speak when you're spoken to.*
ALICE: *But if everybody obeyed that rule, and if you only spoke when*
   you were spoken to, and the other person always waited for you to
   begin, you see nobody would ever say anything, so that . . .
                                        —Lewis Carroll,
                                        Through the Looking Glass

In this chapter I shall discuss the skill of questioning within the context of the formal job interview; you should recognize, however, that all these principles and ideas apply equally well to any variety of information interview (see chapter 10).

Questions take the lid off the interview. They give you a chance to free the interview from a rigidly structured format that may have been used a thousand times before. You will be thanked for this, and you shall get your reward in heaven. The unpredictable nature of questions makes them enjoyable for the interviewer; you even may be asking something new, or at least something not heard in the past few days. Try to make the interviewer happy in this way. Is your question the one that will make him or her wonder how much thinking and background research you had to do to come up with it?

The Purpose of Questioning

There are three major purposes of questioning. The first is to gather information.

>   ***Examples:*** How do you train new management people?
>   In what ways is your product different from your competitors'?
>   What new programs is your department planning for next year?
>   What do you want the person in this job to accomplish?

The second purpose of questioning is to clarify. Your intention is to remove your confusion about a particular matter, clear up a misinterpretation, or illuminate an issue that is important to you.

Examples: Do you mean that the company is planning new foreign offices?

I don't understand how your department's priorities fit with those of the Public Information Office. Could you clarify that for me?

I am unclear about what you mean by editorial responsibilities.

Third, questioning can be used to check on the progress of the interview, and let the interviewer know that you are open to further inquiry.

Examples: What would you like to know about my managerial experience?

Would it be helpful to you to know where I learned about supervisory techniques?

What other information about my public relations background would you like to know?

How does what I've said so far fit with the company's needs?

The word *question* is derived from the word *quest*, "a search." Let this be a reminder that questioning should not be a search-and-destroy mission. If you use questions too boldly, too frequently, or too insistently, you risk alienating the affections of your interviewer.

Questions can be weapons. They can be used to hammer people, bludgeon them, or at least make them a little uncomfortable. Use questions judiciously. A few well-chosen inquiries can be a positive index of your curiosity and intelligent forethought; too many questions can create a dynamic of interrogation from which you will find it hard to extricate yourself.

Questioning skill keeps you from entering an interview flat on your back. It forces you to prepare questions in advance, to decide what is important for you to know. It pushes you to rank your information needs according to priority and decide which questions you must ask first, given the limited time available.

Questioning keeps you in the role of chooser. It reminds you that you are the person who has the most at stake in this search process and that your questions will help you decide whether you will accept an offer if it is made.

Coming prepared to ask questions forces you to concentrate more closely on the flow of the interview because you must look for suitable places in which your questions can be posed. Questioning keeps you from lapsing into a passive stance that might imply: "Go ahead and interview me." You have as much responsibility for the conduct of the interview as the interviewer does, and questioning allows you to assume this role.

Every question you ask requires an act of initiative from you. Do not make the mistake of waiting for the interviewer to ask: "Now, do you have any questions for me?" If you wait for that permission, it will probably be a cue that the interview is just about over, far too late for you to get substantive responses to your questions.

When your question relates to something the interviewer said, don't delay your inquiry; ask as soon as possible. You may even interrupt if necessary, if the question is vital enough to your plans. If you don't want to leap in at once, intervene with: "May I ask you a question?" It's even better to weave your questions into the flow of the conversation. Insert them naturally, as issues arise, if possible.

Effective Questioning

Be sure to pose the questions you regard as most important early in the meeting. This lets your listener know your priorities and minimizes the possibility that you may not get to ask your crucial questions at all. Questions asked in a hurry toward the end of the interview usually get short shrift; they are answered in a cursory manner because the respondent simply does not have time to think about them.

Here are some of the ways to ask questions most effectively:

Ask Open Questions.   The open question is highly recommended because it encourages a respondent to answer in the broadest terms possible. It gives her the freedom to say whatever she pleases, does not restrict the boundaries of the responses. Open questions most often begin with *what, how,* or *in what ways.*

> The open question is broad, the closed question is narrow. The open question allows the interviewer full scope; the closed question limits him to a specific answer. The open question invites him to widen his perceptual field; the closed question curtails it. The open question solicits his views, opinions, thoughts, and feelings; the closed question usually demands cold facts only. The open question may widen and deepen the contact, the closed question may circumscribe it.[1]

Closed questions usually call for a yes or no response. Compare the way in which a single inquiry can be posed in both open and closed ways:

| Closed: Does this job involve working more closely with local newspapers? | Open: How would you want me to help the company relate to the local newspapers? |

Closed: Is the company going to seek new markets?

Open: In what ways does the company anticipate seeking new markets?

Ask Answerable Questions. Be sure you ask a question you believe can be answered without difficulty. It makes the interviewer feel good to have the answer, and you can smile appreciatively at the information you receive.

Be sure your questions actually have answers. Don't ask an impossible-to-answer question just because it sounds clever. The interviewer will regard you as pretentious, and you will deserve every bit of displeasure.

Ask Nonthreatening Questions. Questions that are low in emotional content and do not require deep thought can be used early in the interview to warm yourself to the task of more serious inquiry and to cue the interviewer that you will be active in the process:

Examples: I'll bet it's been a long day for you.
How many people have you spoken with today?
When did the company acquire this property?

Express Puzzlement. A good interviewer reads the puzzlement on your face before you express it in a question; therefore, you should speak up when something is said that you didn't understand. Interviewers appreciate your giving them a chance to clarify some of the more difficult topics or issues.

Ask Well-Informed Questions. Often a good use of a question is to show you have done some homework. Ask a question that demonstrates your knowledge. Generally some questions not only yield good information but also remind the interviewer that you are well organized and self-motivated. Be careful, though, not to push the well-informed question too far. In your haste to prove yourself, you may mistakenly ask a probing question that should have been avoided. A well-informed question, for instance, might be: "How does the company plan to market its new line of ski equipment?" A probing question, on the other hand, is something like: "When did the company decide to take over the southern markets?"

Use Indirect Questions. This method allows you to ask a question without insisting that the person answer it. As Alfred Benjamin says: "The indirect question usually has no question mark at the end, and yet it is evident that a question is being posed and an answer sought."[2]

Example: I'd sure like to hear a little more about that project. You must really be busy with these new departments.

Poor Questioning

It is easy to fall into the trap of thinking that any question asked is a point in your favor because it displays your initiative. An interviewer can usually detect when you are asking a question simply to sound impressive; do not string one nonsensical question after another. Stick to the questions that matter. Anything else will expose your tactic as superficial window dressing.

Here are some other kinds of questions to avoid:

Use of Why. Though *why* is a perfectly legitimate word in our language, it carries an unavoidable risk when it is used in an interview. Simply put, it is threatening and should be used with great care.

Loaded Questions. Loaded questions imply that you have an attitude or strong feeling about the subject and know or suspect what the answer is. They are asked to elicit a particular response. They put the interviewer on the defensive.

Example: Did the company decide to close that office because they didn't want to pay the high wages being demanded?

Double Questions. Probably one of the most common blunders, the double question reveals your desire to get a lot of information fast. You ask the interviewer to answer several things at the same time. Make it easy on your respondent, even if it means you may forget one of your precious questions entirely. Choose the most important question first and trust you'll find a chance to ask the others later.

Curiosity Questions. Don't waste time with questions about things that have piqued your curiosity but have little relevance or importance. It is easy to get sidetracked by something that "crosses your mind," especially in your anxiety to fill the time. That is precisely why you must have your important questions prepared in advance.

Machine-Gun Style. Avoid asking questions in series; the interviewer will feel he or she is in the path of a dangerous weapon and must find a way to divert it. Each question should be followed by nonquestion interchanges. Wait for the interviewer to say something, make a comment based on the response, volunteer some new data about yourself, and then come back with another question.

Shifting the Subject. Be careful not to let your questioning move away from a topic area that interests the interviewer. It may seem that you are deliberately avoiding the topic. Abrupt shifts of topic are less desirable than questions that flow naturally from the previous response.

Intellectuality. In your effort to display the depth of your thought and the way you can tie a contemporary question to a universal concern, you may go too far, perhaps off the deep end. Avoid such pretensions, even if you *are* an intellectual, because most interviewers are not.

> ***Example:*** Could you tell me how Herzberg's theory of internal and external motivators relates to the distribution of work incentives among your professional staff?

Probing. The brother-in-law of the loaded question, this one will hurt you most dearly if you fail to see you are putting pressure on the interviewer. No interviewer wants to be called to task by a job seeker, so if you are in doubt about whether your question touches a sensitive area, drop it. If it even *sounds* probing to you, in all likelihood it will not be welcomed by the interviewer.

Speech

Highly correlated with poor questioning are the ways in which your manner of speaking can intrude upon a free exchange of information. These are some of the key things to keep in mind.

Speak Clearly. If your natural speech pattern is too fast, slurred, garbled, or otherwise fuzzy, give it some attention. No one expects you to be number one on the diction or elocution list, but others have a right to understand what you are saying. Practice with your friends, people who will be honest with you. Play back a tape recorder if you need further evidence. You won't like the sound of that strange voice you hear, but you'll know whether it's understandable or not.

Natural Tone. Within the limits of reasonably good diction and clarity, stay with the voice that is your own. Any effort you make to assume a different persona, through adopting a voice that *sounds* better, will reach the listener's ear as phony, and you will be caught up in your own duplicity when you drop the new voice and return to the natural.

Modulation. Some people talk too loudly; others much too softly, so that they cannot even be heard. Speech volume is important because energy devoted to adjusting ears and body to your abnormal vocal level is energy subtracted from attending to what you are saying and feeling.

Vocal Flatness. Some people believe that it is "professional" to be eventoned, carefully modulated in their talk, not excited about anything because that would sound so childish. Rubbish. If you have feelings associated with what you are saying, it is vital that you express them. Of course, this can be overdone by a screaming cynic or a laughing hyena, but you get the idea. There is nothing professional about vocal flatness—it is simply boring.

You Are Your Questions

The questions you ask are a Rorschach of your career personality. By these inquiries shall ye be judged. If you ask a lot of stuff about salary, fringe benefits, vacation time, you will be spotted as a person who is clearly motivated by the external rewards and less driven by the needs of the employer or your own internal needs. You may not have intended this impression, but your questions will reveal it. If you talk about the company's future plans, you will be tagged as a person who thinks in terms of the big picture. Let your questions create an impression of yourself that accurately reflects your attitude. Imagine that you have only three questions to ask. Which three best reveal the self you would like the interviewer to remember? Avoid the temptation to be pretentious. Choose those questions that clearly represent your highest priorities and speak to the company's strongest needs.

17

Be the Initiator

No one can make you feel inferior without your consent.
—Eleanor Roosevelt,
This Is My Story

To the job seeker, darkness seems to cover this world of work. Imagine a huge pasture in which a thousand people are wandering around at nighttime trying to find each other with lit matches. This gives you an idea of how it looks to both employers and job candidates. Employers have little idea where the right candidates are, and people who want to improve their work situations have even less idea where their talents can be used. Occasionally someone comes along and shines a spotlight on this pasture for a moment, foolishly believing he has illuminated The Job Market. Two minutes later he is gone, people shift their positions, and his picture is already out of date. Such feeble efforts to throw light on "the job market" may be called job clearinghouses or job banks; they fail to capture a restlessly shifting scene.

Most of your self-assessment will be wasted effort, done for naught, if you fail to make connections with employers who need you. Assertiveness is the skill that permits you to make these connections. This vital skill enables you to plug in a number of lights that will illuminate your place in the world of work, allowing you to stand out in the darkness that pervades so much of the hiring process. Assertiveness allows employers to see who you are and permits you to discover what they are doing. Keep in mind that there is no central control switch in this blind-finding-the-blind process known as hiring. If you do not make the connections yourself, you leave the employer cruising the pasture with a flickering match, trying to find her way to wherever you are hiding.

The Advantage Belongs to the Initiator

In every stage of job hunting, you will have opportunities to initiate—gathering information from "experts," finding vital contacts who introduce you to company decision makers, requesting interviews, stating your qualifications, finding out where jobs might be created, or expressing your needs during negotiations.

If you do not initiate, nothing happens. Here are a few examples:

* If you do not ask for referrals, they don't offer any.
* If you don't ask about the job's new responsibilities, they don't tell you.
* If you don't tell about experiences you've had that demonstrate your qualifications, they may not ask you about them.
* If you don't ask what the employers' key needs are, they won't tell you.

Nobody gives you a rule book that says "this is when to take the initiative." You must learn to sense when there is something you need to know, or when there are things about you that you want them to know.

The advantage belongs to the job hunter who is willing to speak up and initiate again and again, in order to make the best connection between what she wants and what the employers need. Put simply, the advantage belongs to those who are assertive.

What Is Assertiveness?

Assertiveness is not, contrary to popular belief, walking up to a bull elephant and asking him to whistle "Dixie" for you. Nor is it bulldozing your mother-in-law into changing the TV channel from her favorite show. These are examples of *aggressive* behavior, which can be defined as taking away the rights of another in order to satisfy your own. People frequently confuse aggressive with assertive behavior.

Assertiveness can be defined for our purposes as (1) taking those actions necessary to put you in touch with the people and situations that appeal to you; (2) asking for their advice, insights, information, and referrals to others; and (3) stating clearly why you believe you're the right person for the job.

Bower and Bower, in *Asserting Yourself*, their detailed treatment of the subject, remind us:

> Some people believe that assertiveness training must turn a nice person into a constant irritant, a rebel, a complainer, and a general all-around pain. Others charge that assertiveness training teaches people to be calculating and manipulative, and helps them control others for selfish ends. Views like these are based on a misunderstanding of the goals of assertiveness.[1]

Assertiveness is the simple act of asking for what you want. It is not a matter of winning, outwitting, bludgeoning, controlling, or even manipulating your foe. The person from whom you seek assistance in your work search is not a foe at all, but a willing participant.

Nearly all the work-search activity in the detective and research stages can be stunted if individuals believe they have no right to do what they are doing. "Why would anyone want to talk to me?" "What makes me think others would want to help me?"

There is an old story about the man whose car has broken down on a deserted rural highway. He walks a mile to a farmer's house to ask for help. During the walk, he ruminates about the farmer's possible responses to his plight. Being of pessimistic bent, the driver creates a scenario in which he imagines that the farmer will be reluctant to help. Thus, by the time our poor beleaguered driver reaches the farmer's door and the door opens, he says: "You can keep your automobile tools to yourself. I didn't want to use them anyway!"

Many of us concoct scenarios of this kind before we approach people to ask them for help with the job search, and these anticipations prevent us from acting. Though there is never any guarantee that an individual will assist you, you always have the right to ask.

Passive, Aggressive, and Assertive Behavior

Let's settle once and for all that assertive behavior is neither passive nor aggressive in intent. Passive behavior will hurt your work search because there will be no search at all; you will snuff yourself out before you start. Aggressive behavior will also hurt your search because you will stifle your listeners, attempt to railroad them into giving you information and leads you require, no matter what their objections. Assertive behavior permits you to ask for help in a way that respects the rights of respondents to satisfy you or refuse, as they please. Since you are not asking for the keys to the safe, the secret formula for Coca-Cola, or a seat on the New York Stock Exchange, you can reasonably expect that most people will try to help you.

> **Example:** *Passive behavior:* I'd better not go in here; they will think I am disturbing their workday.
>
> *Aggressive behavior:* I'm going to find out what the company priorities are, no matter how many people I have to buttonhole.
>
> *Assertive behavior:* Would you mind if I asked a few questions about your job, and the company?

There is a delicate balance between asking for what you want and imposing your needs upon the rights of others. Those I call assertive boors believe they can make requests anytime as long as they preface them with "I would like," look directly at the person, and speak in a clear voice. Assertive boors fail to observe cues supplied by the respondent: that she has not yet finished speaking; that her nonverbal leave-taking behaviors indicate she has no more time to talk or listen; that she shows nonverbally some discomfort with the last question asked. And boors fail to recognize the needs of others in a group to be heard. It is always important to watch anticipatory nonverbal behavior in the people to whom you are speaking; assertive boors usually miss most of it.

Failure to observe your respondent's nonverbal cues can work against you. If you trigger in your listener a "get this person out of here" feeling, by virtue of your insensitive assertion, the feeling will undo any progress you have made, and you may not even get a decent referral to another person.

How to Be Assertive Without Muss or Fuss

How do you steal a piano? By behaving as though you have every reason to be there in the first place. You act in a way that leaves no suspicion about your purposes or your right to be engaged in what you are doing. You walk in the door, enter the appropriate room, set up your moving equipment, and remove the piano with dispatch. Although the ethical dimension is twisted in this analogy, the *attitude* is one that should pervade your assertive behavior. You have every right to explore, question, inquire, volunteer, and be assertive in other ways toward your career objectives. There are four rules you should follow:

State What You Want Without Hesitation.

> **Example:** I want to know what kinds of public relations work your
> firm does, how you go about completing your contacts, and the ways
> in which you are usually successful.

In speaking, face the other person with your body, so you are not turned away at an angle, and do not appear to be looking in another direction. Look at the person directly; your eye contact should be steady but not so fixed that you are staring; occasional glancing away is fine.

State What You Do Not Want. Anticipate any misinterpretations that might stem from what you are saying.

Example: I am not interested in asking you to hire me, and I have no intention of trying to sell you anything.

Be as Specific as Possible.

Example: It would help me to know how you recruit your staff, what skills you believe are most important in effective work here, and what kinds of training and experiences are most beneficial.

Adjust Your Requests as Necessary.

Example: I understand you have less time than we'd originally planned for. Would it be okay to ask you just the few questions I have regarding how you get your contracts and the methods you use to fulfill them?

This last step is particularly important. A juggernaut style of assertive behavior will quickly backfire if you do not pay attention to how the other person is receiving your requests. Each request you make or question you ask must be modified by the willingness of the respondent.

Here are some examples of how assertive language is used with a variety of people.

+ *To a secretary:* I would like to speak personally with one of your financial analysts so I can gather some information about that job.
+ *To an employer:* I would like to know more about your branch services; could you give me the name of one of your branch managers so I can ask a few questions?
+ *To a receptionist:* I would like to know who does the long-range planning work in this company. Could you direct me to his or her office?
+ *To a referral source:* I am interested in speaking with other people who do work similar to yours. Which individuals would you recommend?

Shy People Can Be Assertive Too

Let's assume you are shy. You are generally afraid of people in positions of authority, feel intimidated by secretaries, fall over at the sight of a business suit, and would faint if you had to approach two strangers at the same time.

Try these three simple rules:

Don't Be the Life of the Party. It is never necessary for you to laugh a lot, tell jokes, or otherwise entertain your hosts. Your quiet, unobtrusive attention to their work and lives will be enough to excite their sensors and keep the conversation moving.

Bring Along a Scrap of Information. An easy way to stimulate conversation is to offer a morsel of information about your target employer, and let the conversation carry itself from there.

> *Example:* I saw your new store that just opened across town. How did the company decide to establish a market there?

Use Your Observational Powers. What kinds of material are displayed on the work desk? Trophies, plaques for some kind of service, diplomas, copies of new books you can ask about? What pictures are there on the walls? What do they represent to this person?

Self-Put-downs

Sitting around trying to summon the courage to ask a stranger for advice or information, how many times have you said to yourself: "She really wouldn't want to hear my silly questions." "I'm not interesting enough for anyone to talk with." "He couldn't possibly have enough time for me." "She won't understand what I am looking for." "I know he gets bothered all the time by people like me."

Though there is no guarantee that you will get what you want, you can succeed in eliminating yourself from the game if you let self-put-downs dominate your thinking. Rather than assuming the worst, *let the other people decide.* Don't you decide for them whether a conversation should take place; they have a right to make that decision without your assistance. Ask yourself: "What's the worst thing that could happen?" The most severe consequence of your rash, impatient act would be a simple no, a polite request that you come back later. As my wise grandmother used to tell me: "If that's the biggest problem you have in your life, you'll be all right." And remember, *you don't have to be interesting;* the target people are interested enough in themselves. You don't have to provide the entertainment; just be prepared to listen.

18

Use Writing Effectively

I try to leave out the parts that people skip.

—Elmore Leonard

To write simply is as difficult as to be good.

—W. Somerset Maugham

Words give shape and substance to your thoughts; they bring your feelings to life and create pictures where before ideas were scattered and fragmented. Writing forces you to make coherent sentences of your unshaped flashes of insight. It puts flesh on the bones of your ideas and allows you to capture images that dart to and fro in your mind.

Can the pen be mightier than the tongue? Yes, on some occasions your written communication to an employer can be quicker and more effective than an in-person interview. During the days or weeks (if you are far away) that you wait to see an individual personally, you can penetrate his consciousness with a well-timed note.

The warlords of the working world seek to standardize your written communication in the form of business letters, the résumé, and the formal job application. These are tools you must be familiar with, but you should note that they give you limited opportunity to set yourself apart from the crowd. Thus, I shall leave discussion of formally written job-seeking materials to other publications and attempt to persuade you that your ability to use writing to your advantage depends largely upon the *personal* and *informal* qualities of what you say.

We are all egotists. We wait by the mailbox for letters to arrive and remind us that someone remembers. The mailbox game never loses its excitement because it offers a pleasant surprise, an unexpected compliment, a voiceless hello that you prize because the sender took time to remember you. Don't you still sort through your office and home mail, looking hopefully for an envelope that is personally typed or handwritten to you?

No matter how resolutely and tightly the employment world attempts to depersonalize itself, there will always be individual egos. People will be proud of what they have done and will generally appreciate another person who notices. In view of the numerous impersonal communications that are enforced in a hiring process, the *personal communications* stand out because they escape the trap of formalized language and structure.

The written medium is made to order for those of us who like to think slowly and carefully and say things in just the right way. You can talk to your target person at your own pace. Moreover, you can control the agenda by organizing your thoughts in the order that seems most likely to make an impact. You can make countless mistakes without reprisal and show your audience only the finished product.

A letter affords the receiver the same degree of freedom. He or she can imagine the reply a hundred times, reflect upon your words, turn them over and over, and savor them if they are complimentary. And whatever effect you achieve with your written communication, you have the pleasure of knowing that it lasts and lasts.

Getting Personal

The résumé, application, and other standard forms of written communication are impersonal; they lack the single most potent quality in any writing—a direct connection between one human being and another. Even personally addressed letters can lack this quality. Of the two following letters, both personally addressed, the second—more specific and personal—is far more likely to evoke a positive response and be remembered.

> *Example:* Dear Ms. Jones: I have been reading about your company and would like to know more about its operation. Could you send me literature describing your overseas branches?
>
> Dear Ms. Jones: I have read about the Universal Company in a recent article in *Business Week* magazine. Your work with new metal alloys in foreign markets interests me. Your office told me you recently visited Ceylon to look into these possibilities. Could you send any literature that describes these operations?

I believe a job is a very personal matter. Therefore, I will focus this chapter on methods that will help you cultivate the personal touch in your writing. The more you depend on stiff, aloof, and structured forms of business writing, the more you surrender your chance to reach your correspondent and be remembered, because your letter will sound like everyone else's.

The personal quality can be established by a combination of three approaches in your writing:

1. Comment directly about the person to whom you are writing.

Example: I have read your study of the ecology of local wildlife.

2. Comment about the organization for which the individual works, even if you don't know the particular function of the person to whom you're writing.

Example: I am aware that your agency has been studying local wildlife control and plant technology and would like to know more about your findings.

3. Tell something about your own background that relates to the purposes of the organization to which you are writing.

Example: I have done a study of deer in the local area and am interested to know more about their impact on the ecology of northern California.

A combination of knowledge about the individual or organization to whom you are writing and reference to your own experiences is best because it establishes a basis upon which you can meet for a mutually profitable discussion.

> *You can't straighten up during writing and then hunch back down when you let go of the pen. Writing can teach us the dignity of telling the truth.*
>
> —Natalie Goldberg,
> *Writing Down the Bones*[1]

Behind-the-Scenes Writing

There are several ways you can practice your writing skills without having to take the risk of exposing your words to target employers. Any of the following kinds of writing can sharpen your prose and build your confidence for future writing in the job marketplace.

Letters to Friends. If you can tell a friend why you want to get into a particular line of work, why you believe you ought to be hired, and what you value in this kind of work, then you can say the same things to the employer when that opportunity occurs. But practice first without the threat of being evaluated. As Ernst Jacobi points out:

Writing in the form of a letter to a friend gives you several immediate advantages. It forces you to focus on one specific person, preferably one whom you respect and especially like; this immediately influences your communicative attitude. You will tend to be warm, direct, informal, and spontaneous. You will instinctively take care to stress why you are writing and why you think that what you are writing will be of interest. And you will probably avoid being pompous, stiff, and self-important.[2]

Fantasy Letters. What would you write to a fantasy employer if you had the courage to send this person or organization a letter expressing your loftiest ambitions? Try a letter of this kind, with no intention at all of ever sending it. Assume instead that you have an imaginary reader who will accept and welcome anything you say and believe it as well. Make sure you tell the letter's receiver what you feel about the work but are embarrassed to tell a real person ("I really want to be the sort of insurance salesperson who sells a policy only when I believe the family needs it and who looks after the family's entire financial program").

A Letter to Yourself. Your inner conversations flicker in and out of your consciousness hundreds of times a day. Try putting these exchanges into more coherent form by addressing yourself directly and attempting to convince yourself that your course of action in the work search is justified. Take it even a step further and imagine you are persuading yourself to hire yourself.

Writing Employers Informally

It is a good idea to make written contact with target employers before you formally apply with letter and résumé. Three informal categories of writing can be used to great advantage.

Thank-You Notes. These notes offer you ways of getting across your interest and enthusiasm for the work without professing to be bargaining for a job. Usually the thank-you note follows an information interview. In such a note, you can tell the person how much your talk reinforced your interest in the work, perhaps set the stage for future contacts, and express personal interest in the individual, all in the context of showing gratitude for assistance.

Note from Admirer. For example, an aspiring advertising executive who researches a particular ad agency can identify the name of an account executive, study the ad campaigns for an account he or she handles, and write a letter of admiration for the way in which the campaign has been formulated. Such letters out of the blue are so rare in business communication that the receiver will be surprised to realize that someone actually noticed and thought enough to comment. Be careful not to overdo this kind of letter; make sure you are speaking with definite knowledge and sincerity and that you are not effusive.

Portfolio. In any profession where the work you have done can be shown in writing, this form of communication is an excellent supplement to the résumé because it gives evidence of your résumé's claims and demonstrates that you had the foresight to prepare yourself. Articles, reports, memoranda, advertisements, newspaper copy, training manuals, sales reports, or anything else you have written provide proof of the work you have done. If you do not currently keep a sample book of such materials, now is the time to begin collecting and organizing them.

Warning: Writing Can Work Against You

Like a piece of spinach stuck in your teeth while you are talking, poor writing can distort the quality of your essential message. J. Mitchell Morse cites examples of the written communications he gets from college students: "What is needed is the restoration of confident in fair taxes. The fairest are the sail tax which the rich pay more than the poor because they buy more and are not discriminating against them they feel."[3] The Public Relations Society of America reports:

> Now, bear in mind, the following excerpts are from real letters written by real applicants seeking a real job as editor. Most possessed graduate degrees, many in English! ... "My doctoral program provided an interdisciplinary continuation of the Master's program emphasizing research, management and organization theory and practice, decision making, theory, personnel and business administration, and directed institutional communications." You can't help but like a guy who gets right to the point.
>
> Another Ph.D. in English wrote, "I have become proficient in quick but competent research and apprehension of complex matters." Well, at least he writes shorter sentences.[4]

If you want to use writing skills in your job search but have always been afraid of making errors like these, here are a few suggestions for you. First, write as much as possible in the same style you use in talking. Don't adopt one style for writing and a different one for talking. Use a tape recorder if necessary to hear your conversation or that of others, and do what is necessary to make complete sentences. Second, ask a friend or teacher to serve as editor for your writing; accustom yourself to hearing criticism and learning from it. Third, practice, practice, practice on nonthreatening recipients. Write letters to your sports heroes, politicians, the television networks, and any other people or places you know are not likely to be offended by what you say or how you say it.

Guidelines for Effective Written Communication

Ernst Jacobi, in his excellent book *Writing at Work*, urges that every piece of writing can be improved by attending to several important guidelines. Though his guidelines apply to writing that would be done after you are hired, I feel these recommendations apply equally well to the writing you do in your career search.

Make Every Word Count. Do not write for the sheer sake of writing. Words by themselves are empty shells, signifying nothing, if they are not focused toward a message. Say what you have to say economically. Don't say it again to remind your readers that they might have missed it the first time.

Adopt a Point of View. Try to leave your readers with the impression that you have reached a particular conclusion, so that they know how they and their work have affected you.

> **Example:** It is clear to me that your organization is trying to reach the youth who need help but do not use traditional helping services. This is the kind of effort I am interested in joining.

Watch the Mechanics. Anyone who has ever made a mistake in grammar or shown sloppy syntax will hate me for bringing up the subject, but errors of this kind distract the reader from your intended message. Hence, you are unwise to let them occur. Even typos jar some readers and leave the impression of carelessness. Proofread your writing. Enough said.

Use Strong Verbs. If you want to tell a person you were impressed with her work, try to say a little more than that you "liked" it. Say the work "stimulated" you or "encouraged" you to do additional reading. In describing your own work experience, choose such verbs as *managed, directed,* or *organized* over weaker verbs like *coordinated* or *compiled.*

Give Specifics. If you make a complimentary comment, do your best to back it up with specifics, lest the reader think you are pulling phrases from thin air.

> *Example:* I will remember your presentation on the new laser show because it reminded me of the relationships between physics and art.

Read It Aloud. It has been said that Guy de Maupassant read all his stories aloud to his cook, and if the cook couldn't understand their themes easily, he threw the stories out. Test your writing on a friend, preferably one who has no familiarity with the specific content of what you are saying. See if your writing stimulates interest.

Use Your Own Vocabulary. I cannot emphasize this strongly enough. If you try to adopt words that sound lofty and impressive, your phoniness will be detected. Speak in your own familiar words, as long as they represent plain English, so that you can retain the informal, personal quality of your writing.

Spelling

Spelling errors are a surefire way to unravel all the good you've been doing for yourself in your job search. In your résumé, a cover letter, an E-mail message, a project report, or anywhere you present words that will be read, a word will be remembered if it is misspelled.

Just one spelling error leaps off the page. It makes the rest of your presentation look as though you're not put together right. The reader says to herself: "I'll bet he slurps his soup too. And he probably will be late to meetings . . . and wear spaghetti stains on his ties. What kind of a person allows a spelling error to survive—a sloppy, careless, irresponsible person; he probably doesn't take his garbage out at night either."

Seldom is the penalty so large for a transgression that seems so small. If you blow a word, you've blown it, and it's there for all to gaze upon in wonderment.

People count on spellcheckers on their computers; however, they often miss errors. If your machine allows errors to fly beneath your radar, then your letters and memos are going to make you look like the biggest dummy in business clothes on your block.

Notice I've been talking about single spelling errors. One error all by itself is enough to get your name removed from a list of job candidates. If you make *two* spelling errors on a single page—well, cash it in. One error might be forgiven as a moment of weakness. Two errors mean that you are a persistent goof-up. You wrote the first draft of your résumé or letter and you never looked at it again. Or you think you're so smart that such errors will be tolerated.

If you're committed to never letting a spelling error darken your door again, here are a few guidelines:

1. *Question yourself.* If there are any words that even halfway don't look right to you, say to yourself: "This is a word that must be checked. If there's even a small chance that I have spelled it wrong, I must not let it slip through."

2. *Use a dictionary.* Keep a good dictionary by your side and use it, use it, use it. Every time you see a suspicious spelling, LOOK IT UP in your dictionary. This is your spelling reflex. Even if you're 95 percent sure that a word is spelled right, check out that remaining 5 percent doubt.

3. *Proofread.* Once you have written anything, read it over again completely, word for word. Yes, proofreading is tedious, boring work, and it will test your patience severely. This is good for you. It will hurt your eyes more than a smoke-filled room. But you must proofread. Also, be sure to have a friend proofread for you, since you might have looked at it one too many times to really *see* it.

People who spell words correctly are people who take pains to make sure their work is presented correctly. . . . People who spell well tend to be literate and therefore will communicate well with a far broader variety of people. . . . People who spell words correctly can be counted on to write a memo in your name and not embarrass you.

The thinking in the mind of the interviewer goes like this: "The person who flubs a word on her résumé is the same person who will probably butcher a word when I ask her to write a report to my boss—I think I'll go on to the next candidate."

Some people have the idea that they can delegate spelling to their lesser staff while they concentrate their time on the "big thinking." "Let the secretaries clean up my writing." This approach may work for a while . . . until his boss asks him to check *her* spelling and there's no time to delegate it.

Spelling is one of those things like zipping up appropriate parts of your clothing. You either do it consistently and correctly every single time you appear in public, or else you get a whole lot of attention that you do not want.

Sample Letters

The following sample letters to an employer show the contrast between an impersonal, business style of writing and a more personal, informal style.

First, the business style; note how dry it seems.

Dear Ms. Beaumont:

In your capacity as personnel manager of the Robinson Crusoe Company, you have many occasions to talk with people about the responsibilities of your office. In this regard I would like to request that you let me know whether I could meet with you on an appropriate occasion to discuss matters of some importance to me.

I am interested in requesting information about the nature of your operations, key personnel, organizational structures, and institutional policies. This information would assist me in expanding my knowledge of facilities similar to that which you direct.

I have collected certain background information about your organization that would provide suitable preparation for my visit with you. In my efforts to conserve your time, I have prepared a formal agenda that will not make undue demands upon you.

Could you reply to me at your earliest convenience, so that we can arrange this meeting for our mutual benefit? Thank you kindly.

Now the informal style. Note how the writer uses specific terms about his or her qualifications and language that is personal and direct.

Dear Ms. Beaumont:

I have learned from contacting your office that you are personnel manager for the Robinson Crusoe Company. I am writing to you because I have read about personnel work in the business world for the past few months and would like to meet a person who does it as a professional. I have read several books on the topic and have spoken with relatives who work for International Tool and United Ball Bearing. These relatives told me that personnel work involves a lot of activities similar to what I am doing in college. I am social chairperson for my sorority and supervise the staff of the school newspaper. I like these responsibilities and would like to hear what you have to say about personnel work before considering it as a career.

Perhaps you could tell me how you got into this work and why you feel it is the right field for you. I would benefit a lot from the insight you could give me. I have prepared a small number of key questions I would like to ask you. Would you be willing to see me for thirty minutes?

I have known several people who have applied for and worked at the Robinson Crusoe Company, and they have told me how pleased they are with their jobs. One, John Meharry in the automotive department, wrote you a note of thanks a few months ago, I believe.

I suspect it must be frustrating to be concerned about the welfare of every employee in the entire company. I am interested to hear how you deal with this responsibility and why you like it.

I will be graduating from college within the next year and a half, so your views will be a great help in shaping my own plans. Thanks very much.

Finally, here is an example of a good letter to an employer with whom you would like an interview.

Ms. Carolyn Randolph
Editor and Publisher
Outdoor Education Press

Dear Ms. Randolph:

I read about your publishing company in a recent issue of *Printer's Ink* and was very much intrigued with how you started the business with only one title (your own book) and used your advertising experience to generate contacts with authors so the business would grow.

Since reading the article in *Printer's Ink*, I have read many of the books you currently list because I have considerable experience with outdoor matters and would like to become more closely involved with this kind of publishing. I noticed from the article that you market your books by direct mail and coupon advertising and do not use a sales force to enhance your efforts. I would like to propose that you experiment with the direct sales approach by considering my services.

Before writing to you with this proposal, I tested my idea by phoning or contacting personally twelve different bookstores in our local area. Each told me it would be willing to stock your books if they were more readily available. Hence, I am encouraged to believe that there is sales potential that has not been tapped.

I believe I can help your sales for several reasons: (1) my previous experience (résumé enclosed) as a graduate school representative taught me how to make contacts on large university campuses and the value of the personal approach; (2) I sold computer equipment during my college years and thus learned to be comfortable with selling skills; (3) my experience with outdoor activities includes ten years as an active supervisor of the Appalachian Trail, a term as president of the local hiking club, and occasional articles for the Sierra Club (see enclosed sample).

I believe we should get together to talk about this idea, if you feel it has some potential for you. I will call you during the week to discuss a time we might meet.

Sincerely,
Chris Jones

I have chosen to emphasize writing as a separate communication skill because I believe you can enhance your career search greatly with a personal letter on those occasions when the written form is most convenient and appropriate. A clear and personal writing style is the natural complement to an effective set of interviewing skills. Often the potent and readable letter creates invitations to interviews that would not have occurred otherwise.

19

Try Some Low-Key Public Speaking

The ability to express an idea is well nigh as important as an idea itself.

—Bernard Baruch

You don't usually see a job-search book say anything about public speaking. It's an activity that 5 percent of the population do, not the rest of us. In fact, on the list of things that people are most afraid of, public speaking is the number-one fear; the fear of dying ranks about number six. People would rather die than stand in front of a group and be asked to "say a few words." If you extend this logically, says humorist Jim Pelley, convicted murderers should be sentenced to six months on the lecture circuit.

So, what am I talking about, and why am I asking you to do something you probably don't like and which may even terrorize you? Because "speaking" can be much more broadly defined than paid speeches to large throngs of people. In your career, you'll have many opportunities to speak publicly—as you'll see in an expanded definition of "speaking." If you take advantage of these opportunities, your career will benefit. If you resist, you'll suffer consequences.

Furthermore, being an effective "speaker"—as defined below—is more easily within your reach than you probably believe. I'm not asking that you deliver the keynote at the Democratic or Republican National Conventions. The more common speaking occasions in your career are well within your capacity to handle and do well. You can even enjoy yourself.

Speaking is a natural human endeavor. When you have dinner with four or more people, and you express your opinion on any given topic, you are doing "public speaking." If you make a presentation to a group of prospective clients, you are "public speaking." When you express your views at a staff meeting where several others are present, this, too, is "public speaking." You're also "public speaking" when you make a committee report at your professional association, the PTA, or on the board of a local youth group.

Public speaking, in its broadest sense, is making a presentation to three or more people who are sitting still to hear what you have to say. Extend that to a formal occasion and you have a "speech." But the skills are largely the same.

Anyone can do speaking if they practice it enough. Not necessarily large theater-style speeches, but the kinds of speaking that are described below. Many jobs require these kinds of speaking. People who are uneasy and ineffective at first become comfortable through trial and error. "But the errors are so public!" you say. I recommend starting your involvement in speaking with talks that have the lowest anxiety. Pick the easiest groups to speak to that you can think of. Make your mistakes in front of supportive and nonthreatening audiences.

Ways in Which "Speaking" Is a Part of Job Hunting

Enough of the abstract theorizing. Let's look at how "speaking" often will come directly into play during your job search. If you show your speaking skills well, you'll be the big gainer.

Panel Job Interviews. Increasingly, people who hire are making the panel interview a part of their selection process. This means there will be two or more of them and one of you. Often the panel will consist of five or six people, all staring directly at you. Sound scary? You can handle it. You may be sitting down during the panel, but you're still "public speaking."

Learn to be your calmest and most effective self during a panel interview. If the setting makes you nervous, gather a group of "practice panelists" several times before your "live" interview. Get used to having several pairs of eyes looking at you.

Expect one or more panel interviews even if they don't tell you in advance. Sometimes people will "drop in" to your interview unannounced. Learn to handle that without getting flustered. Regard the panel as a chance to get exposure to more people. Welcome it.

Presentations During the Job Interview. Since presentations are a common part of many managerial, professional, and technical jobs, savvy interviewers like to see a sample of how you perform. They may cue you in advance about what you will talk about and to whom you will speak, or they may spring it on you by surprise.

If you have seldom made presentations before, do some practicing. Take topics you know a lot about. Nobody wants to hear you when you're uninformed. You may know the content, but delivery is another matter. Practice with live groups of knowledgeable people.

Ask for feedback, including both criticism and praise. The more comfortable you are with yourself and your subject matter, the better your delivery will be. People who avoid doing presentations are usually stiff and boring when they speak. You will find and express your personality in front of a group, but only *if* you do it enough to be at ease.

The presentation is a common part of the interview process for many jobs because presentations are vital to the success of many professional and technical people. It pays for you to develop your presentation skills because many companies depend heavily on these skills to obtain funds, impress customers, win contracts, and make a favorable impression on the public.

The job candidate who can speak effectively at the bank, the Chamber of Commerce, clients' offices, the Rotary, and government agencies will be a valuable member of the team. The people who balk at these opportunities will most often not be hired and will not advance in their careers.

Informal Discussions. Sometimes an employer will invite you to dinner or some other social occasion where several people are present—employees, friends of the decision maker, or just others who happen to be around. This is a loose interpretation of "public speaking," but an important one.

At such social occasions, you'll be expected to participate in the discussion. If you sit on your hands and nod quietly, mumbling to yourself, you'll be regarded as a person who has no viewpoint, nothing to say. This is not a good place to be.

None of these three examples of "speaking" requires that you get in front of hundreds of people and hold them spellbound with your oratory or motivational skills. That's for professional speakers who get paid to demonstrate their skills at such events. This is not what is expected of you.

However, public speaking in the terms described above is very much a part of successful job hunting and job keeping. If you are uncomfortable with these forms of "speaking," you can take actions to improve your skills.

You've heard it a lot, so I'll join the chorus—Toastmasters International is a good place to begin cultivating your speaking skills. There are many local chapters in towns and cities of all sizes. Choose a Toastmasters Club that fits your personality. The practice and feedback are highly valuable and supportive.

Here are some guidelines about effective speaking, regardless of whether you're giving a stand-up presentation to twenty-five managers, speaking to a panel of five during a job interview, or voicing your opinion at a dinner party:

1. *People appreciate realness.* Speak the same way you talk when you're having a friendly conversation. Don't try to put on airs or sound like a "speaker." Talk as though it's over the back fence. Don't ever talk down to your audience.

2. *Know when to stop.* Perhaps the most common mistake that people make when speaking is to ramble, go on too long, revealing that they don't exactly know how much is too much. Insecurity leads to rambling. Practice and feedback eventually can cure this problem.

3. *Do mental rehearsal.* When you know there's a talk you're going to give or a statement you're going to make at a meeting, play it over in your mind when you're taking a walk, taking a shower, lying in bed, or otherwise relaxing. Imagine yourself with the audience. What are you saying to them? What are they responding to? Run through the key points several times. Your imagination will help your speaking muscles to be ready when the time comes. Arnold Lazarus's book *In the Mind's Eye* gives excellent guidelines for mental rehearsal.

4. *Develop your natural sense of humor.* Everyone has a sense of humor, but many are afraid to let it out when speaking to a group. This is *not* about telling jokes, because jokes are not recommended. Humor will often emerge from the immediate things that happen during your talk. Someone sprays a tray of paper clips. You stumble and fumble over certain words or phrases. A tray of dishes is dropped in the back kitchen. Someone in the audience says something funny. You recognize something humorous in what you're saying. Let the natural humor out when it occurs to you or your audience. People like to laugh and they'll appreciate you when you encourage it.

5. *Do the first three minutes well.* Anxiety tends to peak in the beginning of a talk. If you're nervous and ineffective at the start, it will affect your entire presentation. Speaking coach Lee Glickstein urges that you allow thirty seconds of silence before you begin speaking, taking in the positive energy of the people assembled, feeling the pleasure of being there. Glickstein and many other coaches recommend telling a story about yourself that relates to your topic, so the listeners can identify you with the presentation. Whatever your approach, do something that enables you to look forward eagerly to the first three minutes, because that is where you set the emotional tone of your entire talk.

6. *Tell stories.* Brief stories. A well-chosen story often makes a point better than an abstract explanation. These can include stories about work you've done, about lessons learned, funny stories, poignant stories, etc.

7. *Get feedback.* Whenever possible, ask people for criticism (and praise) about your speaking. You and everyone else has blind spots, things we do wrong that we're not aware of. Some of us mumble. Others talk too fast. Some people are into pontificating, they're full of themselves, and it drives their listeners nuts.

Some people "uh" and "ah" a lot when they speak, and it is distracting. Others say "ya know?" and this verbal tic is distracting as well. There are many other speaking flaws. Find out what yours are and correct them. Practice helps, because you get a lot of immediate feedback from faces in the group or audience—sleepy faces, puzzled frowns, enthusiastic eyes, smiles and nods, and that wonderful look that says "tell me more."

> *Example:* Carla never thought of herself as a speaker and never saw the need for it. Then she applied for the job at the Middletown Zoo. They brought her in for the "interview" and said: "You have thirty minutes to tell these bears, giraffes, monkeys, and mountain lions why we should hire you." After two minutes of awkward silence, Carla was led away, babbling to herself.

Unfair? Goofball hiring method? Not really. The zoo wanted to see what was inside Carla, how she expressed herself, and what feelings about her work would emerge naturally. Even if Carla had had time to prepare, she might not have felt "ready" for this presentation.

The zoo put Carla in an impromptu situation, an unusual one. How could she have been "ready"? By talking about her career ideas to enough different groups that her "philosophy" and "viewpoint" pop out whenever anyone asks. Carla can have a two-minute version, a ten-minute version, and a longer one when called for. She could be so familiar with her ideas that it doesn't matter if her audience is a panel of interviewers, a dinner party of executives, curious opossums, or wild turkeys.

If you are comfortable enough with your ideas and yourself, you can begin speaking on the spot to anyone. Speaking will become a part of your daily routine when you do it enough. The higher level of advancement you aspire to in your career, the greater the chances that you frequently will be called on to "say a few words" at a moment's notice or in a prepared presentation. Make speaking part of your work and life.

Part IV

Skills
for Selling
Yourself

How to Sell Yourself
with Dignity

Selling? Most people would rather avoid it. Selling is not held in high esteem, and it asks for qualities that most people don't believe they possess. Salespeople? You probably try to keep them at a distance. Heaven forbid someone should suggest that you become one. They're often pushy, devious, and unscrupulous, and they're always twisting people's arms to buy something they don't want. The image of selling has been discolored by underhanded tactics in general and used-car salespeople in particular. You probably wouldn't want your son or daughter to grow up to be one.

We sell all the time in our lives, but we prefer not to recognize it as such:

"Would you go to the movie with me? I want your company, and in exchange
   I'll give you mine, and besides you'll like this movie, because . . ."
"Would you be my valentine? I'll treat you well, love and respect you . . ."
"Will you come sit for Johnny while we're away? We have lots of movies you
   can watch and I'll make your favorite meals. . . ."

This chapter will describe three principles that enable you to be as good a salesperson as possible: (1) Apply transferable skills from past experiences to future ones; (2) present your transferable skills in the form of stories; (3) build your social skills to support your job search.

These principles will allow you to sell yourself with comfort and with your dignity intact. You will recognize selling as a "natural" human activity where you can be honest and respectful of those considering buying your services. Selling yourself is a straightforward exchange of value for value. This chapter tells you how to do it.

Don't Blow It Now—You've Come Too Far

They won't know if'n you can't tell 'em. They won't divine your full potential from your résumé; they won't assume your academic credentials mean you are the greatest; they won't stop you in the grocery store and say: "Wait a minute, that face, that hard-driving look, that can-do expression, we gotta have it!" Even when you work hard to get into job interviews, the interviewers will not look deeply into your eyes, feel your pulsating forehead, and say: "You're just what we're looking for!"

To get their attention, you have to show more than paper credentials. Selling yourself in job interviews is more than giving stock answers that sound positive but mean little:

+ I want this job. (So what else is new?)
+ I'm really good with people. (That's better than being good with amphibians.)
+ I'm a hard worker. (Did you think we wanted a sloth?)
+ I'm a high-energy type of person. (Are you a battery?)

These are useful sentiments, but they are not enough. While they may sound fine to you, the interviewer has heard them a thousand times before. He or she wants to know what is special about you, and how your background is suited to the job. Fortunately, this is easy to accomplish, because you get to talk about the one topic in the world that you know best—yourself.

Selling yourself is your payoff for all the hard work you've done so far. You've done a great job of finding the jobs that you're a candidate for. You've probably already spoken to people with whom you'd like to work, and will talk to many more of them. Don't lose your momentum now. Give them the information they need.

An Easy Three-Step Process

If you cultivate the following three easy and enjoyable skills, you'll have the tools you need to do well in any job interview. There is nothing mysterious about these skills; they do not require complicated techniques and they are not related to the high-pressure methods that are taught to insurance salespeople and other sales professionals. These are simple, everyday skills that all successful job hunters use. As you read them, you'll see that you have probably already practiced these skills in your previous job seeking.

1. Make Connections Between your Past Experiences and Future Aspirations

You must make the fullest possible use of your past experiences when seeking a change of work; otherwise you are judged on the basis of superficial credentials and other external criteria, such as test scores, manner of dress, and prestige of previous employers. Your ability to communicate your worth is a function of your ability to recognize value in your own experiences and see how it can be translated into new capabilities.

The key links between your past and future experiences are transferable skills. Since the skills that matter most are almost always "transferable" in nature, you can look to your past for clues about selling yourself for new jobs. You will see how past skills can be applied to new kinds of work, perhaps entirely new careers. Here are some examples:

✦ *John Was a Plumber and Became a Stockbroker*
John ran his own plumbing business for seven years. What's he doing in the stocks and investments field? Just fine, thank you. John applied his skills with customers, his ability to acquire information and research materials (to be on top of things in plumbing, you have to organize and read all those technical manuals), and his social skills in the community (how do you think he got all the customers?). John had a good sense of how to build a client base at the same time he was developing knowledge of investments. It took him three lean years, but now John has a "book" of clients and is profiting from his new career.

✦ *Amanda Went from Music to Real Estate*
Amanda the Panda was a guitar performer and vocalist for six years, living the ups and downs of looking for the next gig and enduring "day jobs," but loving the life of a musician just the same. Eventually the life wore her down. Amanda realized the gigs would never get to the level that would enable her to think about buying a home, so she started looking elsewhere. Homes and properties beckoned to others as well as to herself. There was money to be made, and maybe recording dates could be financed for her group, PandaMonium.

How did Amanda make it as a real-estate salesperson, with only musical experience to draw upon? She had had plenty of contact with the public and had developed strong social skills, mingling skills, and ability to engage people quickly. Her years of life in the poor lane served her well in withstanding the low-income months before she developed a home-buying clientele. Amanda had kept the books and managed the performance dates for her group, so she could do the paperwork and handle telephone calls. Sheer persistence and endurance—required of any musician—were in her favor in pursuing real-estate customers. Amanda built a comfortable sales record and has made a down pay-ment on her home, with a large basement for PandaMonium rehearsals.

✦ *James Left Political Lobbying and Shifted to Termite Inspections*

Termite inspections?? Hey, it's a good business, if you don't mind crawling under houses. James had ten years of the lobbying whirl in Tallahassee, Florida's state legislature, and that was enough. Fun while it lasted, but no more of the frenzied halls and last-minute deals. James wanted out, out, out. Termites seemed about as far as he could get from the various forms of wildlife at the state capitol.

James applied his organizational skills to starting a business. His physical-endurance skills (gained from all-night sessions at the capitol and his personal hobby of rock climbing) helped him acclimate to the demand of scrambling under homes. His interpersonal skills played nicely in attracting customers and developing good relationships with them.

"Termites don't make complicated deals and then shift their viewpoints at a moment's notice," says James. "They're pretty straightforward. If they're there, you remove them. They may come back a few years later, but they don't change their minds every four hours."

The termite inspector general said:

> "What? You're applying for a license? Go back to the legislature where you belong. You'll never like this business. It takes a certain kind of person."

The new termite-meister said:

> "Send me to Outer Mongolia before you stick me back in politics. I can work with homeowners and the undersides of their houses. I ran a lobbying office. I can run a business. Come around in six months. See how many customers I get."

No matter what your previous work has been, you will discover that you have been using skills that can be applied to new jobs or careers. Even if the career you aspire to is very different from what you did before, several skills will still be transferable.

You can develop a plan for moving from accounting to oceanography, from print shops to making false teeth, or from college recruitment work to archae-ological expeditions. In some cases, you'll have to acquire technical skills (or perhaps a degree) to gain entry, but in a larger proportion of situations you can make the shift without additional formal education, by applying skills you've used before. Whatever change of work you contemplate, *first* talk to people in that field to see how your past skills apply.

Even if your transferable skills are not enough to carry you into a new job or career, here's how you should approach it: (1) Your transferable skills give you the foundation for developing expertise in a new field; (2) you begin getting direct experience in this new field as soon as possible (as a volunteer, temporary worker, contract worker, or otherwise); (3) you start acquiring knowledge of this new field to boost your qualifications. If your skills are strong enough, you may get hired and do this on the job.

Do not be discouraged by employers who say: "You don't have enough experience." Your transferable skills are your primary sales tools. Once you have looked at a new job and say to yourself, "I can do this," refer to your skills (and supportive stories) to demonstrate why you believe you could meet the employer's objectives. Make your best case for yourself, and then if you aren't hired, develop your strategy for acquiring knowledge and building skills where you may be lacking. But, above all, go forward with confidence that you can use your skills and learning abilities to qualify for new fields of work.

2. Needs Assessment

Every good salesperson knows that needs assessment—identifying what the customer is most willing to pay money for—is at the heart of the selling process. Let's see how this applies to job hunting. You must have an idea of what employers want before you can sell it to them.

An employer doesn't hire someone just to get a job done. She needs the job you do to accomplish certain objectives. How do you find out what these objectives are? Any way you can. Certainly information interviews are a main tool. Talk to your contacts, read about the company in the press, etc. Sometimes you have to just consult your intuition, think as though you were the head of the company—"What would I want done here if I were the CEO?" Here are two examples of how needs assessment propelled job hunters into being hired:

◆ Sam learned that Spanish-speaking staff at a local hotel were quitting right and left. Service schedules were falling apart. They needed a manager/supervisor to restore morale among the workers. Sam put together references along with his Spanish-as-native-language background, showed where he had been employed successfully as a supervisor, and offered this as his presentation on the phone and in person. He was hired and has received commendations for his work.

◆ Lydia found out through her research that a large office-supply store was alienating its customers through poor service and rude treatment. She learned through her contacts that a sourpuss manager was at the bottom of the problem.

Lydia figured "I have nothing to lose," went to the store owner, and offered her services as a "customer service consultant." They hired her for three training sessions and obtained modest but noticeable improvements in customer response. Two months later the owner dumped the manager, and guess who was hired to give it a try?

3. Tell Them Stories About Yourself

The second major step in selling yourself is storytelling. No, not sitting around the campfire telling tales about Indians, nor seeing how many bold and creative lies you can construct, nor entertaining the listener with narratives about the great Southwest.

The stories I want you to tell are stories about *you*. Talking about your transferable skills is a good start, and most necessary in attracting your listeners' attention, but it is not enough. You want to give a fuller picture of your capabilities. And the easiest way to provide this fuller picture is from stories of your past experiences.

Anyone who hears you say "I can do this . . . I can do that" will be likely to ask: "How do you know you can do that? What makes you say that you can?"

Essentially, your listener is saying: "Prove it to me." Your best support comes from the things you have done before. That is where the stories come in. If you tell me you are good at something, but you cannot tell me where you acquired the skill or how you come to have the knowledge, I will have a hard time believing you. So tell me a story.

> *Examples:* I think I would be a good computer programmer, because it involves logical thinking. I got my logic skills from philosophy courses in college. I am also good at chess and won an analytical thinking contest during college. One time I spent three days and nights working through a math problem that no one else could do, but I did it.
>
> ▶ I have always been able to work under the stress of deadlines, as this job calls for. I was a news editor in my hometown and was continually assigned the late-breaking stories that had to be covered, researched, and written up in a matter of hours. I also worked summers at the local plant, where packages had to be completed during peak periods, with a lot of the workers complaining, and being interrupted by telephone calls, too.
>
> ▶ Probably the best reason to consider me for this accounting job is that I was financial manager of my fraternity. When I took over, the books were in a total mess. With only the introductory accounting

course under my belt at the time, I got the whole system in order, including purchasing, dues, investments, and a complicated loan arrangement with the local bank. I got the job done with almost no supervision, and enjoyed working out the problems.

▶ I think you should hire me as manager of member services here at the racquetball/fitness center because I understand how to keep members happy. I used to work at a tennis pro shop and developed many tournaments, deals on equipment, social events, and clinics for injury prevention. I would hang around with the members a lot and find out what they were complaining about, then try to develop a program to satisfy them. One year I had them all out there doing stretching and conditioning exercises when they complained about getting tired late in their matches.

Stories are easy to listen to, especially if they are told concisely and they are convincing. Stories beat trying to "explain" in analytical terms why you are good at something ("I'm good with people. They like me . . . they come to me . . . I'm just *good* with them, you know what I mean?").

Stories explain without having to explain. They *show* you as a problem-solver; they reveal what you have done and lead the listener to believe that you can do it again.

In many cases, people will lack direct experience ("I have never worked with that type of problem or customer before"), but they will have indirect experience that can be related to the new job.

Example: You want a job as a retail store buyer.
Story: I have been manager of purchasing for the community theater. In this job, I have purchased costumes, and done a lot of negotiating with the merchants. I know what it's like to cut a deal, and how important it is to develop relationships with people. I have never been in retailing, but I think I can apply my experience and do a good job.

When a story is needed, almost any story will do. If you think you may be unqualified but you want the job badly, reach back for a story that demonstrates some positive quality that you think will get their attention.

Example: Linda wanted a job as director of the women's center at the community college, where the job called for working with inner-city students, many of them older than traditional-age students. The idea of the job was to develop programs highlighting the career potential of women. Linda had never done anything like it before. However, at one time Linda ran a day-care center. She told the Women's Center interviewer: "I worked with a lot of older women when I took care of their children. I found out a lot about their ambitions to advance careerwise. I encouraged many of them to apply to school after their children grew up a bit. That makes me think I can do this job, because I know what their problems are and how to handle them." Other candidates had more experience on paper, but Linda's timely story got her the job.

The listener wants some evidence that you can back up what you have said about yourself. A story is convincing because it is believable and provides concrete examples of skills you have used and problems you have solved. Come armed with the stories you need to demonstrate your qualifications.

Develop Your Social Skills

Life is a contact sport. . . . People deal with and help the people they like. Learning how to become likable is what developing social skills is all about.

—Jack Falvey,
"Developing Party Skills"[1]

At least half the business of the world is conducted in social settings—at social events, golf courses, tennis courts, cocktail parties, church suppers, awards ceremonies, and so on. Job hunting is very much in this flow. In social settings, you meet employers, contacts, and people who may give you job leads and other valuable information.

To make selling work, the more social contact you have, the better. It's perhaps asking too much to have you change your social habits dramatically, but see if you can give it 20 percent more oomph than usual.

Some readers may think it's unfair that job contacts are so often made socially. This is not so. People always prefer eyeball-to-eyeball contact with each other in order to evaluate who has possibilities. It's more "fair" than other methods in that you get to be seen as a live person, not a disembodied voice on the phone or a name on a piece of paper. Social occasions are often set up with that purpose in mind. Get used to it. Adapt to it. Learn to love it like a lost brother or sister.

You don't have to be a party animal, but you should learn how to handle yourself smoothly and positively in mixed company. The least mentioned, but important, part of selling yourself is the fine art of being liked by those whom you want to hire you. Given a choice, employers will always try to hire the people they like best. "Likability" impressions are formed from the informal contacts you have with interviewers and with everyone else in the work setting.

While you are telling stories about your past experiences, people will be forming impressions about you:

Is he easy to be with?
Does she seem to get along easily with everyone?
Is there anything about him I am uncomfortable with?
When she talks with me, do I feel she's really interested?
Do I think I could trust him if I worked with him?

The answers to questions like these may affect your chances of being hired as much as the content of what you can do for the job and the organization. Sometimes a person who is more congenial is hired over someone who has better experience and credentials because the latter made people feel uncomfortable, or "acted like he wanted to run over us," or "seemed too task oriented, not interested in us."

It is hard to judge how much these factors weigh in the hiring decision. You might as well assume they are key variables and give the social dimension your full attention.

If you're feeling short on any of the above factors, what can you do about it? Consider your social skills. People practice their "likability" by being around each other, being out in public, and interacting in as many ways as possible. Here are some things you can be doing.

Informal Partying. Going out to boogie with your friends and a few strangers is a good place to start. Even though this stuff is strictly for fun, it helps you to practice being with people. If you don't do it much, now's the time to get hopping. If not dancing, go to house parties, or picnics, or cocktail parties, or tailgate parties . . . or *something!*

Formal Partying. The norms and ways of socializing at work are important. Often they will be part of a job interview, to see how you mingle with people and how well they like you when the structure of the interview is let down. Such events usually include eating, where it's easy to make mistakes.

What you eat and, especially, drink at a party are important. Try eating something before you arrive so you aren't hungry. Practice moderation in drinking. Most business social gatherings aren't parties even though they look like it. "Parties" are for doing business standing up.[2]

Get some experience with this kind of partying. If you have no other access to it, try your family members in the working world or other contacts. Get them to invite you to such events, so you can learn how to handle yourself there.

Take a Contact out to Lunch. Lunching is part of socializing, and an easy way to get comfortable with the social skills that are part of the working world. Try this with your easiest contacts first, and then invite to lunch some you know less well. Take them to unfamiliar restaurants, so you can get used to new situations. Invite a contact someplace where you will run into her friends, so you can get accustomed to the unexpected encounters with other people.

Give a Party Yourself. This is not always within people's means, but where possible, creating your own social events is a good way to improve your ability to mingle with others and get to know them. Once again, be careful not to let eating or drinking get in the way of your interacting.

Many a job has been lost because the otherwise qualified candidate did not do well socially and was vetoed by one or more of the office staff. In such cases, the rejected person is often not told that social skills were at the root of his problem. How do you tell someone they turned people off, or they did not project much warmth? Instead, the candidates might be told they were simply "not as qualified as others."

The social dimension is easy enough if you're comfortable with it, you do a lot of partying, and people usually like you. But if you back off from socializing at all, check out your social skills in one or more of the following ways:

◆ *Ask for feedback from interviewers.* Once hiring decisions have been made, it is all right to call an interviewer and ask: "Can you give me an idea of my strengths and weaknesses in the interview? Was there anything in my interpersonal style that you'd recommend I change?" Sometimes this kind of honest inquiry will yield helpful advice.

◆ *Ask your friends for feedback.* Do I interrupt when others are talking? Do I sometimes express myself hesitantly? Am I a good listener? Do I get my point across firmly? Is there anything in the way I speak that makes it hard to listen to me?

◆ *Be true to your own personality.* We are not asking for a personality transplant here. If you are a low-key person, then go on being that way and communicate in the style that is comfortable for you. However, pay attention to things you do that may make it more difficult for people to talk with you.

Maybe this all makes you feel self-conscious. Well, in a way it should. Socializing does not come naturally to everyone but it is a necessary factor in anyone's job search. If you jump into the social pool more often than you are used to, and take the ups and downs that come with unrehearsed talk, you'll be a new and improved socializer before too long.

Ask Without Pushing

If you want the job, say so. If you believe you can do the job well, tell the interviewer.

In selling, they call it "closing." Closing the sale. Asking for the business. In job hunting, it's called "asking for the job." Closing is what distinguishes successful from unsuccessful salespeople. Many in the selling field go weak in the knees when it comes to closing. They do everything right up to that point, and then they punk out.

Similarly, job hunters may do a lot of things right and then lose their confidence when it comes to asking for the job.

Asking for the job has several elements in it:

1. A clear statement about the value that you bring to the company.

2. A very brief summary of your experiences and skills that support this statement of value.

3. A direct expression of your interest in the job and your belief that you can do it well.

4. Nonverbal behavior that supports your statement—a strong and steady voice, expressiveness, enthusiasm, and a calm and confident manner.

"Asking for the job" is your way of saying confidently that you believe in yourself. Here are a couple of examples of what it might sound like:

> "I believe I can be an effective assistant manager of your pet store, and this is the job I want most. My past experiences show that I can attract and keep customers and that employees are productive when I work with them."

> "I believe I can do the job you need here. This job as a bookkeeper is the one I want. I've saved money for other companies with my

efficient record-keeping system, and I have supervisors who can tell you about my positive effect on other workers."

If you don't ask for the job, the employer may think several things, none of them good:

"Maybe he's not sure he's the right one for this job."
"I need a person who's confident. I'm not sure about this one."
"How do I distinguish this person from the others?"
"Is he waiting for me to ask another question? I've run dry."

Asking for the job does not involve being pushy at all. Pushiness would be characterized by overbearing behavior, in which the person might say things such as:

"You really need me here."
"I'm the best person for this position. I'm sure of it."
"Why don't you make me the offer now."
"I've told you everything. What else do you need to know?"

When you "ask for the job," don't expect an immediate answer. You'll probably get a vague, noncommittal verbal response like this:

> "Well, thanks for your statement. I appreciate knowing that you're very interested. We'll take all this under consideration and be in touch with you soon."

Nonetheless, it's good that you said it. You gave the interviewer a concise summary of why you believe you should be hired. Even though she gave you a noncommittal response, you may have observed nonverbal signs that were positive, such as a smile, a nod of agreement, or general warmth in the interviewer's demeanor.

Asking for the job is a good way to conclude your comments about yourself. You can combine this with asking:

> "What other information about me would you like to have?"

This indicates that you are open to further communication. Your "summary" does not mean that you have closed the book regarding your statement of value. You would be pleased to add to it, if requested.

Make Job Offers Come to You

How would you like never to have to look for a job again? That may be the nicest gift this book could give you.

No matter what the books say—be optimistic, be persistent, organize yourself, do this, don't do that—the whole job search is an injury in search of a victim, a knee-deep pile of rejection, and an endless set of chores. You've heard "finding a job is the toughest job you'll ever have" until you want to croak. That message does not encourage you to get started. It makes you want to hide and pray for redemption.

Ever run into people who have jobs offered to them? People who seldom have to send out résumés, pound the pavement, or wonder about where their next job offer is coming from? Don't you wonder how they do it? Are they just lucky, do they have great connections, are they extraordinarily talented, or simply in the right place at the right time? Wouldn't you like to be one of them? They are engaged in the No-Search Job Search. These people have learned how to function so that job opportunities occur in the natural course of their lives. There are more such people than you think. This approach is very much within your grasp. Many of the principles in this book, when followed faithfully and done well, lead logically to the No-Search Job Search. In this chapter, I will describe more deliberately how you can set yourself up for future job offers and understand what it means to say: The best job search is no search at all.

Reasons to Avoid Job Hunting

First let's examine what can be wrong with the ordinary job search. While it is difficult to eliminate entirely the need to initiate a formal job search, here are three key reasons why it is better to avoid it whenever you can.

1. Perhaps the worst place to be evaluated for a job is in a job interview. If you have had very little prior contact with the interviewer, the interview is guess-work, and you both know it.

It is difficult to go for interviews where you have to perform your act in thirty minutes. You're downright lucky if the interviewer happens to divine most of what your capabilities are. We teach people interview skills, but it is always a struggle to portray your key experiences, motivations, and talents when the interviewer has no other information about you.

2. The process of the job search can be debilitating. No matter how much we dress it up and equip you with tools and tips for success, a formal job search, where you are the supplicant and the jobs seem to continually elude you, is a grinding experience. The formalities of job hunting deserve some attention, but I maintain that, as Finch says regarding the Company Mailroom in *How to Succeed in Business Without Really Trying*, "It is a place OUT OF WHICH YOU MUST GET." I have suggested ways in this book to recapture some of the enjoyment of job hunting, but I believe the most pleasurable job search is one you conduct without résumés, without formalized interviews, and without the wearisome planning and record keeping that most job-hunting books urge upon the reader.

3. Given the choice, most employers would rather recruit you informally than through a formal search process. The more employers know about you prior to an interview, the happier they are. They know that formal interviews are a guess-ing game too, and it's hard for them, because they have a lot at stake. They would rather contact you through informal channels because they'll either have greater exposure to you, or the reference will come from more trusted sources, or both. This chapter will tell you how to take full advantage of infor-mal avenues.

The No-Search Job Search

You are doing your best job hunting when you are engaged in something else besides job hunting. And job opportunities pass in front of you every day, even though you may not think about them. Consider these two ideas:

1. Everything you ever do is noticed by somebody. Every nail you hammer, memo you write, or job you complete affects someone, and a great number of people see you at work as you are lining things up, working toward your goals, and putting out the final products. All of these people form judgments about you and how you do your work. Since it is a small world that we live in, any one of these individuals might one day have the chance to comment about your capabilities, and your potential for doing the next job you might be seeking. In other words, everyone you run across is in a position to help you with your future aspirations.

2. *Your next job may be right in front of your eyes.* Often the job you will seek next is one you are only dimly aware of when you first see it. You don't know you want to be manager of that department across the hall when you first walk in there. Your awareness develops over time. You don't know you have a flair for association work the first time you call them up to get some information. It may only hit you later after repeated contacts. Often we are drawn naturally and unconsciously to the areas that interest us.

The No-Search Job Search does not happen automatically. Many people will miss their chances, either by not recognizing them or because they act too passively. Learn to make use of these three principles of the No-Search Job Search:

+ *Principle 1: Positioning*

It is one thing to do a good job. It is quite another to do the job well and have key others know that you have done it. Adele Scheele[1] calls this skill "Positioning," and it is crucial to the no-search job search. Positioning means finding a way that you can be useful in that "place where I want to be," and then getting them to let you do it. People who aspire to political positions and volunteer to work on election campaigns are veterans at positioning. If I work at a local college but covet a position at the largest flower shop in town, and I give the flower store information about how to appeal to students needing flowers for formals and other special events, then I am positioning myself for future possibilities. "Positioning," in its broadest sense, is putting yourself in situations where others will have face-to-face exposure to you and your work. When people observe you firsthand, their impressions are far more valid and lasting than if you had only a brief interview with them.

+ *Principle 2: Timing*

The earlier, the better. Positioning and other aspects of the no-search job search work better if you practice them long before you ever think of changing your work. Doing these things just weeks before you want to make a change is less effective. It is too little and too late. People with whom you have contact will not offer you jobs at first sight. Their knowledge of you and confidence in you will grow over a period of time.

✦ *Principle 3: Genuineness*

Positioning doesn't mean much when you are trying to get someone's attention in a self-serving, manipulative way. If you want a job with me one day, be interested in what I am doing without regard for what I might do for you. Don't just try to "win points" with me, because I will figure that out before long.

An Example of the No-Search Job Search

Let's suppose you work way uptown for a small bookstore, but you really want to have a management position with the Metropolitan Transit Authority, the city agency that deals with bus systems. One job has nothing to do with the other. How can you possibly position yourself to be offered a job with that agency? Thinking as far ahead as possible, you might do any of the following:

- ✦ attend the public board meetings of the MTA, where you can learn more about what they are doing, where their activities draw the public's attention
- ✦ request informal meetings with anyone in the agency who will talk with you
- ✦ volunteer to do some informal research in your neighborhood regarding use of the bus system, complaints, patterns of commuting
- ✦ compile a listing of current books (remember, you work in a bookstore) that illuminate the problems of cities and their public transportation systems; then abstract these publications and request a meeting with one of the MTA managers to present the information

Surely you could think of even more things to do. No one of these by itself will necessarily yield a job offer, but each brings you in contact with key officials of the MTA, and each gives them an opportunity to know more about you.

If anyone asks you, in the above example, why you are doing these things for the MTA, you can answer: "I am very interested in public transportation and think I would like to get into this kind of work one day." You are admitting your career inclination without making formal application for a job. If any members of the MTA want to encourage you along these lines, they are free to do it.

Will You Never Have to Look for a Job Again?

You *can* increase the number of job offers made to you, even though you still have to initiate job searches when necessary. Time pressure and economic necessity may force you onto the streets, but that does not undermine this basic principle of the no-search job search: people who know and respect your work, your work habits, and your motivations best will create opportunities to work with you, because it is to their great advantage to seek known quantities rather than take their chances with people from the vast, anonymous labor pool.

While résumés, job interviews, application forms, and job-notice boards will never disappear, you can become less dependent upon them. The no-search job search emphasizes that job seeking can and should be a natural and informal process of people getting to know each other, not a parade of hoops an applicant must jump through to attract an employer's attention.

I believe that three themes make the no-search job search possible and practical for anyone who wants to use them:

✦ *Theme 1: The Jobs That Are Appealing to You and a Good Fit for Your Talents Are Definitely Out There Somewhere*
This is one article of faith I will ask you to accept in this book. You can assume that jobs are out there that appeal to you, and that you have a decent chance of being hired if you make yourself available.

Detective work is easier than you think. The "small world problem" (see page 103) explains how you can find *anyone* in the working world, any job no matter how remote, faster than you thought possible.

An important corollary of the above theme is this: *A potential job opening can be anywhere, often in a job that is currently occupied by someone else.* You should look at any job, no matter who is in it, regardless of whether or not the job is "open." Because a certain amount of *turnover* (people leaving their jobs, sometimes unexpectedly) occurs continually in all sectors of the working world, what appears to be a filled job may become vacant before too long. It has been noted[2] that 30 percent of the American work force has been in their present jobs one year or less.

Thus, if you can find it, you might get it. If you don't get it, you'll probably be put on the trail of something similar. If you still don't get it, you have learned more about your job market than if you sat home and hoped for the best. It saves you the wear and tear of sending letters and résumés and waiting by your mailbox in frustration. Detective work keeps you active rather than passive, and puts you closer and closer to your goals. Your job(s) are waiting out there for you, but someone else will find them if you don't.

✦ *Theme 2: Many of the Most Effective Job-Hunting Skills Are Not Thought of as Such*
It will interest you to know that you are doing some mighty effective job hunting even when you have no idea you are doing it. How is this possible? Because job-search skills are not like mechanical skills, or computer skills, or gardening skills, for which specific, structured manuals can be written. The job search

involves people, and the decisions people make about hiring are not scientific, structured, or done with laboratory equipment. People are on display every day, at various times, not just in job interviews. Thus, there is much daily-life activity that introduces the job seeker and the jobs to each other, long before an employer evaluates a job candidate. As a result, these skills can be viewed as job-search-related:

1. Partying. Social skills contribute greatly to successful job hunting, and where is socializing more obvious than at party time? Fraternity boys and sorority girls have known this instinctively for a long time, and in fact make many of their job contacts through such socializing. These opportunities are available to you as well.

I am not trying to make your playtime into pressure occasions, where you have to worry about how many people you are meeting, or whom you are impressing favorably. I don't want you to feel like an actor who must always be "on." If you get used to parties as natural points of contact, the benefits to your job search will accumulate without unnecessary pressure or forcing.

2. Reading. As in reading books and journals that relate to the fields of work that interest you. If you want a job in advertising, you should be reading *Printer's Ink*, *Advertising Age*, and a couple of the best books on the topic. Jobs will not jump at you from these publications, but they will give you valuable background on the field. Reading is an indispensable skill in job hunting, because you can learn so much about a field through easy access to a library or the Internet. Without such information, you are a sitting duck in any job interview. Reading also can give you names of people you may want to contact—authors of journal articles, newsletter editors, etc.

3. Cleaning Up Your Room/Your House. Getting the drawers unstuffed, sweeping up, finding things you thought were lost forever, going through the books, magazines, and papers lying around. Why is this helpful? It's time to get a little organized, to see what names, addresses, materials, files, books, or other things you might have that will help your job search. Looking through your belongings also helps stir your memory about what your interests are. Cleaning up your home helps to clean out your mind, and gives you a fresh start for deciding what your job direction will be. It's good therapy, and doesn't cost anything. Try it. You'll find it's a form of unconscious job exploration.

4. Painting a Few Rooms. Or getting involved in some other project around the house that takes a few hours and takes your mind off your job-search troubles, giving you a chance to mull over job or career ideas without having to do anything about them. Creative thinkers call this "incubation time," time when ideas can be shaped slowly before they appear in a sensible form. Let your mind relax. Paint the kitchen . . . fix the bicycle . . . even clean the oven (ugh), and you'll come up with a few thoughts you did not expect.

5. *Walking Around the Neighborhood.* Or any neighborhood where you might see things that spark your curiosity, and talk with people about their work or their opinions on anything at all. You need access to a wide variety of people whose work differs from your own. You're probably in your own rut— you see the same people every day, and hear the same opinions. Check out your neighborhood or someone else's and be sure you meet people whose work is different from yours. Think of this as outdoor partying, without a formal invitation.

6. *Writing Letters.* Especially when you are at a distance from the work that you would like, this can be a useful skill. Sending résumés is not an especially successful method, but writing personal letters can have a greater payoff. For example, get acquainted with the author of an article that you read about gardening. Or send for the literature of a new company that you heard about. Get the name of a department head before you write, so that he may give you a personal reply. Or write to a friend who works in another town or city to find out what his company is like. Or write to a professional association to get advice about how to enter that profession. Or write a personal letter to someone whose work you admire, and ask her for a lead or advice.

I am not talking here about the stiff, formal "letter requesting a job interview" that appears in so many job-search books. I am suggesting a more informal letter saying something like: "I have heard/read about your work/your organization and would like to know more about ———. Could you tell me? Can you suggest other materials I might read? Many thanks . . ."

7. *Playing Sports.* Like anything from volleyball to racquetball to bodybuilding to aerobics to sailing. Or any other recreational pursuit that you might prefer, ranging from bird watching to needlepoint to skydiving. Recreational activities are great places to meet people, and chances are they represent a wide variety of kinds of work. You are not joining the group deliberately to make "contacts," but they will happen naturally if you do.

◆ *Theme 3: There Are Many Ways to Attract Job Offers Without Résumés, Job Interviews, Reference Letters, or Application Forms*
This is the heart of the No-Search Job Search. It's the art of using your present circumstances—present job, community activities, professional activities,

personal and recreational interests—to set yourself up for future job opportunities, without embarking on a formal job search. Advancing your career is often much more effective when you are not submitting yourself for formal evaluation (as in job interviews). Instead, you are simply going about your business, doing what you do. All the while, you are using some of the detective skills in this section, but *you are not job hunting*. If you use these informal methods well, the formal job search will become just that, a mere formality, because your informal activities can produce the same results.

Perhaps you are imagining that these informal methods are ones that high-powered, well-placed people use, but how could they possibly be relevant for little ol' you? You do not have to be a high-level honcho to use them. These approaches apply to anyone in any job field at any level, because people are continually observing each other at work and at play.

You have probably not used these informal methods before because you mistakenly believe that in order to look for a job, you have to look for a job. "Looking for a job" refers to all the formalities of the job search (résumé, etc.), but in fact many jobs are learned about, people are evaluated, and job offers made long before a formal search process is begun and completed.

Each of the following is a powerful means of advancing your job and career opportunities. Note that each of these is potentially more beneficial than formal job-seeking behaviors because it allows a job seeker and a possible employer much more intensive contact with each other than would ordinarily take place in a formal search process or brief job interview. Integrate as many of these as possible into your habitual activities. The more you use these methods, the less you will have to depend on job-search formalities.

1. Be Active in Your Profession

A person looking for people to hire will always prefer a known quantity over an unknown. Professional involvement is the easiest way to become known to a large number of your colleagues, some of whom you may want to work for one day. This does not mean that you must run for elective office, chair committees, or do other heavy work involved in leading an organization. Attend programs, go to conferences, choose a committee or two if you are interested, present papers, get to know people in your local area who do the same work you do. Keep up with new information, through journals, programs, and meetings. Much of the best information in a profession passes by word of mouth. Friendships made at meetings become trusted contacts later. Get to know people in your profession, break bread with them, and you will find that you hear about job possibilities long before they are advertised. It is no accident that so much job hunting occurs at conventions and conferences. Face-to-face meetings make it much easier to evaluate people. Résumés and the usual formalities become much less important.

2. Become Active in Someone Else's Profession

Other people's work can be terribly remote and foggy until you meet the people who do it in person. It can be enjoyable to acquaint yourself with a new profession by attending one of their meetings and being there to talk with their practitioners. Read their journals before you go there. Be familiar with the current issues. Ask questions about them, and you'll feel connected to this group soon enough.

If possible, find some reason to be there that relates to your present work. You're an accountant and you are curious about the National Association of Social Workers? Let's say you want to become acquainted with accounting procedures in nonprofit agencies. Any excuse will do. Or if you're thinking of changing professions, just go ahead and admit that. You're not job hunting. You're just learning about a new profession. But, if someone happens to mention a job possibility—or a good part-time work opportunity—you're there to hear it.

> *The faster you get real job experience, the better your chances of building your dream career.*[3]
>
> —Bob Weinstein, *"I'll Work For Free"*

3. Volunteer Your Services

You cannot try every job in the world, but the next best thing to being there as a paid employee is being a nonpaid worker in your spare time. Sure, you don't have much free time, but if you want to sample a new kind of work, there's no substitute for doing it. The word "volunteer" has come to have overtones of hospital aides, and various people referred to as "do-gooders," but don't let that image derail you. Many fields of work have opportunities for offering free help. If you work there, you get a taste of the challenges involved, make contacts with key people, and probably hear about openings when they occur.

Volunteer positions are easier to get than paid part-time jobs, and the employer is usually grateful for your services. A volunteer worker can often have all the responsibility that a paid employee would have, because the job is there to be done, regardless of the pay involved.

Example: Marc wanted a job as a writer with *Philadelphia Magazine*. He couldn't land anything paid, so he volunteered to do office work for them. After three months, the magazine gave him a trial writing assignment; he did a good job and the piece was published. He contributed six more articles (all unpaid) in the course of the year. Finally, a staff writer job came open and you can guess who was first in line for the position, and had the credibility and experience to be hired.

4. Do a Project with Someone in the Profession

What better way is there to know someone's capabilities than to work with that person closely on a project for several weeks or more and count on his/her contribution to get the project done?

The old concept of an apprenticeship was a sound one, and it looks positively brilliant today next to the chancy and impersonal methods of personnel selection. Though we seldom call for apprentices anymore, it is still possible to develop such an arrangement for yourself in almost any field of work. Sometimes we call these internships, or collaborations, or research projects. It doesn't matter what you call it, just find a way to assist a person with some of his/her work, and that person will learn more about you and your capabilities than could be learned in a hundred job interviews.

If you help a person build a house, he/she will undoubtedly remember you. Wanna work for the local newspaper? Help a reporter write a three-part series about your neighborhood or the company you work for. Wanna work for the local historical society? Assist them in organizing and mounting a fund-raising campaign, and I assure you that you won't be forgotten.

In many cases, this can be job hunting at its finest. Yet nary a résumé changes hands, and you are not being interviewed. Just the same, if a job opens in his/her setting, you will be in a great position to hear about it and should be a prime candidate.

5. Find a Link Between Your Present and Future Jobs

Your present job can be a bridge to different fields of employment long before you may decide to make a change. Let's say you're working as an insurance underwriter, but you really want to be in the recreation and leisure fields. Check out the insurance needs of some parks and recreation departments or leisure organizations. Make yourself useful to your present employer while looking into possible new ones. Let's say that you are a technical writer for

IBM, but you have your heart set on managing a plant nursery. Review some gardening manuals to see if their style and approach might help you in designing the manuals that are used to train computer workers.

Suppose you are a bank loan officer, but you would prefer to be in the music business. Investigate and review loan applications for music publishers, learn something about their financial situations, and gather some information that will help you to decide when and how to pursue a change of jobs. With a little stretching of your imagination, your present work can be made relevant to almost any other occupation that you might want to enter.

6. Do Your Present Job Well

Often the best advertisement for yourself is a job well done. That may sound old-fashioned and trite, or like a page out of the Scout Handbook, but it is still true. When you perform your job, others see you do it. They form an impression of you, and many of these individuals are connected to other job possibilities that you might want. *Everyone* you meet and work with is a possible link to the next position that you may want to be considered for.

The methods I am describing here may help you to eliminate the use of résumés and other job-search materials, and may help you to minimize the number of formal job interviews you must endure, but they will probably not allow you to sidestep the reference check. Regardless of how much you may dislike your present work (and sometimes you feel you're being treated unfairly), this job can help you make progress toward a future career if you impress the people around you. Good words from them will always work in your favor. ("She's a class person. She didn't like it here, but she always got the work done.") No matter what your job, do it well and it will always be noticed.

7. Write and Speak About Your Work

Do you know which people are most likely to be remembered in any profession? Those who speak publicly on a variety of occasions and those who write books and articles for professional journals or popular publications. If you want visibility for your views among other professionals or members of the general population, go public with your ideas. From such visibility job opportunities will develop.

They won't be interested in you if they've never heard of you. Other than having worked with you, the only way a prospective employer might have an impression of you is through your speaking or writing.

Example: Clarissa worked as a staff member for a member of the City Council, but always wanted to move to the Mexican-American Chamber of Commerce. However, she could not figure out how to meet a member of that board and make a good impression. She decided to write a newsletter for her council members and send it to various civic groups, including the Mexican-American organization, and also spoke to civic groups whenever possible. She used her role as newsletter editor as an excuse for requesting an interview with the board president; her name recognition got her in the door and gave her the chance to request an interview. Two months later she was offered a job and a chance to use her writing and speaking skills.

Look for opportunities to become a spokesperson for your employer, in your professional organization, and in your community work. Be interviewed in the newspaper. Write for journals, newsletters, or other publications. People who represent themselves or their organizations in print or in public speaking are presumed to know a lot about their field. Often you will be accorded the role of "expert" on a given topic simply because you have been quoted, invited to speak, or receive a byline for your writing.

Volunteer your services. Don't wait for someone else to ask you. It is not cocky or presumptuous to do so. All publications are looking for new material to publish, and many groups need speakers to stir the interests of their members. In terms of potential career advancement, one well-placed article or speaking engagement can be worth ten reference letters. Be the one they're talking about when someone says: "Oh, yeah, I've heard of him," or "I read something she wrote, just the other day."

8. Do Community Work

There is no general category of activity that offers a greater range of contacts and experiences than community work. This category includes anything you do outside of your employment that contributes to the betterment of the town or city where you live. Service organizations (Rotary, Kiwanis, Jaycees), hospitals, boards of directors of businesses and other organizations, United Way, Salvation Army, youth groups, recreation departments, private industry councils, humane societies, child guidance clinics, and many others all need help.

We all know that community work is for the good of your fellow man or woman, and certainly that is the main reason you do it, but there is nothing wrong with getting some benefit from it yourself. How does doing community work help you? (1) It exposes you to an excellent cross section of people in a wide variety of professions and fields of work, people who can introduce you to new career possibilities. (2) Community involvement provides you numerous forums for becoming known to others. Without having to ask them for job interviews, you have many chances to show what your skills are, and show that you are responsible and hardworking. (3) It gives you many reasons to get closely involved with people without being overtly engaged in the process of job hunting. (I would much rather consider you for a job if I had shared committee tasks or other projects with you than if you are simply a name on a piece of paper.)

Is All This "Sneaky Job Hunting"?

All of the eight methods above are highly useful in opening up job possibilities for you, and they all can be done at any time, not just when you are looking for a job. Furthermore, they are more effective when you are happy in your present job but exploring possibilities for the future. Thus, they constitute the No-Search Job Search.

However, these methods may have a distinctly unpleasant flavor to you. They may strike you as being sneaky, aiming at career progress even though you are not saying so. You may prefer to be more open about your intentions. Do not regard these approaches as deceptive, because they are not. You are doing all of these things because you want to do them for their own sake—attending professional meetings, writing articles, contributing to projects, etc.—to broaden your thinking, to expand your range of experience and information. Sure, they are good public relations for you, but your involvement grows out of your genuine interest in your profession, the work of others, and the problems of the community. If you weren't drawn to these activities, you could not sustain your interest simply for career points. Get involved in these things, because a lot of others are already doing them. Don't hide your light under a bushel. If you would rather be up-front about it, then tell everyone: "I'm doing this to set myself up for a future job." This may release someone else to say: "Well, bully for you, so am I."

The No-Search Job Search Is Compatible with the Rest of This Book
The normal job-search process and the no-search job-search approach are integrated with each other. Self-assessment skills, connecting skills, and communication skills (parts 1, 2, and 3 of this book) are all used in the NSJS approach, and all are used in the deliberate job search as well. *The more you can put these informal methods into practice, the less you will have to devote time to the formalized job search.* Connecting skills in general carry the flavor of the NSJS,

since they emphasize that 80 percent of your job-search progress can be made before you engage in the formalities of applying for jobs.

I recommend that you incorporate the no-search job search as a continuous part of your routine, because these involvements will generate more and better job opportunities for you than a metric ton of résumé writing, job interviews, and application forms. When you hear a person say: "I did not actively seek this job. They found me," odds are that person has been using several no-search job search methods as a regular practice.

Doing It Your Own Way

This book is full of structure, advice, and rules, like most other job-search books. You know you're not going to do half of what I say. Oh, you'll agree with enough of it to get inspired for about two hours, and then you'll settle back into your usual routine, saying "How am I gonna DO all this? . . . It's harder than I thought. . . . I never liked school anyway."

Well, let's just say all rules are off. I don't want to set you up for frustration and disappointment in yourself. Don't worry about the way it is *supposed* to be done. Don't follow any programmed approach (do this, then do that). The only way you will do a job search successfully is your own way. Use your own unique methods, because you have learned some good ways to get things done in life and you should not abandon them now.

No two people do job hunting the same. You will choose the parts of this book that you like and incorporate your own strategies. You'll do some things as prescribed, and others you will finesse or sidestep, because that's the way you are. I'm not going to try to change you, and you shouldn't either.

Here are just a few of the individual ways that certain people go about their job search. Some of these may even apply to you. More likely you will add your own special approaches to the list.

Each of these strategies is a distortion of my advice in this book and a lopsided view of any textbook job-search model, but it *works* for the particular individual who uses it, and it works a lot better for them than "doing everything right." Therefore, I encourage you to find the lopsided or skewed strategy that works for you. Be creative, and above all, ignore the parts of this book that look too tedious or awful to do.

> *Examples:* **No phone calls.** I hate the telephone. It's too impersonal, and it makes me nervous. I would rather deal with people face-to-face, which is more natural. So I just walk in and talk to people or I meet them someplace, and one thing leads to another and . . .

All phone calls. The telephone is my ally. I keep on the phone for days and weeks until I get ten solid leads or interviews. No pavement pounding for me; this is more efficient.

I only go to parties. I don't do anything else to look for a job. I have a good time. I know where the people hang out. I check things out, lay back, listen, talk some more, until someone gives me a job lead. I'm patient, and it happens. It sure beats making phone calls, answering ads, and all that other stuff that's just a pain.

I offer to work for free. I figure out who I'd like to hire me, and I give them some free help. Not everyone takes me up on it, but eventually I strike a deal. Then I can prove myself through day-to-day work, instead of going through the artificial messiness of applying for jobs.

I go to the mountaintop. I go directly to the head of the organization where I want to work. I want the person in charge to know who I am, and I need to find out what his/her priorities are. If the leader likes me and what I have to offer, then I don't have to fool around with anyone else.

I send letters or make phone calls to my most trusted contacts. These are the only people I ever tell that I'm looking to make a change—the people who know me best. This is all that I do. If I threw myself onto the open market, it would be a waste of time. I tell my friends and contacts what I am looking for, they give me a few leads, and I eventually plug into new possibilities.

I never talk about jobs. I seek out projects with people whose work I like. Sometimes these projects are related to my present job, other times they are side interests. Usually I do this while I still have a job that I plan to leave. Lo and behold, people offer me new jobs. It doesn't work right away, but this is more fun than the résumé-rejection scene.

I research a field of work intensely. I find out everything there is to know about a new field, through library research, the Internet, and in-person detective work. I read annual reports, study industry trends, know key statistics, and stay abreast of recent happenings in the companies where I want to work. I get all this in my head before I ever show up for a job interview.

I contract my services on a part-time basis. I want them to know about me before I go for the full-time appointment. So I offer them a sample of my work through part-time contracting. If they buy it, they usually like it and I'm in a good bargaining position for a more permanent connection.

Each of these methods makes sense for the people who use it. Most of these methods are not so oddball after all. Each takes advantage of a job seeker's strength.

Notice that many of these methods seek to reduce the amount of time spent in the formalities of job searching. These are wise people, because they know the do-everything methods can be wearisome and frustrating. The less time spent in sending résumés, completing applications, or suffering through screening interviews, the better.

You probably know some people who seem to hear about jobs without even trying. Some of these folks practice the so-called oddball ways described above. They're not dumb. They would rather dig a tunnel to China before doing everything recommended in a job-search manual. Find and cultivate the methods that work best for you.

In general, the more you apply no-search job-search approaches, the more you will have job offers presented to you, and you'll have much less involvement with the formalities of job hunting. You can probably already see the no-search job search operating in your life. If so, keep doing what you're doing.

22

Sell Yourself Long-Distance

You are fifty to three thousand miles from where you wish your eventual employment to be and are wondering what exactly to do about this stark reality. Of course, it is very difficult to conduct a work search at a distance. Scattering résumés across the landscape yields little, and you must wonder what else is worth doing. You cannot expect to receive job offers by mail. As noted later in this chapter, your long-distance job search must lead to one or more in-person visits (at least a week at a time) to your target town, city, or area.

You may wonder whether it makes any sense to do long-distance work searching. Keep in mind these two things: First, very few people do any preparation at all before they set foot in their target areas. Thus, any advance work you do will put you that much ahead of your competition. Second, every day you are in your target area, you will be hungry and anxious to find work, so you will be sorely tempted to skip much of the recommended detective work and research. Hence, it pays to do as much as possible before you go there.

This chapter assumes you have chosen a target geographical area, preferably a town or city, and that you have a goal statement that describes the kind of employment you are seeking.

> **Examples:** I want to work with flowers or plants in Ashland, Oregon.
> I am seeking administrative work in a college or university in the Boston area.

Long-distance job hunting can be frustrating because you won't often make a lot of progress until you're "there," on-site. When you're there you can apply the connecting skills detailed in chapters 8 through 14. Until that time, there are three forms of contact you can make while you're in your present location—writing, telephone, and in person.

Writing

Write letters requesting background information about work available in the area. Direct these letters to chambers of commerce, United Way, or other groups that exist to provide this information.

> *Example:* (letter to United Way): I would appreciate your letting me know how I might obtain a listing of social service agencies in your area that relate to senior citizens.

Write letters requesting information from a target employer.

> *Example:* I would like to know about the programs and services of the Community Health Clinic and would be pleased to pay for any publications you may have available.

Write letters to individuals who work at your target employers. You will have gathered these names either from previous literature or from inquiries by telephone. Write to a person whose job title intrigues you, even if you know nothing about his or her work.

The advantage letter writing gives you is that people are flattered to receive personal attention by mail. When you receive a letter from someone who is aware of your work and has taken the time to study and think about it, you assume the person is impressed by what you and your organization are doing.

> *Example:* Dear Ms. McShain: I am writing to you because you are director of programming for the Community Health Clinic and perhaps you can tell me a bit about the kinds of programs you offer in a typical year.

Write follow-up letters to everyone who responds to you. Be sure to research whatever information they have provided in their replies—key articles, books, other information. Include in your reply an example of your work, if possible. Ask for permission to make an appointment when you arrive in the target area. You can enclose a résumé, but emphasize that you are not asking for job help, and are simply including the résumé as a convenient summary of your background.

> *Example:* I read your report on the year's programs and was intrigued by the variety of field trips you take within a limited budget. Could I arrange to visit you, when I arrive in Minneapolis, to ask a few more questions?

Writing letters by E-mail to prospective employers is, of course, possible, but I don't generally recommend it since you have not met the employers and you don't have permission to access their E-mail. It's better to use conventional mail than risk a breach of employment etiquette.

Telephoning

Request printed materials you may have mentioned in your initial letter to the organization. A phone call will probably hasten the arrival of these materials by several days. Ask for the public relations office, the public information office, or some similar department title.

> *Example:* Would you send me a copy of your annual report and any other publications or brochures describing your activities?

Request the names of key officials mentioned in the annual report, company newsletter, or similar publication. Ask for the personnel or public relations department if the operator is confused about where to refer you.

> *Example:* Could you tell me the name of the vice president for finance?

Speak with a target person and request one or more of the following: (1) an appointment to see him or her when you arrive in Target City; (2) suggestions about additional reading you might do to better understand the individual's profession; (3) recommendations of names of other people in the profession whom you could write to or see when you arrive there.

> *Example:* Thanks for the letter you sent me about investments work in the insurance industry. I read the book you recommended—can you suggest similar titles? Would it be possible to meet with you when I arrive in Hartford? Before I arrive, are there other investment analysts there you would suggest I write to?

Your request for a meeting could be for either an information interview or a job interview, depending on where you are in your job search. I would prefer that you do information interviews first, to better understand the employer's needs; however, you may already have enough information to request a job interview.

In Person

In-person meetings in your local area can be very beneficial to you before you make a trip to your target location. Your present town or city is like your target city in the following respects: It has many of the same kinds of organizations you're interested in; it has many employers where your skills are needed and values can be satisfied; the process you use to reach employers in your present town is the same as what you would use in your target city. You should (1) obtain printed materials—newsletters, magazines, annual reports, and so on; (2) visit these employers in order to practice your information interviewing; (3) practice the process of getting referrals from one employer to another, perhaps even a referral to someone in your target area, and ask about branch offices in other cities or towns—maybe the headquarters of the organization is located in the place where you are going.

"But I Don't Have Any Contacts"

The importance of having contacts cannot be overestimated. When you don't live where you want to get a job, you need people in the new area to serve as guides for you. Even if they do not know where jobs are, they can help tell you who the employers are in that town, how small or large they are, and give you names of people to seek for advice and orientation.

So what makes you think you do not have any contacts? Sure you're all alone and far away, but remember the Small World phenomenon (chapter 9). With a little effort, working through people as links to other people, *you can reach (just about) Anyone, Anywhere.* That includes the mayor of the city, or the local TV star, or the woman who runs that fancy-sounding boutique, or the publisher of *Power Tools Unlimited*, that magazine you just heard about.

What makes me think so? A contact is simply a person who will talk with you for five minutes even though he or she does not know you, either because you called him up, walked into her office, or got referred by a friend. You don't expect the contact to get you a job or throw a party for you, just move you along toward a new source of information and get you a little closer to target employers. Now, that's a modest enough expectation, isn't it?

If you still think you have no contacts, try this. Ask anyone in your present town or city:

Who do you know in ——— (target city)?
May I call ——— and say that you suggested I call?

That person will probably be in a different line of work from what you want. No problem. You're just trying to get the chain started. Ask the first contact:

Can you tell me something about what it's like to work in ——— (city, town)?

I'm looking for work in ——— (field of work). Can you suggest any organizations I should know about or people I could talk to?

If you don't know anyone in that field, who can you suggest that might be close to that field in some way?

By keeping your demands minimal (you just need a name or two, or a suggestion about where to call next), you can keep the chain going, and before too long, you will find someone who knows someone who works in your target area. At the same time, you can also do the Direct Approach. Call one of your target organizations directly and say: "I'm moving to the area and am looking into work in the ——— field, and would like to know something about what your organization does. Could you tell me your main programs and services?"

There are no rules against this. Commercial air travel and geographical mobility have been common for long enough that people know people all over the map of the United States, and the cross-connections increase every day. Your job is to tap into them.

The Loneliness of the Long-Distance Job Searcher

Life on another planet is no fun. You're here, thinking about how to get there. Your friends and everyone else are now seeing you as pulling away or already gone. You're excited, they're not. You're looking, they're not. It can make you feel awkward, and not very much a part of either place. What to do?

* Cultivate colleagues there. Start a correspondence with any contacts you've met on the phone who sound particularly interesting, or whose work you'd like to know more about. This probably should not be someone in a target organization, but someone else who may become a friend, a person there in a different field with whom you might share some mutual interests.

* Build bridges to people here. Make a special effort to cement a relationship with people in the local area with whom you intend to maintain a connection. Take them to lunch, show interest in their career problems, try to get information that will help them.

* Have a timetable for getting out, a target date for moving there. Try to squeeze in a trip to the new locale before you move there, so you can reinforce your telephone contacts with in-person visits.

Loneliness is not a long-term ailment. If you stretch the ropes between here and there right now, these will become lifelines, and they will still be in place when you are there. So, when you're there, part of you will still be here. Got that straight? These "ropes" are people who help you get there and follow your progress after you have moved.

When You Should Move to Target City

You probably should not move permanently to the target area for your work search until you have accomplished the following. First, you need to have accumulated a list of at least fifty prospective employers, using employer directories, telephone books, and other resources. You need this many to convince yourself that there *are* more than a handful of possibilities there.

Second, you should have reviewed enough printed and Internet material from the specific employers, the commercial press, and professional organizations so that you are reasonably prepared for a job interview if one should occur the day you arrive. A detailed review of this kind should focus on the top five employers on your prospect list.

Finally, it's not a good idea to move permanently until you have at least five specific places of possible employment in the target area where some individual is personally aware of you as a result of your correspondence, a direct referral from a person in your present area, telephone communication, or any combination of these.

Does "Being There" Electronically Help You?

In these days of being "wired" for instant communication to any location, you may be tempted to think that long-distance job hunting is "no problem." Guess again. Communicating electronically is not going to transform your job hunt into a "right next door" process.

Some job hunters think that "employers will make a lot of hiring decisions electronically, so it's not important for me to be there." Not true. Employers may screen candidates via the Internet, video interviews, etc., but they will almost always reserve final judgment for in-person meetings. Job candidates will learn to "look good" on the Internet and TV, just as they've learned to inflate their résumés. All the more reason for employers to meet people face-to-face for a more thorough evaluation.

Distance is still your enemy. You can do some things to help yourself at a distance, but whenever you have a chance to close the distance gap, do it. There is still no substitute for face-to-face contact.

If and when the day comes that people are hired without face-to-face meetings, it will be a sad day indeed. It has an Orwellian flavor. Do you want people making inferences about your motivation, your character, your key skills, and your creative imaginings without having met you? Keep these points in mind:

+ Personal chemistry is a major factor in almost every hiring decision.
+ As a prospective employee, you want to emphasize your motivation, your key skills, and your creativity. Always persist in demonstrating these in person.
+ It's a must for you to see the place of business and experience the downtime between interviews.
+ You want to experience the personalities of your prospective boss and co-workers on a firsthand basis.

When and Where to Begin Your Long-Distance Search

As you must suspect by now, long-distance activity cannot wait until two weeks before you intend to move. You should probably begin six months before you intend to move. This means you will be researching, writing, phoning, and talking in person long before you have resigned your present position.

All the following sources are good places to begin your efforts:

+ *Newspaper subscriptions.* Lay out the funds for out-of-town newspapers to be delivered to your doorstep or post office box on a regular basis. This will acquaint you with the newest developments that may have work potential for you. Such items as "New Plant Opens Up" or "Government Contract Renewed" tip you off about employers you didn't detect in the phone books.
+ *Regional magazines.* Currently many regions of the country produce magazines that focus on topics and people of local interest. In the East, for example, you can find *New York*, the *Washingtonian*, *Philadelphia Magazine*, *Pittsburgh*, the *Bostonian*, and others. These publications will keep you abreast of regional currents of change that may suggest employment opportunities.
+ *Polk's city directories.* If the phone book for your target city is not available, try the local library and ask for Polk's. It gives you the same information as a regular telephone book, and it locates the people and employers for you by section of town.

Anticipation is important, but it takes time. The more time you allow yourself between long-distance activity and the eventual change of location, the less anxiety you will feel and the more chance there is that productive connections will happen.

What if You Have Several Target Cities and Towns?

What if you're looking at job possibilities in several far-flung cities and towns? That's no excuse for staying at a distance. Fling yourself out to where you think you most want to be. Establish your geographical priorities and act on them.

How Do I Get an Employer to "Fly Me In" for an Interview?

This is what we all hope for in seeking jobs at a distance—to create enough interest that the employer will fund our trip. Here's how you might establish enough credibility so they will invest the time and money to "fly you in":

1. Establish your qualifications through paper or electronic résumés, in response to announced positions.

2. Uncover an unannounced vacancy—through your personal referral network—and contact the company in a timely manner.

3. Request or respond to a telephone interview, in which you cite key qualifications that fit with the employer's needs.

4. Identify a specific high-priority need of the employer (a reason to want you). You establish this through your research and/or intuitive reflections on what you believe the company might need.

5. Ask your references to call the employer to indicate why you're a good candidate for the job.

If you can establish that you have skills that will give promise of helping the company achieve a key objective, then paying your plane fare and hotel is a very small investment, compared to the potential value you may bring them.

When Your Target Is Narrow, Broaden Your Possibilities

When you have your sights set on working in a particular location, often you are limited to that particular town, city, or area. Either your spouse has just gotten a new job there, or the family has decided this is the right place to live, or you decided to move back home near your parents, or some other reason. Thus, you must take the work that is available in that location. You may not get the job that you had before, and may feel some keen disappointment about that. However, it is possible to take an optimistic view about what this might mean.

Because your geographical scope is now limited, you can open yourself up to a broader range of types of work. Now may be just the time to be creative about how your previous work experience can be applied. It was harder to do before when you had a regular job, but now circumstances allow you to consider other possibilities.

Suppose you are a nurse with administrative responsibilities. Consider how your background might be applied to health insurance companies, health maintenance organizations, or even to the health and fitness programs of local businesses.

You may find new kinds of work that you would not have thought of before. A new job can make you stronger overall, because several kinds of work experience will make you more marketable. I'm not saying this just to make you feel good while you go through a difficult transition. People who have the gumption to change their work usually come out ahead in the long run because they learn more, adjust better to change, and tell more interesting stories.

Part V

Interviewing
for Success

23

Give Them Some Reasons to Want You

*Life would be so much better, I realized after watching a performance
of "Tosca," if I were an opera singer. . . . I just know that everything
would go much more smoothly for me if at the end of the day my coworkers would rise from their desks and applaud me wildly. If they
would only applaud, and shout "Bravissima!!" and pelt me with long-
stemmed roses, it would make a really big difference.*
—Andrea Behr, *San Francisco Chronicle,* 8/31/98

Who is this person and what spaceship brought her here? The "standing ovation" is not so far removed from your reality as you might believe. "Ovations"
are given to those who see their role in the employer's picture as larger than
their jobs.

Here is an expression that captures the very essence of successful job hunting*: Give Them Some Reasons to Want You. The employer is frantically
looking for prospects, rummaging through her filing cabinets, seizing people
in the hallway, pressing her ears to the wall, rooting through her desk drawers,
asking plaintively: "Where have all the good job candidates gone? Wherever
can they be? Why are they hiding from me?"

You have it within your very hands to solve this woman's problem, but she
won't know about you if you don't tell her. You have to do something to get
her attention.

Just being the happy, industrious, eager scout of a job candidate is not
enough. To the employer, candidates often look alike. They smile, they explain, they babble, they plead, they grovel. Your mission is to set yourself
apart from the preprogrammed pack. You will do that by "giving her reasons
to want you."

What are these reasons? Ways you can help her solve problems, which are
those of her company. What problems, you ask? Forsooth, the problems and
"needs" you have identified in the diligent research that I know you did prior

---

*This phrase was suggested by Ms. Susan Engleking, Austin, Texas, Chamber of Commerce.

to seeking job interviews. You did those information interviews, didn't you? You know, the ones where you asked inquisitive questions so you know what they're looking for? I know you just loved those. Not at first? But after you got used to it, they were easy.

Here are a few examples of how your skills may become "reasons" to hire you:

✦ You're a good technical writer and this home appliance company is way behind in production of their technical manuals, recruitment literature, and instruction books for consumers. You show them a portfolio of your writing and express your willingness to work on their publications—voilà!—they have a "reason to want you."

✦ You have research skills that were sharpened as a history major and a staff member of the Library of Congress. The nonprofit nutrition association Eat Your Way to Heaven needs you to research grant opportunities and state-of-the-art nutrition research studies. They especially need the grants, and you'll help them find the money sources. Zounds!—they have a "reason to want you."

✦ You are a veteran backpacker and have some knowledge of bears and how they may be a threat to people who come across them. In your research of outdoor organizations, you learned that Outdoor America had been sending out groups of schoolchildren, only to have serious problems with the bears. They need someone to teach the leaders and children how to prevent bear problems. You are the person with the answers—but of course!—and they have a "reason to want you."

"Why Should I Hire YOU?"

This is the main question of any job interview. Now consider how people often answer that question:

"I'm a really hard worker."
"I really, really need a job."
"I'm a quick learner."
"I have the skills for this job."
"I have a degree that relates to this field."
"People will just love working with me."

Observe how these candidates do not even mention the needs of the employer. They simply state their own attributes, without referring to the employer's priorities. It's like saying: "Hire me because I need the money. In fact, I'll go crazy if I don't have a job soon." The interviewer says to herself: "Never mind about your situation. What are you going to do for *me*?"

Your task is to find out what the employer wants and needs, because this is what they're willing to pay money for. Once you know what they're looking for, you can speak directly about your value.

The "reasons to want you" are typically very practical—they refer to things you can *do* to help the employer. Which means if they hire you now, you can start helping with their problem right away.

Don't be shy. Do not hesitate to tell them what you can do. Now is no time to leave the employer guessing. Follow this structure:

1. *The Problem.* Tell the interviewer what you have identified that you believe they need help with:

> "I understand the children in your groups have been bothered by bears and the staff are not sure what to do."

2. *How You Can Help.* Tell them what you will do if you're given the chance:

> "If you hire me, I'll teach the staff and the children how to prevent any bear problems, and what to do in the rare event that unexpected difficulty occurs."

3. *Your Past Experiences That Support Your Claims.* Tell them what you've done before that leads you to claim your skills:

> "I've been a forest ranger for three years and a member of the Backpacking Society for ten years. I've sighted bears many times and have frequently found ways to head them off and avoid trouble."

"Giving them reasons to want you" is *not* being pushy. It's exactamente what the interviewer wants to hear. Encourage them to say "Yes, we will benefit if we hire this person."

The "Me First" Attitude

When job hunters have a me-first attitude, they are ineffective in the job market. Some job hunters have been accustomed to taking a *microscopic* view of their responsibilities in the marketplace:

"I do the job and you pay me."
"I do what you ask and you reward me."

"I stick to the job description and my boss is happy."

"Workers" can become so oblivious to the purposes of the organization that they think of their jobs as "entitlement":

"I show up and you pay me."

Many workers are absolutely mystified by the view that they must contribute to the bottom line. Such people, when laid off or changing jobs, have the maximum difficulty in selling themselves to employers.

The me-first and me-only viewpoints may also reveal why marriages and other relationships have a hard time making it. Successful partners ask questions such as:

"What do you need from me to make your day better?"
"What do I not understand about you that I need to understand for our relationship to work?"

In the best of marriages, these questions are either asked and responded to overtly, or the partners anticipate each other's needs.

"Me First" in Everyday Life

I used to know a guy whom everyone called "I'll-pencil-you-in Ben." Anyone who asked to meet him for lunch, a movie, or anything was told: "That sounds okay. Let me pencil you in."

For Ben that meant you were in a "hold" status until something or someone better came along or he simply lost his enthusiasm for meeting with you. Ben did not keep friends for long.

What does Ben have to do with job hunting? When people have little, cursed habits of relating to others, do they tend to show up in other spheres of their lives? Of course they do. "But I would never play movable chairs with a job interview appointment," Ben says. So it's OK to play movable chairs with me? Ben, you'll do it with an interviewer if you're given half the chance.

If everyone else in your firmament is a chess piece to be moved around according to your shifting priorities, then sooner or later you'll exhibit these behaviors in your job hunting and job performance. You'll ignore one meeting where you said you'd come in favor of another that sounds "more profitable." You'll accept a job offer but then renege on your agreement because something better comes along before you start work. You'll start a project for your boss but put it on the back burner when a future prospective boss asks you to look into something.

When I get a phone call from someone like Ben who cancels an appointment the same morning or day that I have arranged to meet him (he has done this before), and I listen to the voice mail message ("I just have things I have to get done"), I cringe. As I tune in to the "apologetic" voice, I say to myself: "I would never hire this person."

Going Above and Beyond

Stretch your imagination a bit. Rather than bumble silently along as a "me-firster," suppose you did any of the following to help your employer:

+ You got hired because you saw a way that a mortgage loan company could help people understand refinancing options easily, you wrote a trial advertisement, it got a big response, and they wanted to have your services "right away." They didn't ask you to write the ad, but you approached the job as an "owner," saw a need, and did something about it.
+ You got hired as a career counselor at the local community college because you proposed a series of group workshops that enabled the Career Center to attract more students.

A job hunter must conceive of herself as one who can earn "wild applause" by doing something that everyone in the organization benefits from. Here are a few more examples:

+ The computer whiz applicant who recognizes that the company needs to have staff meetings (they're a bunch of techies who never thought they needed to communicate on a regular basis) so that people could share information, be "on the same page," and work toward common goals; the company hires him and profits go up, because clients are served better.
+ The bookstore applicant who increases traffic in the store by arranging highly popular poetry readings and appearances of celebrity authors. She has the knack for getting these people on the phone and charming them into appearing. Many ovations.
+ The toy store job hunter who figures out how to help customers negotiate the maze of toy options (she shopped in the store; it took her four hours to get what she wanted; she said to herself: "I can do this better"); business skyrockets, management shares profits. Everyone stands and applauds.
+ The stockbrokerage applicant who designs a system for funneling research data to clients while brokers are busy on the telephone; trades increase, clients are happy, business booms, everyone gets a raise. Cheers abound.

The Interviewer's Perspective

The job interview is not a courtroom, where lawyers fight over the right and wrong of what you are saying. The interviewer is not your adversary. He or she is on your side. Interviewers want you to succeed, do well in the interview, because it makes their job easier. Of course, they are not always perfectly congenial or clear about what they want, but that is because of their imperfect interviewing skills. Fundamentally, they hope you are the best candidate for the job, because if you are, their task is completed.

Say I'm the interviewer, and I am looking for that something special or different about you that the other candidates may not have—a reason to be interested in you. So your job is to help me find it. Put an idea in my head. Give me something to chew on, something that would help me to justify choosing you, something besides your degree and bland statements such as "I love the business world." Say something that attracts my attention, and draw it directly from your understanding of yourself and your understanding of the job in question. Speak to me.

> *Example:* I would be good at organizing your data projects because I have done that several times before.
>
> I think I could do well in your economic development area because I have had experience with our university's Bureau of Business Research.
>
> I believe my writing ability would help in that division because there are so many reports to write for different audiences.
>
> I could use my experience as a grants administrator for the government to help your department apply for new grants.
>
> I am comfortable working with quantitative data and statistics, so I think that research analyst job would be a good one for me.
>
> I have a lot of patience with difficult people, and am sure I could help out in the customer service department.
>
> My work as a camp counselor taught me a lot about how to manage children. I could apply that to what you are looking for in the Parks and Recreation Department.
>
> I know where to get many of the building materials you need for that construction project, and I can get them at good prices.

You would not pull any of these statements out of thin air. Each would come only after you had analyzed the job at hand and related it to your particular background.

The first rule of selling yourself is to find some way to distinguish yourself from the competition. State something that is unique about yourself that the others cannot offer. If your "reason to want you" is sound and reasonably stated (you don't have to be excessive; it is not necessary to say you are the best ever at a certain task), most interviewers will want to know more about you.

Example: Susan wanted a job with ABC Instruments, a national computer technology firm. But she had a liberal arts degree in history, did not want a sales job, and couldn't figure out how to attract their attention. With a little research (a skill honed in history courses), Susan discovered a job as a junior management trainee that involved studying new product designs and reporting on their potential to higher management. She didn't know a lot about technological products, but decided to make her pitch as follows: "I have strong writing and research skills and, if you'll teach me the technical things, I can produce and write very clear and useful reports." It happens that ABC had been complaining about the reports developed and written by other junior management—they were not clear and the data were often incomplete. They bought Susan's "reasons to want me." She worked there for four years and then, on the basis of her contacts with local industry, was hired by the chamber of commerce to be vice president for technological development. Her career had started modestly enough—with a job for which she might have been seen as "unqualified" if she had not given the employer a specific rationale for hiring her.

In Conclusion

"Giving them some reasons to want you" keeps you in the right frame of mind. An employer has no reason to talk with you unless he believes you can help the company or the organization do its job better. The more clearly you can state how the company will benefit from your skills, the more attention you'll receive.

24

Show Rather Than Tell

What more compelling way is there to convince a manager to hire you than to do the job the way he wants it right there in front of him?
—Nicholas Corcodilos,
The New Interview Instruction Book[1]

There is a fundamental flaw with the job interview: the difference between what a person *says* she will do and what she will actually do if hired. No matter how convincing and articulate a job candidate may be, the interviewer wonders: "Will her deeds match her words?"

The difference between what you say you can do and what you will actually do introduces a measure of doubt into the interviewer's mind. This is why interviewers sweat and worry as much about interviews as you do: "What if her actions do not measure up to her words? Then I'll be making a mistake if I hire her."

There is a way that you can close some of that gap between words and deeds, and therefore increase your chances of getting the job you want.

What if it were possible to *show* the interviewer what you would actually do if hired, so she could see with her own eyes the results that you would achieve? Does this sound like putting you in a time machine and projecting you into the future?

Actors/actresses, dancers, and musicians are accustomed to "auditions"—defined by the dictionary as "practical demonstrations of suitability." Will you be singing and dancing your way to the top? Will you be taking to the stage to get your next job? Not necessarily, but in the most general sense we're on the stage whether we like it or not. Might as well show 'em what you can do, rather than answer questions posed by interviewers who secretly whisper to themselves: "I wish I could see what he will actually do on the job, so I can make a better decision."

If you can make your job interview into an "audition," you'll go a long way toward increasing the interviewer's confidence in your ability to perform the job.

Ask yourself this question: "How might I be able to demonstrate during the job interview some of the skills that I would use if I were hired?"

How would this be possible? Consider the following:

1. *Demonstrate skills during the interview that would be a part of your projected job.* For example, any job interview is going to call for a certain amount of speaking skill. In all likelihood, your job will also require you to communicate orally. How you express yourself in the interview is thus a "sample" of what you'll be like on the job.

Listening is also a skill that is found both during the interview and on the job. If you listen carefully and show the interviewer that you've understood her, you can be expected to listen well to customers, coworkers, company suppliers, and others.

Perhaps recalling technical information is a necessary skill required for the job you want, and you can demonstrate this during the interview by citing your memory of technical details or procedures. Be careful with this one, because if you overdo it, you will seem pretentious.

Consider what other skills of the job you might demonstrate in the interview—research skill (demonstrated by your knowledge of the company's recent history), diplomatic skill (shown by your handling of sensitive topics), analytical skill (demonstrated by your response to complicated questions), think-on-your-feet skills (shown by your response to questions you hadn't thought about), and poise (demonstrated by your dealing with a panel interview).

2. *Send in advance or bring with you to the interview samples of your previous work that relate to the job.* Such "samples" might include brochures you have developed, reports you've written, flyers of programs you have planned, drawings or designs you've done, or videotapes of work you've completed. Your previous employers may have had handouts describing their work. If any of these reflect your skills and experiences, consider which of them to bring with you to the interview. Don't just dump these on the interviewer's desk. Ask her: "Would you like to see a description [or brochure, or summary] of the work I did previously?"

3. *Consider how you might give a "live" demonstration of your work during the interview.* As Corcodilos says in *The New Interview Instruction Book*:

> How can you do a job before you're hired? Act like you have the job. Don't treat the interview as an interview. Go to the interview as though it's your first day on the job.[2]

To do this, you might say to the interviewer:

> "I have done a lot of work explaining technical procedures to other employees. I'd like to give you a demonstration with a group of people who work here. How might I get an opportunity to do this?"

"I know you're looking for someone who can organize a filing system. If you show me your setup, I can show you how I would organize it and explain that to members of your staff."

"You told me that you need someone with mechanical skills. Show me something here that needs fixing and I can demonstrate what I can do."

"Customer service is very important to your operation. May I have your permission to show you how I would greet and interact with customers here in the store?"

"I really want to work in this veterinary clinic. Let me handle the dogs for a while, and you'll see that I have the right temperament and I can deal with their problems."

"I know that I can find buyers for your real-estate agency. Give me a chance to get on the phone for a few days, and I'll get results."

The following are ways that you can benefit from demonstrating your skills in a "hands-on" manner:

✦ By proposing a skill demonstration, you are vividly expressing your confidence that you can do the job. It also shows your assertiveness, a quality you will undoubtedly use on the job.

✦ If the employer sets up the opportunity for you to show your stuff, you have a much better chance of making your case than if you had never asked.

✦ The interviewer may think of other ways you can demonstrate your skills. Any opportunity to show what you can do is likely to work to your advantage.

✦ Your suggestion to demonstrate your skills may also be a request for a full-blown "trial work experience." You might say:

"I know it's hard for you to determine from a brief interview [this is exactly how the interviewer is feeling, so you're empathizing accurately with her] how I will perform on the job. Let me suggest this: Give me a couple of days or a week here to show what I can do. Put me on the job and I think you'll see I have what you're looking for."

Once again, this is an expression of your confidence in yourself. If the interviewer offers you any kind of a trial work experience, consider taking it. There is some debate on this. Would the employer be getting "free work" from you? Is that fair? I leave it to you to judge the integrity of the employer before suggesting that you offer a trial work period. My own view is that you have far more to gain than lose by demonstrating your skills for a week. So what if you work a week for free? In all likelihood, someone will notice you who can recommend you for future opportunities.

If you cannot leave your present job without giving notice, do your best to "show" your skills during the interview. You can also request additional interview time:

> "I'd like to show you some of the things we talked about, if you'd be willing to see me for an additional interview."

John wanted a job as a salesperson in a sporting goods store. He had some ideas about how to arrange the merchandise for best in-store marketing, but he needed an additional interview (he had to wait a week until he could get time away from his job again). His ideas attracted the interviewer's interest enough that he was granted a second interview, and John was offered the job.

In general, if the interviewer extends your interview time to include any of the "demonstrations" you propose, do them.

Showing is more powerful than telling. Whenever you have a chance to demonstrate, take it. Not only is showing more persuasive, it also increases the number of hours of exposure you have to the interviewer. The longer the time of your overall interview, the better your chances. The more they see of you, the better.

What if you blow it when doing a demonstration? There is always that chance, but the odds are with you, not against you. You'll get points for simply requesting and doing the demonstration in the first place. They will allow for your nervousness, and you have these skills or else you wouldn't be there, right?

4. *Talk about what you would do during your first weeks on the job.* Instead of simply saying that you can do the job, ask the interviewer: "Would you like me to tell you what I would do if I were hired, to begin accomplishing the results you're looking for?" For example, you might say:

> "To generate more customers for your title company, I would do the following: (1) Call listings of real-estate agents to develop leads. (2) Join the Real Estate Appraisers Association to develop contacts, from which I would generate more leads. (3) Begin developing relationships with financial consultants, whose clients can be referred here. (4) Get myself established in two or more community-service

organizations, to further expand my contacts. (5) Do a personal survey of real-estate agents in order to develop them as referral sources and get their advice on where to look for customers."

It is especially powerful to describe what you would do during your first weeks on the job. Corcodilos recommends:

1. Define a simple strategy for solving a problem:

"I can improve your customer service here in the hardware store by redesigning the traffic flow and the front counter space."

2. Describe specific tasks:

+ "I will design the blueprint and floor plan."
+ "I will consult with counter furniture suppliers and report designs to the staff for evaluation."
+ "I will begin training sessions with staff once the final designs are selected."

3. Show your special skills:

"I will use these skills: spatial design; negotiating with suppliers; understanding of customer service; training and supervision."

While these are simply words too, they give evidence that you have thought a lot about the job and that you have a strategy for working toward the results they're looking for. This is more advanced thought than most job hunters ever devote to their interview preparation.

Interviewers are aware that some job candidates are good talkers but may not come through if they're given the job. They fret anxiously that you will not live up to your credentials. The idea of making such a mistake is an interviewer's nightmare.

Therefore, you should look for opportunities to give the interviewer firsthand evidence that you truly can do this job, so that she can see for herself that your words are not empty ones. You're saying, in effect: "If you don't believe what I'm saying, let me show you." Put showing into your job search. It's far more powerful than telling.

Showing does not fit into the usual mode of job interviewing. Interviewers habitually just ask the applicants why they believe they're suitable for the job, and accept what they say.

You will attract the interest of other interviewers when you ask to "demonstrate," because they'll see an opportunity to close that gap of uncertainty between what you say and what you will do, and they'll be intrigued by your forthrightness. The closer you can model your interview behavior to what you would be doing on the job, the more effective your presentation will be.

The motto of Harry Truman and the state of Missouri—"Show me"—has always been a persuasive one. In the future, I expect that successful interviewing will evolve in the direction of asking job candidates to "audition," because interviewers will need to reduce the mistakes they make by listening to what interviewees say they will do. The trend toward hiring temporary workers as a selection technique is evidence that this is already happening.

25

Remember, Interviewers Are Irrational

Come into my parlor, said the spider to the fly. You wiggle around and hope to escape the interview with all your limbs intact. When you're the fly, interviews don't look like a party experience. But, truth to tell, the spider is just as uneasy about the whole affair as you are.

Interviewers are supposed to choose the "best" people, the people with the "right" qualifications. How do they know who is best for a given job? They don't. Interviewers have a lot at stake, and they're still guessing. It's a forty-five-minute roll of the dice.

Never let it be said that interviewers make their decisions on a rational basis. Rather than hire individuals who are objectively "the best," interviewers often choose the ones they *like* best. How do they justify their choices? As John Krumboltz, a longtime authority in the career development field, once said, "When a reason is needed, any reason will do."

In truth, many so-called irrational decisions by interviewers result from evaluating factors that lie beyond objective competence.

I've known people who were hired based on each of these factors alone:

+ She tried to spear a cherry tomato and it landed on the floor; she handled the moment with ease by saying, "That one had a mind of its own."
+ He gave her his seat on the subway, and found out later she was president of the company where he was interviewing.
+ She did magic tricks while waiting for the interviewer, who was delayed for three hours.
+ He spilled the entire contents of his briefcase on the floor and laughed so hard the interviewer got caught up in the hysterics.
+ She just outlasted the other candidates: "It was an endurance contest by the time we made the decision, and she was left standing."

- She was six feet one and found ways to make the five-two interviewer comfortable with her height.
- He and the interviewer laughed about the ugly building where the agency was located.

What do all these anecdotes tell us? That personal qualities often outweigh "paper qualifications" in the hiring process. If these factors are "irrational," then so be it. How you are is sometimes more important than what you know or can do.

These may seem like odd justifications for hiring; however, each of these mini-stories reveals legitimate "data" about the job candidate, and all of these factors are "emotional."

So don't expect that you will be hired just because you have Wow credentials, a Pow suit, and a Zowie résumé. Interviewers make their decisions in mysterious ways.

In chapter 23 I made a case for having "reasons to want you." I most emphatically support that viewpoint, but sometimes even the most compelling reasons are not enough. Why not? Because every interviewer responds to a job candidate emotionally as well as rationally. While you're talking with your head, he may be listening with his heart.

It may seem unfair to evaluate you in emotional, irrational ways. Not necessarily. The nonrational influence in an interview is very important. While companies certainly want people to have as much competence as they can get, competence isn't everything. The most "competent" person is not necessarily the best individual to hire. Emotional factors relate directly to job performance. What kinds of emotional responses are we talking about?

1. *Interviewers hire people they like.* They do so not only because they want people around who make life more enjoyable for themselves, but because likability is a significant clue about how well the person will get along with other employees. This is no small factor. A person who's easy to work with will tend to enhance the productivity of everyone around her. The likability factor is on the interviewer's mind every minute of the interview.

Be yourself. Laugh if you do something awkward—and you always will. Acknowledge the pressure of the interview situation. Be humble even while you are telling about what you can do for the company. Relate to the interviewer comfortably, even if she acts stiffly (she's nervous too). Show that you like her before she has decided to like you.

What should you do about being likable in your job interviews? Consider the interview the beginning of a relationship with the interviewer. Empathize with her situation. Hiring is not easy. She doesn't want to make a mistake. Show her you have some understanding of what the company needs.

2. *Interviewers respond to enthusiasm.* You may not have all the best qualifications for the job (nobody does), but if you complement your skills with strong desire, interviewers will take notice. There are people who try to fake enthusiasm. Don't you be one of them. If you genuinely feel it, show it. If you are *not* excited about the job and the company, don't show up for the interview. When you are enthusiastic, the interviewer says to herself:

> "This person's drive will be infectious. Others will be energized by her attitude. She will be dedicated, and we can expect her to work to improve her skills and grow."

You don't have to jump up and down, screaming, "Hire me and I'll take you to the mountaintop!" But you should not suppress your motivation, either, in the interest of business formality and presumed protocol.

There is such a thing as quiet enthusiasm—a sparkle in your eyes, your eagerness to know more about what the company is doing, and your modestly expressed belief that this is the right place for you.

Enthusiasm is the motor oil that makes everything else in the engine work smoothly. Interviewers know it's not a good idea to hire a highly competent person who is only moderately turned on by the job. They'd much rather have a person who is fired up and has the potential to learn new skills.

3. *Interviewers are always looking for the fit between you and the company.* Is this a place where you'll be happy? Will you like it here? Will you stay a good while, so they won't have to look for someone else in a year or two?

How does any interviewer know if you're a good fit? They don't. Once again, they're just guessing. Help the interviewer with this, especially if you're coming from a different industry. Tell the interviewer how your past work experiences connect with this job:

> "I will like working here in the computer industry, because I once had a job where I enjoyed the contact with technical people. They're good to be around because they're always coming up with new ideas."

Give the interviewer some reason to believe this company fits your personality:

> "This mortgage and title company is a good fit for me, because I like keeping track of lots of paperwork and making sure everything is in order. I like knowing that things are done efficiently. It was the same way in the lawyer's office where I worked previously."

A "good fit" may be focused on other things, such as telephone contact:

"Here at your financial consultation company, I noticed when I called for interviews that everyone here is very responsive on the telephone. I give a lot of attention to how I treat customers on the phone. I'd be happy to demonstrate this for you."

4. *Good interviewers always look for signs of trouble.* Does this candidate seem egotistical, argumentative, withdrawn, cynical, or cryptic? Are there any signs that his or her personality may rub people the wrong way?

There are always people who have the competence, but they're a pain to work with. Sometimes their competence can override their personal traits, but all things being equal, the decision maker would rather have employees who feel right to them "interpersonally."

What should you do if you suspect that you're on the wrong end of some of these trouble factors? Maybe you wonder if you're egotistical, or you've been told before that you're cynical but that's the way you like being, or you can be withdrawn at times, or you just don't feel completely comfortable mingling with people in office situations. Can you change your ways of being and cross over the bridge to more positive attributes?

I wouldn't ask that you change your personality, because you want to be true to yourself. I'm not in favor of trying to change your general ways of being, because you wouldn't want to do it, and even if you did, it would probably be transparent to others and awkward for all concerned.

Nevertheless, you do want to look at any features of your behavior that may either turn people off or leave them feeling indifferent toward you. Why walk directly into difficulty when you might avoid it with a few minor adjustments of the ways you act with people?

And I do mean *act*. That notion may sound odd; however, part of being a socialized human being means that we all act at certain points in our lives for one reason or another. We present certain behaviors in order to be "agreeable" and try to get what we want. When you don't throw spitballs and stick your tongue out, people tend to like you better and listen to you more.

Adjustments

What do you do if you're on the short side of some of these factors that are so important to interviewers? This is covered also in chapter 26 ("Find Out What Your Blind Spots Are"), but it will help to summarize a few key points here:

1. *Go out of your way to solicit feedback.* There's that computer word that has wormed its way into our daily vocabulary—"feedback." It would be better to call it "bounceback." You want some of the impressions that you make on others to bounce back to you. Since you might be oblivious to the negative ways you may affect others, you have to ask a wide-open question:

"What ways do I act that might be a turnoff to interviewers?"

Or, if you have a suspicion about what you do that is ineffective, you can ask a very direct question:

"Am I sometimes cynical, and if so, how do you think this affects people?"

Ask these questions to anyone who is interested enough to try to help you—friends, other job hunters, teachers, even people who have interviewed you. Sometimes people who know you well can make helpful observations.

2. *Try acting contrary to your usual ways, and see if you notice any different result.* This means you suspect what the little culprit might be, so you act to negate it, or even behave the opposite. For example, if you suspect your tart sense of humor might be a turnoff, you turn it off, smile more, and listen more. That may be a struggle, but see if it elicits any different responses.

"Why, Grudlee, you seem different today. You haven't made fun of me yet. It's kind of a relief."

3. *Ask the interviewer questions that will "take the emotional temperature" of the interview:*

"How do you like what I've said so far?"
"What else is important in deciding how good a fit I am for this job?"

Interviewers won't often comment directly on your personality, but these questions might give you some clues:

"How do you think my personality would fit here?"
"How would you compare my personality to others who have done this job?"

Very often any of the above "irrational" factors can carry the greatest weight in a hiring decision. If you are an interviewer, you certainly want to hire as many compatible, likable, and enthusiastic people as you can, and one argumentative, secretive, or egotistical person can be one too many.

Even when the interviewer is bound to a tight interview structure, and he's been told to hire according to certain factors, he will still try to hire the person he "feels" best about. Hiring can become a very personal thing pretty quickly. An interviewer can feel very attached (or unattached) to your candidacy, and then he will concoct all manner of "reasons" to justify his selection.

26

Find Out What Your Blind Spots Are

I blow interviews. You blow interviews. We all blow interviews. You will blow more interviews in the future. But it's OK. Interview blunders will be good for you.

The interview is a forty-five-minute finger snap designed to forecast how productive you'll be over the next several years. It's a pressure-cooker atmosphere little better than tea-leaf reading, where the interviewer tries to "read" what you're saying and translate it into on-the-job productivity. For your part, you somehow try to portray your abilities and predict how you will perform if they hire you.

Interviews go wrong. They ask you the wrong questions. They ask you things you did not expect. You fumble around. You feel awkward. You say whatever comes to your mind first, desperately trying to fill the silences. You just know they were hoping for more. The interviewer sits looking inscrutable. "What *are* they thinking? Did I say anything right?" You can't imagine they could hire you based on how you answered those questions.

And they don't. You blew the interview. You just *knew* you would mess it up. What might you have done differently? Who knows? Interviewers don't tell you in advance what they're going to ask, so how do you keep from bungling the next one, and scrunching the next one, and . . . ?

You don't really know if the interview went wrong. It just feels that way. Given that the interviewer doesn't say much about how she's rating your responses, your tendency may be to assume the worst. Sometimes you can tell things are going OK if she's smiling or nodding affirmatively, but that may be standard interviewer behavior for all you know.

The truth is, you probably *did* do some things wrong. But you have no idea what they are. And you may well continue making these mistakes, simply because you don't know what else to do. These are called "blind spots." You're blind to certain flaws in your interview behavior because you're not aware that they are mistakes. Blind spots. You have 'em. Everyone has 'em.

It's vital to identify your blind spots because you'll continue to undermine your job interviews if you remain unaware of them. Everyone has things they do or don't do that get in the way of communicating clearly their ability to do the job.

Here is a sample of typical blind spots:

+ talking too fast
+ dominating the conversation (it's recommended that you talk 50 to 70 percent of the time, but more than that, and you may be overdoing it)
+ talking too slowly
+ not looking at the interviewer
+ being too modest or self-effacing
+ speaking too well of yourself
+ laughing too often and inappropriately
+ not listening well
+ nervous hand gestures
+ verbal tics, such as frequent use of "you know," "like," etc.
+ giving overly brief responses
+ little enthusiasm or expressiveness

Of course, your blind spots can be even more substantive. The following is a sample list:

+ did not know enough about the job
+ did not prepare adequately regarding the nature of the company's objectives
+ didn't know what the key needs were for this position
+ did not have a key competency required in the job
+ does not know the industry well enough
+ does not express himself clearly

It's difficult for you to gauge just how well or poorly you did in a job interview because the interviewer does not send you a "score." The only index you have is whether or not you received a job offer. This is not an especially accurate measure of how well you did. You need feedback. You need some evaluation of how well you presented yourself, so that you can identify your blind spots and overcome them. How do you get feedback? Here are some possibilities, and I strongly urge you to take advantage of them. If you keep making the same mistakes, you will be a very discouraged job hunter somewhere down the line.

1. *Ask interviewers for feedback.* Call on the telephone. Ask to meet with them in person, if possible. If not, ask your question on the phone. Here's a good way to ask for evaluative comments:

> "I want to improve how I present myself in future job interviews. Could you tell me what my key strengths and weaknesses were in my interview with you?"

By inquiring about both your strengths and weaknesses, you give the interviewer a chance to give you balanced feedback. Either praise or criticism by itself is so one-sided that the respondent might feel uncomfortable giving it.

Not all interviewers will be willing to give you feedback. Some are afraid of lawsuits; others are not sure their bosses would think it's OK. Nonetheless, keep asking. Appeal to their interest in helping you. If even one out of three or four gives you some feedback, that's well worth your effort.

It's usually not a good idea to ask for the evaluative comments in writing, because that demands more of the interviewer's time and he has to be more committed to his thoughts when he puts them on paper. The fear of lawsuits is a factor that will discourage written replies.

2. *Ask your friends for feedback.* People who know you will be able to offer thoughts about your "blind spots." They may not know for sure, but they can make reasonably valid guesses about what you might do in job interviews that would work against you. Why? Because they have had a lot of experience with you. They can be even more helpful if you role-play some job interviews with them. Why not role-play the interview you just had last week, or the one you're going to have a week from now?

When you role-play, create conditions as close as possible to "real" interview circumstances. Set a time limit, prepare your friend regarding what questions to ask, and ask her or him to adopt a serious, businesslike attitude.

Coach your friends to ask you the questions that you find most difficult to answer. Create a set of "nightmare questions"—the ones you least want to be asked. Then be prepared to answer these. Be sure your "interviewer" asks these questions and is at least as tough on you as a real interviewer would be. This may introduce some anxiety into your role playing. That's good. Get used to the demanding questions and learn to overcome the bumps you have in answering them. This will reduce your anxiety in the real interviews.

3. *Practice on video before your next real interview.* It's not usually fun going through an interview on videotape and then watching yourself. However, it will enable you to observe any blind spots you may have. Ask several people to view the video and give comments on how you presented yourself. This will help to "average out" any particular biases that your respondents may have.

Video interviews may have a somewhat unrealistic flavor, since both you and the interviewer will be self-conscious about the camera. However, video still gives you tangible, visible evidence of areas where you need improvement.

4. *Ask employers to give you practice interviews.* Let's say there's a general field where you want to find a job—for example, real estate, computer systems, or publications. Identify some employers in this field to whom you will *not* be applying for jobs, and ask them if they would provide you practice interviews. A good way to find such employers is to be active in a professional association and meet people there on an informal basis. Tell them exactly what you're up to:

> "I want to practice my interviewing and find out what I'm doing wrong. Since I won't be applying to your organization, I thought you might give me some feedback on my general ways of responding to interview questions."

These employers will know some good questions to ask you, and they will have definite observations about the quality of your responses. They may see your blind spots right away, and even if they don't, this is excellent practice for future interviews.

You may think it unlikely that interviewers will do practice interviews for you, but you will be pleasantly surprised. Interviewers like to be helpful when they can, and it enhances the image of their company to do these kinds of things.

Interview Styles That Don't Work

There is no particular interview style that works best. In fact, any attempt you make to change your personality is sure to fail, because you will be trying to be someone else. However, there are certain personalities that people believe are effective, and they are *not*:

The Chatterer. Never a moment of silence with you. Any lull in the conversation is cheerfully rescued by your witty, inquisitive, anecdotal, charming talk, talk, talk. You believe an interview should race along at top speed, so the interviewer is overwhelmed by your conversational talent. This approach will fail because the interviewer will feel overpowered, perhaps even insulted, by your need to display your talking ability.

The Counterpuncher. You don't commit or expose yourself by leading with your jaw. You wait for the interviewer to let you know what is wanted, then you give a short, careful response. You show only as much of yourself as you have to, because you are terrified you'll make a mistake. This careful bobbing and weaving will offend the interviewer because you are so difficult to engage in a two-way exchange. Your caution will turn sour because the interviewer wants, above all, to know you in some genuine way.

The Data Blabbermouth. You provide as much evidence as possible that you're knowledgeable. You bludgeon the interviewer with facts and figures, drop names, and try to impress with the breadth and depth of your knowledge. While gathering data is vital for preparation for the interview, an excessive display of knowledge can distract the interviewer from other purposes of your meeting. Information is good to have, but the interview is primarily a two-way exchange.

The Inoffensive Diplomat. You were well-mannered as a child and carry into adulthood the view that diplomacy succeeds where insensitive blundering fails. Your task is to never offend and take care to treat people with maximum gentility. This motif distorts the entire purpose of the interview and ultimately makes you appear an obsequious fool because you avoid answering any question that has the faintest trace of risk, and you're unwilling to take enough control to ask questions or say things you need to say about yourself.

The Tiger. You take charge at every turn and show your willingness to assume responsibility and be a self-starter by asking leading questions and proposing your own agenda for the interview. This attack posture will ultimately turn on you, because you will have taken away the interviewer's power to assume control when he or she wants to do that. Assertiveness is prized as a quality in job applicants, but, taken to an extreme, it becomes a display for its own sake rather than a skill that facilitates further discussion.

Aberrant Factors That May Lead to Blown Interviews

Interviews are unpredictable affairs. If you have a bad one, it will not always be due to your own mistakes. When you feel your interview was unsuccessful, consider that either of the following might have happened and factor it into your evaluation of yourself:

1. *There are bad interviewers.* Lots of them. Many people are thrown into the interviewer role without wanting to be there and without a clear grasp of what they're looking for. They don't know how to interview, but they have to act as if they know what they're doing. They may do any of the following that

would skew your performance in the interview and perhaps lead you to feel you have blown it:

+ They ask the wrong questions because they are poorly informed about the job you're seeking.

+ They dominate the conversation, leaving you little opportunity to talk about yourself. This seems illogical and perverse, but some interviewers just don't know how to stop talking.

+ They feel their job is to put you under stress, to see how you react. So they ask you unnecessarily tricky questions. Unfortunately, this kind of tomfoolery still occurs at times, so you have to deal with it. React with poise. If the question is unanswerable or you don't have the answer, say: "I don't know."

+ They don't know what to ask you, so they throw the ball to you. This is actually a good chance to say everything you want to say, but the interviewer's awkward silence may leave you feeling you've done something wrong. Take the lead and keep talking as long as the interviewer seems to want you to do that (this is an exception to the 50 to 70 percent guideline mentioned earlier in this chapter).

+ They react strangely to your responses, either because they don't understand the job or because they're just strange individuals. When you believe you have a bad interviewer, tell your story about the value you bring to the company, regardless of what the interviewer is saying. If the interviewer talks too much for you to tell about yourself, politely interrupt and say:

"Before our time is up, I want to be sure there are certain things you know about me. . . ."

Don't be distracted or upset by whatever the interviewer says or does. Demonstrate your professionalism and unruffled demeanor by smiling and staying on course regarding your self-presentation. If they don't know what to say or ask, take more responsibility for the interview. Ask the questions they should be asking you and then answer them:

"You're probably wondering what experiences I've had that will enable me to help the company. There are two I'd like to tell you about. . . ."

If an interviewer asks you questions that don't relate to the job or your goals, use these questions as "bridges" to the questions you want to answer:

"Yes, I was raised in Louisiana and learned to do a lot of fishing there. Fishing and my work at the local foundry taught me the importance of patience and detailed preparation for tasks. I can tell you about other jobs where I have shown these qualities, which I believe will help me do a good job for you."

2. *There are interviews that get disturbed or derailed by circumstances.* Examples: The interviewer gets an unexpected and crucial phone call that distracts her. . . . In a group interview, one person asks dumb questions and throws everyone else off track. . . . The interviewer is late and unprepared because she had some other company business to attend to. . . . A computer crashes and everyone in the company is trying to figure out what to do because a project deadline is that afternoon. Your interview is the last and least thing on their minds.

When things happen like this, roll with them, maintain your poise, and don't feel put upon that they're giving you less attention than you deserve. Your ability to respond calmly and professionally to the "circumstances" will win points for you, in terms of your patience and understanding.

In the above cases, interviewers are making it harder for you to communicate fully and clearly your ability to do the job. Nonetheless, even when interviewers are not on target, or circumstances alter your interview, you can still ask these interviewers for feedback after you have seen them. All the feedback you can get about yourself is to the good. One of your jobs in job hunting is to learn, grow, and discover where you need help. Blind spots remain blind until you, with the help of others, discover what they are.

The Eight Factors of a Successful Job Interview

Interviewers are merely professional gamblers who have been pro-vided a thirty-minute tip sheet analysis to help them decide on which candidate to place the bet.
—John L. Lafevre,
"A Peek Inside the Recruiter's Briefcase"[1]

The formal job interview is usually handled with great care. It is treated as though it were a sacred event, with high ritual. Many believe it has mystical qualities, that the interviewee must tune in to the special wavelength of inter-viewers, adopt certain magical techniques, or present a new personality.

In truth, this view of the employment interview as a formal presentation is heavily distorted and surely oversold by those of us who teach others how to conduct the work search. The more you are led to believe that an interview demands acting talent, intense rehearsals, and decoding the interviewer's re-marks to trigger the "right" responses, the more deeply in trouble you will find yourself when you talk with a prospective employer.

We must demystify this thing we call the interview process. Your success in an interview is a direct result of conversational habits you practice in your routine daily interactions with friends and others. An interview is nothing more than a conversation between two people who desire information from each other.

You Conduct Interviews Every Day

Every time you speak or listen to what someone else is saying, you are most likely engaged in an interview. A job interview is simply a special, artificially contrived example of an ordinary two-way exchange. You can bring your interviewing skills into play almost anytime, because these skills generalize to meetings with prospective employers. Practice interviewing in everyday situa-tions like these: asking the restaurant waitress how to get to the theater across town; trying to discover why your children strewed toilet paper throughout the house one hour before guests were to arrive from the West; questioning your tax accountant about how to plan your next year's expenditures; resolving a quarrel with your companion, lover, or friend; explaining to your professor why you've chosen such an arcane topic; or negotiating with your family about a summer vacation trip.

By being the "interviewer" in such situations, you come to appreciate clear and helpful responses and learn what interviewers say to elicit further information (see chapter 16—"How to Ask Questions"). Practicing the "interviewer" role helps you to be a more sharply tuned respondent. The frustrations of interviewing also teach you how important it is to give specific answers to the questions that are asked.

The job interview is almost always the centerpiece of the job-search process, your chance to show your stuff, the place where your motivations and the employer's needs come together. So let's find out what goes on inside those cubicle walls and inside the interviewer's heart and mind.

Is the interviewer just a heartless villain dedicated to dismembering your well-laid preparation and ripping away your careful facade to uncover the real you lurking somewhere under the surface? Or is he/she a friendly confidant who will give you every opportunity to show your best side and try mightily to discover your most glorious abilities and potential? The interviewer can be both of these extremes at times, but mostly he or she is like an earnest and congenial detective who is trying to solve the mystery of who you are by looking for clues in your responses to questions. The interviewer is also looking to see if he/she wants to spend further time with you beyond the initial interview.

There is a hidden agenda consisting of eight items in every job interview, regardless of the nature of the job or the type of industry. I will outline how you can respond most favorably to each of these themes. Eight sounds like a lot of factors, like a ton of things to worry about. Will your mind be filled with so many do's and don't's that you can't relax? It's less complicated than you think. When the interviewer asks a question and you answer it, you're often covering several factors at the same time. Being aware of these themes helps cue you about how the interviewer will evaluate you. You won't score perfectly on each point (nobody does), but your awareness will help you understand "Why did he/she ask me that?"

Why be afraid of this little devil, the interview? The other candidates have as much anxiety as you do, and probably more if they have not read this book. The eight qualities below give you eight different ways to shine. Of course, you will make mistakes, some of them so clumsy that you will laugh at them later.

You've had bad interviews before, and you'll have them again. So what? There's no great Interviewing Scoreboard in the Sky that says: "Ding Him

Forever Because of Previous Interview Sins." In this game you get plenty of times at bat, and eventually you will become confident and handle the interview process well.

Some of these eight items are openly stated in the interview, and others are not. Certain aspects are difficult to address openly, such as "likability." But you can be sure this is a factor in selection, even though it is judged only indirectly. Others may be stated clearly if the interviewer chooses, such as "Tell me about your leadership experiences." However, just because an interviewer does not name a factor does not mean he/she is ignoring it. "Leadership," "communication skills," and others can be inferred from your general responses to questions, so keep all of these themes in mind. If you are not sure whether a particular aspect has been covered, you may want to bring it up yourself: "I'd like to tell you why I am motivated to pursue this job."

How Are These Eight Factors Combined?

Who knows? If there were a formula for combining job selection factors that predicted successful job candidates with any degree of accuracy, we'd all know it by now. But, fortunately for the sake of individual judgment, there is no such formula. All we know is that every item on this agenda is important, since each taps some dimension of your job potential.

However these eight factors are combined, the result is wholistic and subjective in the mind of the interviewer. He/she may even use an interview scorecard, but the final decision will still be an intuitive combining of all themes. Therefore, you should treat all eight elements as being of equal importance and give your attention to each of them.

1. Personal Impression

What the Interviewer Is Looking For

"I wonder if this person will be an effective representative of our organization. Will he look professional, serious, dress attractively? Will he socialize well, make clients feel at home, make the customer/student/visitor want to be involved with us? Does this person display confidence, warmth, interest? If I were coming here for the first time, would I be impressed by him?"

What You Should Do

First of all, dress appropriately for the interview. Do enough research to know what is suitable for that work environment, and then dress about 10 percent better than the norm. Enough has been written about dressing for success that I need not rehash it here. Neatness, grooming, and a professional look are the keys. Have more experienced people check you out if you are not sure whether your appearance will make the grade.

Personal sociability is important in almost every job. Generate friendliness, warmth, and enthusiasm as much as you can, without portraying someone other than yourself. First impressions do matter. Your ability to move into new situations and meet new people comfortably contribute to how you are first received. If this is a difficult area for you, practice placing yourself into new social situations, at offices, parties, and elsewhere.

Take a look at some of your nonverbal factors, such as vocal quality (do you speak clearly, firmly, not too fast or slowly?), body posture when sitting or standing, hand gestures, eye contact (a strong indication of your assertiveness and ability to relate confidently), or facial expressions. If you are unsure about any of these, get some advice from a career counselor and practice any skills in which you are weak.

2. Competence

What the Interviewer Is Looking For

"Can this person do the job we have here? Has she had related experiences? Can I detect skills in her background that will help in this job? What can I ask that will cue me about her abilities? Maybe she can do the job minimally, but how good is she? Can she tell me things that will reveal her capabilities?"

What You Should Say

An interviewer will already have some idea of your competence if you have submitted your résumé, but you should assume that he/she wants to know more, or have some verification of what the résumé says. The best thing you can do is tell stories about your past experiences that reveal your abilities to perform the job. Don't make the interviewer work hard to find out what you can do. Anticipate what the job calls for (with the help of your research), and make connections between your skills (as derived from past experiences) and the skills the job requires. Don't be modest. Give some idea of why you believe you can do the job *well*. Interviewers like confidence as long as you don't overdo it. We're not talking about bragging here, but simple declarative statements such as: "I am a good supervisor, and the reason I know that is my work last summer at the _____, where I oversaw the entire operation of _____."

In many cases, the interviewer is looking for multiple competencies, your ability to perform many tasks well. Anticipate as many different competencies as you can and be prepared to talk about them.

> *Example:* I can organize data projects, supervise staff, and do research in the technical libraries. I can also do public speaking when needed, and I like to write reports for management in clear language. I know this job calls for a lot of different skills, and I have had some experience with all of them.

Sometimes you will be referring to your previous experience in the same type of job, but often you will be applying for a different type of work, and will have to make connections or "translations" between one job and another, between your past experiences and the responsibilities of the new occupation: "In my job as a data processing manager I took care of the budget and managed the department's resources, so I believe I can do those things well in this job as a purchasing agent."

In general, the more clearly you relate your past experiences and present motivation to the job you want, the more an interviewer can believe that you have the capacity to do the job well.

3. Likability

What the Interviewer Is Looking For

"Would I like to work with this person? Is he enjoyable to be around? Will he get along with the others here in the office? If I ask him to work with a wide variety of people, will he handle that okay? Does he listen well? Will he relate smoothly to the higher-ups? Does he have some fun about him, or is he all work and no play? Is there anything about this person that might affect his attitude or moods on the job?"

What You Should Say and Do

How do you go about being likable? Well, there is no easy answer to that, but we'd better pay attention to it, because this is a powerful yet always unspoken factor in hiring decisions. Unless there is a strong argument to the contrary, people tend to hire people they like and find congenial. They do so for a variety of reasons:

+ It is more enjoyable to work with likable people
+ Relationships in the office will be better
+ Likable people tend to get more cooperation, and thus more work is usually accomplished

✦ Such people tend to have greater potential for advancement

There are things you can do to stay on the right side of this key factor.

a) *Be genuinely interested in everyone you meet,* from bosses through staff people, secretaries, receptionists, and anyone else. Word gets around fast in the office, and everyone has a say about "what's this person like?"

b) *Be a good listener.* Easy to say, but hard to do when you are focusing on what you are going to say next. Pay attention to the questions you are asked, the statements your interviewers make, the feelings they show between the lines, and even their attitudes toward each other. Maybe what they are saying is even irrelevant to the job. Listen anyway. Listening, more than anything else, begins to cement the relationship with a person. Let them know you are listening by rephrasing or summarizing what you heard them say.

c) *Be as at ease with people as you possibly can be, given the circumstances.* They are not going to bite your head off, and you will not fall into a deep hole somewhere, never to be heard from again, if you don't get this job. Try to imagine you are at a party and you are getting acquainted with some people you think you're going to like.

d) *Be loose.* Take what comes. Interviews can have unexpected little wrinkles in them, like phone interruptions, mistaken arrangements (so what if they lost your plane ticket, or gave you the wrong directions to the office), encounters with people you were not prepared to meet, spilled coffee, and maybe even a fire drill. The questions interviewers ask can be oddball and perhaps even designed to rattle you. Maintain an upbeat attitude no matter what answer you give. "Poise and Maturity" below discusses stressful questions in greater detail.

e) *Don't be manipulative.* Don't try to endear yourself to anyone by making an obvious play for their approval, such as excessive comments about the pictures on their walls or the trophies in their offices. These ploys are recommended in other books, but most interviewers will view your comments as transparent and thus discount them. Worse yet, such attempts to curry favor may work against you.

f) *Avoid negative talk.* Don't be critical of former employers or indulge in stories about people you don't like. Even though your criticism may be legitimate, it casts a negative light on you. Sometimes an interviewer will even bait you, because he/she knows that your former boss is a difficult person. Don't be tempted to tell war stories, because the interviewer may assume you will be just as critical of his/her operation if you are hired. Don't be negative with anyone.

Interviewers may show you where you stand on likability by their smiles or other nonverbal responses, but they will seldom tell you directly. You need not press hard with your likable behaviors. Just avoid the traps implied above, and remember that congeniality counts.

4. Motivation/Enthusiasm/Commitment

What the Interviewer Is Looking For

"I wonder how badly she wants this job. Is she fired up about it? Does she project this enthusiasm to me? How hard a worker is she likely to be, based on the intensity she is showing me? Is she really interested in this field, or is she just looking for a job? If we hire her, will she be with us long enough to make a real contribution? I wonder how I can find out what she really wants from her career. How do I know if this job is her first choice?"

What You Should Say

Depth of motivation often makes the difference between an ordinary employee and a great one. How can you demonstrate it? If they ask whether you want the job and you say yes, that doesn't quite settle the matter.

a) Show your enthusiasm verbally and nonverbally. Don't be stiff. Let them know you like the job and would be very energized by it.
b) Relate this job to your previous experiences. This is another place where storytelling comes in handy: "I have done projects like this before, and have really thrown myself into them. For example . . ."
c) Talk about your ambitions, your desire for future growth in this field of work. Give some general idea of how you hope to progress with this company, and why such advancement appeals to you.

Motivation can be done to excess, of course. Jumping up and down screaming "It's me! This job is me!" would be a little over the line. But I know I can count on you to be tasteful.

A good interviewer will ask you about your motivation and potential commitment, so be prepared to answer. Interviewers usually try to see how this job will fit into your career history. If you are changing careers, you will have to give the interviewer some insight into why you are moving in this direction and how it fits with your larger career goals and ambitions. When the applicant is leaving one field for another, motivation is always a significant issue for the interviewer.

Interviewers usually believe that the most motivated applicant will do the best job, even if he/she has a little less relevant experience or needs a little more training. Thus, even if you have the qualifications on paper and you have answered questions satisfactorily in the interview, *don't be cocky or complacent*. More than one job offer has been lost by candidates who said: "I thought I had it made."

5. Leadership

What the Interviewer Is Looking For

"Does this person have potential for taking responsibility in our organization? What makes me think so? Do I see evidence that he has been a leader in other settings? Does he seem to want to move ahead and be in charge of things? Would he be a good example for the rest of our staff?"

What You Should Say

Leadership is one of private industry's favorite words. It also gets high marks from nonprofit employers. In fact, everyone likes leadership and tries to get as much of it as they can.

First let's agree that "leadership" refers not only to being the head of an organization, or club, or committee, or team; it also refers to taking responsibility for a project, even when you are not the appointed leader of a group. Leadership is a broad concept that denotes seeing a goal and bringing together the people and resources to achieve that goal. Often leadership will involve supervising or managing other people, but that is not always so. Leadership can mean building a boat by yourself in your backyard, or lobbying the city council to do something on behalf of the homeless.

Interviewers would like to see some evidence that you are a take-charge person who makes things happen. They believe that such qualities will pay off for the company, because you will exert the same leadership skills on the job. Thus, you should call attention to any significant responsibilities you have had, even if the results were not completely successful. Failures can be as important as successes: "We got the board of trustees to agree to have a basketball team at my college. I organized the effort, lobbied the board, called the referendum, and met with the president. . . ." Tell interviewers about your leadership roles, even if they do not ask. Identify skills in your leadership positions that will help you on this job. Leadership usually is a good sign that you know how to get along with people and manage them. The interviewer is looking to the future as well as the present. The entry-level job may not have leadership in it, but the interviewer envisions bigger things for you. Show that your thinking is ambitious and that your previous leadership experience was no accident.

6. Communication Skills

What the Interviewer Is Looking For

"What evidence do I have that this person writes clearly and effectively? Would she represent our organization positively as a public speaker? Is she a powerful communicator? Will she communicate well to other staff members? Could she write a speech for our president if she had to, and could she deliver it if necessary? How much writing and public speaking has she done before?"

What You Should Say and Do

Writing and speaking skills are highly valued in a wide variety of jobs, particularly for jobs that lead to greater responsibility. Organizational leaders are always required to communicate effectively, in writing and in person. Therefore, you should go out of your way to provide evidence of these skills. Offer examples of your writing style—perhaps management reports, publicity materials, or newsletters that you have produced. Take care that your résumé and cover letters are well written; these are obvious examples of your writing talent. Any problems or sloppiness in these materials will be interpreted by the interviewer as a sign that you cannot write well.

Every time you open your mouth you give evidence of your speaking ability. If you have done public speaking, say so, but don't overemphasize this, lest it sound like bragging. The interview itself is a prime example of your speaking skill. Speak concisely yet with sufficient detail, don't mispronounce words, and work on your vocal quality if you speak too softly, too rapidly, or in some ineffective way.

Don't try to impress the interviewer with your speaking style, but make sure that you answer questions with conviction and speak with a tone of confidence. If this is a problem area for you, it can be corrected or improved through speech classes, Toastmasters clubs, and practice in your daily life.

7. Poise and Maturity

What the Interviewer Is Looking For

"Can this person handle herself under pressure? Does she have the depth and maturity to deal with questions that are almost impossible to answer? How would he project himself as a representative of our organization under trying circumstances? Could she handle difficult customers? Will he come apart when things get crazy around here or people challenge his ideas? How would she do in a heated argument? Is he calm under fire?"

What You Should Say

This is the area where the interviewer may turn to stressful questions and lovely thoughts of how to rattle your cage. Interviewers most often do *not* do this, but they may create some stress if they feel the job requires your ability to deal with pressure and they need to know how you conduct yourself. Sometimes your prior experience will reveal your ability to work under pressure, but if the interviewer is not sure, he/she may create some tension or uncertainty on the spot to see what you do with it. The interviewer may ask questions such as:

What would you do about our sales problems if you were the president of our company?

What is the biggest mistake you've ever made, and why did you let it happen?

Tell me why you think our company is so hot when you really know very little about it.

Who's the worst boss you've ever worked for and why?

Above all, remember that *how* you answer the question—your calmness, your reasonableness, your ability to remain positive and congenial—is as important as the content of your answer. Grace under pressure is a virtue, and the interviewer wants to see that you have it. You can admit to a bit of uncertainty before answering (a pause to give yourself time), but do so with poise, because that is what people in leadership roles are called on to do frequently.

The interviewer may try to argue with you and get you to admit you are wrong, perhaps even badger you about a point of view. This is a test of your diplomacy and ability to engage someone on a difficult issue, maintain their respect, and still get your points across. "Winning" the argument is not as important as having a constructive, peaceful discussion, even if the interviewer is trying to rile you.

Stressful questions are not standard parts of an interview, but you should be ready for them. Sometimes stressful moments will occur, even though they are not planned. An interviewer may misinterpret something you say, forcing you to clarify yourself in a tactful way. Or the interviewer may make a joke about something you said and you don't think it's funny. These incidents call upon your poise and maturity, your ability to manage the conversation with style and self-control.

Poise and maturity is another item on the agenda that is seldom stated (No interviewer asks, "Are you mature enough for this job?") but often noted. It contributes greatly to your overall impression, so don't let little glitches in the interview process get you upset. If you stumble around, or get caught in a misstatement, what's important is that you handle the mishap with honesty, dignity, and calmness.

8. Outside Interests

What the Interviewer Is Looking For

"Is this person one-dimensional, or does she pursue things away from the job? Does she show any flair or originality in her outside interests? Do I see signs that she can get intensely involved in something, that she is productive, works hard toward goals? Maybe I can understand more fully who she is by considering the other things she does. Do these show any strong convictions? How about an ability to organize herself? Is there any evidence of achievement in her outside involvements?"

What You Should Say

Whether you are a passionate handball player, a rock collector, have a collection of quilts you have sewn, or you make wine from your own vineyards, it is generally okay to talk about your personal interests, especially if you are asked. Don't push these interests into the conversation where they don't belong, but be alert for opportunities to point out skills you have developed or knowledge you have acquired in your hobbies that may be related to the job you want.

> *Example:* I take geological field trips and have made maps of the area. This has developed my drawing skill, and I have learned a lot about the Surveyor's Office. I think this background will help me as a junior planner here at the Office of City Planning.

Even if your interests are not directly related to the job, your involvement in them can be a positive sign of enthusiasm and your ability to organize your energies. Interviewers often like to know more about you and may ask: "What do you do in your spare time that you really get fired up about?" The interviewer is trying to determine if you have a spirit of dedication and intensity that may carry over to your involvement with the job. People who organize themselves for maximum efforts in their personal interests usually can display this kind of self-management and commitment in their careers.

While some interviewers might want you to say that you have no outside interests, because you are fully dedicated to your career, this is an unusual point of view. It is more common for an interviewer to prefer a balanced individual who works hard but also gets involved in personal activities.

If you have not had any recent strong interests, either because you were involved in school or had family obligations, it is fine to talk about interests that you intend to pursue in the future. Even a little exposure to an outside activity should give you enough to talk about, if you are asked.

Follow-up

In job hunting, it isn't necessarily over when it's over. While you concentrate your attention on a job interview, and breathe a sigh of relief when you're out of there, there is still more to be done. You can make some of your best progress after the interviews have been completed.

Job hunting is an ongoing process, not just one brief appearance on the interviewer's stage. Interviewers can call you back for encores, and they can be helpful links to the rest of the job market, so consider the things you can do to enhance your prospects:

If You're Still in Contention for the Job

Write a letter to the interviewer. Graciously thank him/her for the meeting, say what you learned from the interview, and reaffirm your interest in the job. This is an opportunity to state more emphatically why you want the position and why you think you are well qualified. They say in theater, "Always leave 'em laughing." Translated to job hunting, you might say, "Let the last word they have from me be a good one." You can also be a bit more personal in this letter, since you have met the employer and can recall key things he/she said.

Ask one or more of your key references to call for you. You don't always have to wait for the interviewer to call your references. If there is one who you believe will say especially good things about you, ask him/her to call the interviewer. Tell the reference what you know about the job and why you believe it is the right one for you.

Send any materials the interviewer asked you for. If there are examples of your work, reference letters, or other materials he/she mentioned during the interview, send them right away and accompany them with a thank-you note.

Call to ask how the selection process is going. "I'd like to know the status of my application, and reaffirm that I am still very interested in this job" is a good way to say it. How soon after the interview should you call? If the interviewer has not told you when to call, anywhere between one and two weeks is good. How often should you call? Take your cues from the interviewer's timetable. If you're unsure, ask when it would be all right to call again.

If you have received an offer of another job but you would prefer this one, it's good to call right away and tell them when you need to make a decision. Then you will negotiate regarding the selection timetable and you will have to decide whether or not to take a "bird in the hand."

Follow-up gives you several ways to demonstrate that you—like your job search—are well organized. If an employer has several forms of positive contact from you, he/she is likely to recognize that your interest in the job is quite serious.

If You Have Been Eliminated from Contention

Why bother if you have been eliminated from the selection process? Because any employer can be a link to other job opportunities. Consider the following things that you can do:

Ask for feedback about your strengths and weaknesses. If you believe you had a decent interview, call or visit the interviewer to ask about how you presented yourself. Both the praise and the criticism are important to you. A little news of what you did right helps to keep you going, and criticism cues you about what you need to change. Often interviewers enjoy helping you improve what you are doing, especially if they want to encourage you to continue in their line of work.

Ask for referrals. "I'd like to continue seeking work in this field. Could you suggest who I might talk with, or where job possibilities might generally be?" While you may draw a blank on this, it is worth asking. Especially in tight fields where professionals know each other, you may get a strong lead if you made a good impression during the interview. At other times the interviewer can tell you the kinds of organizations best to approach, or give you other useful information.

Send thank-you notes. You're beginning to see the all-purpose value of reconnecting via the thank-you note. It is the best means you have of reinforcing a positive impression, so use it with anyone you hope to see again. A well-stated and friendly letter is remembered long after the selection process is over. If you write ten of these letters to interviewers you liked, odds are you will have some beneficial future contact with at least two or three of them.

The ability to follow up well separates the confident and enduring job hunter from those who are sticking their toes in the water but are ready to get out.

Early interviews are just preludes to better interviews. Sometimes interviews circle back on themselves. The person you talked to three weeks ago (who rejected you, but you did some follow-up anyway) is the person you meet on the street who tells you about a new company she just heard of. The interviewer does most of his/her thinking about you long after your conversation is over. If you follow up well, they may give you the edge in the final selection, or they may call to tell you of another opening, or refer you to a good contact in the industry.

Follow-up also sharpens your persistence skills, your ability to keep moving toward a goal even when the initial signs are cloudy. There will be many moments when you want to give up or settle for less, but follow-up reminds you that every contact you make has some potential. It sounds corny, but the person you least suspect might help you can become the one who gives you the lead you're looking for.

There are memorable stories of follow-up told among job counselors and job hunters. One concerns a new college graduate named John who wanted a job with a financial newsletter on Wall Street, and wrote this letter after interviewing with ABC Company on his campus:

Dear Mr. Feinstein:

It was a pleasure speaking with you when you were here at the University of Pennsylvania last week to talk with me and other members of the graduating class. Your visit reaffirmed my interest in joining the ABC Company. I learned from you the importance of reading the key financial journals and how to sift the reliable information from other, more speculative data.

The job with ABC Company is still my first choice. I have been talking with other financial newsletters, but believe that yours is the best, because of its depth of analysis and professional growth opportunities. Even if I am not offered a job by your firm, I will improve my writing and analytical skills by following your many recommendations. I am also beginning my studies for the Chartered Financial Analyst examinations as you suggested, and will take key courses to help my preparation. I am quite convinced that this field is right for me, and plan to continue my efforts to do newsletter work in the Wall Street community.

Since you are an alumnus of the university, you may want to consider returning for Alumni Weekend on April 17–18. We will have a series of social and cultural events (program enclosed) that should interest you. I would be available at that time if you should wish to speak with me, since I am on the planning committee for that weekend.

Many thanks for your helpful recommendations regarding my career plans.

Sincerely,
John Sartoro
Class of 1987

Arlo Feinstein did return to campus for the alumni weekend, though he did not intend to meet with John Sartoro. He spent most of his time with old classmates, but as luck would have it, he wandered into the university gymnasium during a few free hours and sought out a racquetball game. Standing around the gym, just having finished a game, was our man John. You know the finish of this story. Arlo remembered John's appreciative letter, they talked after leaving the gym, and John found himself a member of the newsletter team two months later.

John's letter was not a sales letter; he decided to take a different approach. He restated his strong interest in the job and backed it up with concrete evidence that he was determined to succeed in the financial analysis and newswriting field. He wrote a letter that stuck in the employer's mind. It seemed that luck worked in John's favor, but he did a lot to establish a positive image in Arlo's mind. He played the follow-up game in a deliberate yet professional manner, and it worked.

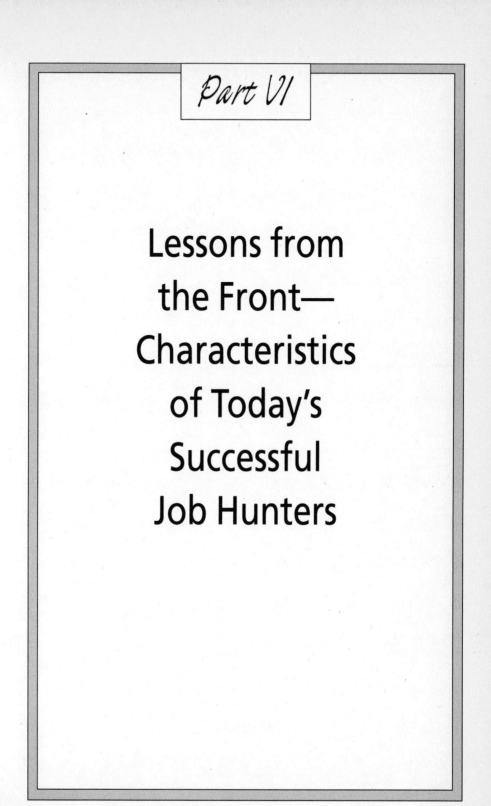

Part VI

Lessons from
the Front—
Characteristics
of Today's
Successful
Job Hunters

28

Hide Your Résumé

The idea of the perfect résumé is to everyone's job-search fantasy. Here is the fantasy: (1) You craft your résumé into a carefully worded document that portrays you as the "candidate most likely to succeed" at the job for which you're applying. Your qualifications fairly leap off the page and into the employer's waiting arms. (2) The employer reads your résumé with glowing eyes and shouts: "Egad! We've found her! This is the person we've been waiting for!" (3) You are invited to the interview and you prove to be the living embodiment of all the promise offered by your résumé. You're offered the job and you and the company ride happily into the sunset.

Here's what really happens: (1) Your résumé is lofted into "The Pile" with many others. It looks like many of the other résumés. It is one more piece of paper that crowds an employer's files. (2) When they read your résumé, they don't know how much to believe; after all, people are inflating, puffing, and outright lying on résumés every day. They're more likely to look through your résumé for factors to remove you from contention than they are to look for reasons to hire you. (3) You sit waiting by your mailbox for a reply, and your frustration grows. Employers barely have enough time to look at The Pile, and the likelihood that your résumé will rise to the top is slim indeed.

Receiving résumés is a bureaucrat's idea of how to manage a selection process. The résumé is used far more often as a device to *eliminate* people than to hire them. Once you surrender to this administrative nightmare, your résumé will be breezed over, dissected, and eventually dismembered. The paper version of your glorious self is tossed into some machine that chews on the verbs and nouns and spits it out in favor of someone else who lucked into the right combination of words.

Sending in your résumé is a passive process. You have almost completely relinquished your control of how you're being evaluated. Passive people do not get jobs.

The Flaw in Anyone's Résumé

Posting a résumé to a prospective employer is sometimes like sending a dead fish through the mail. It will not tell your story in a way that livens up the employer's day. Your résumé is old news. It doesn't tell what you *will do*. It's a dull recounting of what you have done. It does not speak to your present energy, your ambitions, your present goals, and your enthusiasm for the job that you want. A résumé is a barely flopping flounder, because it tells nothing about who you are right now.

People Don't Like to Hire Pieces of Paper

Would you get excited about a piece of paper if you were doing the hiring? No. You can't see the person, you don't know who wrote the résumé or what it really means, and it looks like everyone else's.

Hiring a piece of paper is risky. You feel as if you're closing your eyes and guessing. "Who is this guy?" . . . "Did she really do what she said she did?" . . . "Does this job mean that she was in charge or not?" . . . "Why did he leave this job for that one?" . . . "I don't know anything about this company. It must not be very good." . . . Judgments such as these are made all the time, and you have no chance to counter them.

The résumé is a passive document. It sits there like a lump and tries to sell itself, but readers can evaluate it any way they want, and you can't fight back. The résumé does not smile, it does not act energetically, and doesn't make any pitch for itself beyond the bare words it offers. It's a shy wallflower in the ballroom dance known as the job hunt.

Therefore, the résumé should not be the card you pull first off the top of your job-search deck. Employers are more likely to trust what they can see with their own eyes. The implications for you, as job hunter, are clear:

1. You must lead with yourself rather than your résumé. Let your person be the first thing they see, rather than the paper version of you. Keep your résumé out of the loop until they have met you. You can accomplish this in any of several ways, which have been noted earlier in this book under the concept of "positioning": information interviews, temporary work, contract work, volunteer work, association meetings, or connecting with employers through community work.

The résumé can work for you when you've already had some face-to-face exposure to the person doing the hiring. However, when you're a complete unknown, your résumé is more likely to work against you than for you (see "bad things" and Knockout Factors later in this chapter). A small number of people get interviews by sending résumés, but your odds are far better if you make personal contact first (information interviews, temp work, volunteer work, contract work, etc.). Face-to-face exposure gives your résumé greater credibility. They've met you and are curious to see what your résumé says about you.

2. After they have some idea of your capabilities and your personality (which can be determined only through in-person contact), then show your résumé when it's requested. Having had some exposure to you, they'll be ten times more likely to: (a) read your résumé, (b) believe what's on it, (c) like it and like *you*.

What About When a Prospective Employer Insists on Seeing Your Résumé First?

Do everything you can to avoid this by "positioning" yourself, as explained earlier (chapter 21). However, sometimes you have no choice. They require that you send the résumé first. In such cases, send it in, but do one or more of the following:

1. Hand-carry your résumé to the employer's office. Dress the same as you would if it were a job interview. When you're there, say:

> "I just wanted to bring my résumé to you, introduce myself, and see what the office looks like."

At the very least, this gives you a chance to meet the receptionist, or whoever is there to take your résumé. You may get lucky and encounter someone else in the office. Your presence gives you an opportunity to come across as a real person rather than a piece of paper.

2. Ask for an information interview with anyone in the office who will talk with you, either that day or at a later time.

3. If it interests you, ask if either contract work or temporary work is available.

4. Ask one or more of your references to call the employer and offer a brief word of support for you.

Thus, even though you've been jammed into the bureaucratic mill, you're still using your options for in-person contact to get some face-to-face exposure.

These options are far more active than simply mailing your résumé and never being seen in person by anyone.

The Bad Things That Can Happen When You Send Your Résumé

Prepare a résumé, but hide it. Don't use it until you have to. When you send your résumé to employers, any number of bad things can happen and often do:

+ Your résumé is lost in the company's system for processing paper. A secretary misfiles it, or a manager puts it in her in-box in and forgets about it for a few weeks. Why do people lose or forget about your résumé? Because they have other things to do. It's only a piece of paper. Out of sight, out of mind.

+ Your résumé is misunderstood. You think it tells why you can do a particular job. Others read it and think otherwise. They judge you based on their own biases and interpretations.

+ Your résumé is stacked against those of others who appear to have more experience, more skills, or more something. You are "eliminated" before you have a chance to state your case.

+ Your résumé is put in a "hold" file until others candidates' résumés have been obtained. This process could take weeks or months. Why do companies take so long to review and process résumés? Because the real selection process is taking place somewhere else. When your résumé is the only thing they know about you, you're in the pool of "unknowns," and that is probably where you'll stay.

Try not to let the résumé be the first thing that an employer knows about you. If you do, you might suffer from the dreaded "Knockout Factors"—reasons that people can eliminate you based on a first reading of your résumé:

Knockout Factors

+ *Any mistake on a résumé.* Make a spelling error, a grammatical error, a typographical error, or other simple blunder, and your résumé may be discarded.

+ *Résumé scanning.* Many companies scan résumés for "key words" that pertain to their work; if your résumé doesn't have enough of these key words, you may be eliminated. This is a pretty chancy way to have yourself evaluated.

+ *Poor layout and design.* If your résumé doesn't happen to strike the reader as especially attractive or well laid out, he/she may put yours on the bottom of the pile. How much does this have to do with your ability to do the job? Very little, unless you're applying to be a graphic designer.

+ *You have experience different from that of the person reading the résumé.* Yes, people often like to hire people the same as themselves. It leads to inbreeding and lack of creativity, but they do it anyway. What can you do about your experience on paper being different from the person evaluating you? Nothing.

+ *The "wrong schools," the "wrong affiliations," etc.* Employers have their favorite schools, and schools they don't like; they have companies they like, professional groups they like, and so forth. Your affiliations are at the mercy of their judgments when all they're reacting to are the labels.

+ *Gaps or discontinuities.* Anything different from a straight line of past experience in the field where you're applying will be questioned. They can evaluate it any way they please. Sample employer comments: "A year away to do research? Sounds like a boondoggle to me." . . . "Five years in the hotel field prior to applying for work in health care? What does one have to do with the other?" . . . "Your years as a homemaker? I don't know how to interpret that."

+ *Ambiguity.* Anything vague or the least bit ambiguous can be held against you. If you worked on an archaeological research trip and it would take pages to describe what you were doing, the reader may give up on your one-paragraph summary (all there's room for on the résumé) and assume "this is probably not relevant to us."

By not being present, you cannot tell the résumé reader why your past jobs have taught you skills that you need for the present job. Your résumé attempts to explain that. Why don't they believe you? Because often they choose not to. Résumé readers are conservative. They assume that 30 to 50 percent of your résumé is inflated, because so many of them are. You're honest. But they don't know that. When companies receive hundreds of résumés for a job opening, as they often do, their first impulse is to throw all the résumés to the Human Resources (HR) Department and tell them to eliminate 90 percent of them right away, so the decision maker will have less of a task. Guess what your chances are of making the cut? Are they throwing out potentially good employees on the basis of caprice? Of course they are.

The résumé is an administrative tool designed to make life easier for the employer. It will seldom make the best case possible for you. The résumé fails to reveal:

+ your full understanding of why you are confident you can help the employer achieve the organization's objectives
+ the intangibles that can only be perceived in a series of job interviews or by a trial work experience—your motivation, your personal qualities that reveal what you would be like to work with, and the personal chemistry between you and prospective coworkers
+ your future aspirations and how they may be relevant to the job for which you're applying

◆ how well you fit or do not fit with the culture of the organization where you're applying

How to "Hide Your Résumé" to Best Advantage

Successful job hunting is getting as much in-person time as possible *before* you present your paper credentials. The more employers have had face-to-face contact with you before they see your résumé, the greater attention they will pay to your résumé and the more they will believe what it has to say. Why? Because people tend to trust what they see in front of them; they trust their in-person judgment. Thus, use your résumé as a document to "support" the in-person impressions that you have already made. As much as possible, use these guidelines:

1. Try not to send your résumé through the mail. That gives employers and HR people many opportunities to eliminate you.

2. Have your résumé ready, but try not to show it until you've had as much in-person contact as possible.

3. If people ask for your résumé first, do your best to get them to meet with you in person before you send your résumé (or ask if you can meet and bring your résumé with you).

4. If in-person contact is not possible, hand-carry your résumé to the company, so that at least you will meet a receptionist or other person who works there. Go to the department where the hiring decision will be made, not to Human Resources.

5. Revise your résumé based on what you learn about the company, and its needs, from in-person meetings. Ideally, you should customize your résumé for a particular employer and the specific job you want.

Plan and negotiate the many ways you can present yourself in the job search. Do not let bureaucratic procedures dictate how you will be evaluated. An active personal presence is more likely to get you serious attention than a passive résumé that arrives quietly in the mail.

29

Maximize Face-to-Face Contact

I've always marveled at how good dogs and cats are at getting interviews. Nobody has to write a book telling them how to get out there and network, make contact, and present themselves. You don't hear a word about the shyness problem among kitties and canines. They don't claim that interviewers have long noses. Once dogs and cats decide that things are safe, which usually doesn't take long, they're in each other's faces, interviewing up a storm. They don't mind rejection. If you're not available, they'll go to someone else. No loss of self-esteem. No trip to the analyst's couch. Admittedly, they don't have to call each other for appointments, but you get the idea.

Whoever said that humans are the superior species? Somebody says "Boo!" to us, and we go into hiding. We meet the slightest resistance and we're ready to give up. In job hunting, dogs and cats can hang out their shingles and give lessons to the two-legged creatures.

What is wrong with us humans? Why are we so afraid of each other, especially in the job search? Why do we have to write books urging people to seek connections with others? Furthermore, why do people bend every effort to avoid in-person contact in job hunting? Job hunters write letters, send résumés, read job ads, prowl the Internet, and do everything *except* where their time should be concentrated for the best results—face-to-face contact with other humans. Is this evolution in reverse? What's the story?

You might say that it's a bureaucratized world and people have been oppressed by "the system" into believing they must send paper materials first before getting permission to see employers. This is a big mistake, because it leads you to be passive in your job hunting. "Waiting for permission" is a frustrating place to be, and it is very nonproductive.

The system can be handled. What worries me more is that you have learned to be afraid of people. This fear will fracture your job chances, because face-to-face contact is still by far the method of choice for those who make hiring decisions.

Follow the 60–30–10 Rule

Sixty percent of the energy you allocate to job hunting should be devoted to face-to-face contact. At least 60 percent. I would prefer that it be 70 or 80 percent, but I'll settle for sixty. The remaining energy will include 30 percent allocated to technology (telephones, computers, etc.) and 10 percent to writing.

Job hunters often try to do the reverse—60 percent for writing letters and sending résumés and 10 percent in-person contact. After the completion of interviews, they run away as fast as they can. They avoid social occasions where they might meet new contacts. They fail to expand their networks. Instead they go to the same places and see the same friends or acquaintances time and again. How many new people have you met in the past month? How many opportunities for meeting new people have you passed up?

Maybe you think there's a lot to be afraid of:

"I'll get rejected and I'll feel even worse than I already do."
"They'll say something that will humiliate me."
"I'll make a fool of myself."
"I'll find out I'm worse than I already think I am."

May as well put a few blankets in your closet. With that kind of talk, you'll be making a permanent home in there.

Woody Allen has said: "Eighty percent of life is showing up." In your effort to emulate the neighborhood animals, remind yourself there are plenty of reasons why employers and other people want to see you in person. Writing letters is not "showing up." It's more like hiding.

Getting in to See People

Many readers would protest that they're OK about talking to people, but they can't get in to see them. In this age where people hide behind their latest technology, decision makers often seem impossible to access. First, remember that people who hire *want to* find individuals who can help them and their organization. But they act remote because they are besieged by tons of job seekers.

Therefore, it is not your task to simply request face-to-face time with a decision maker. It is your job to "give them some reasons to want you." This phrase has been discussed in chapter 23, but a little extra emphasis here won't hurt.

A decision maker has to believe that you can help her further the company's goals; otherwise it is a waste of her time and unproductive to talk with you. Consider some of the possible reasons that she might want to see you:

+ You have a skill (writing, researching, telephone selling, computer repair) that might fit into a temporary work slot. A lot of "temp" work these days is professional in nature.

+ You can help the company complete a project they're working on. You can be an independent contractor. (What projects are they doing? Do your homework. . . . Do information interviews. . . . See chapter 10.)

+ You have skills that can be applied in volunteer work positions. (Why work for free? Because many people get their first breaks that way.) When you hear about projects during your information interviews, ask if you can become involved.

+ You believe you can speak to one of the company's primary needs—attracting new customers, retaining present customers, saving money, enhancing the company's reputation, improving productivity or morale of present workers. How can you do this? Talk to people at the company. Relate their needs to your skills.

If any of these rings a bell for you, the decision maker wants to talk with you. Don't be shy. All they can do is say no. If you can give them a reason to want you, you're way ahead of most applicants who simply say: "I need a job."

Reluctant Dragons

Hesitancy to confront the ups and downs of face-to-face contact remains the single most common roadblock that job hunters put in front of themselves. Sending résumés is soooo much easier. Many job hunters regard the prospect of job interviews as though they're going to be the worst blind dates they ever had.

Job hunters are afraid of being chewed up and spit out. Instead you should recognize that the more face-to-face contact you have, the better you're going to do.

Rejection

Is it better to take the lumps of rejection that are inevitable in face-to-face encounters, or only go to those job interviews and information interviews where you know you'll be well received? You know the answer to that one.

Rejection is the entry fee to the house of career advancement. Are you going to be a Reluctant Dragon or will you get out like the neighborhood cats and dogs and make things happen? Shyness is no excuse. For comments about shyness, see the next chapter.

The "60 Percent Rule" includes all forms of face-to-face contact, not just formal job interviews. In fact, the majority of in-person time should not be job interviews. The best kinds of face-to-face contact are information interviews, temporary or part-time work, community work, and participation at professional meetings. You've often heard people say: "I just got that job by luck. I happened to meet . . ." In all likelihood, they were doing one or more of those things noted above.

When you get yourself out of the dark room and into public life, remember that most of the people you meet will be as nervous as you are. Many of them are happy if you start the conversation. They'll wonder how you learned to be so straightforward.

There will always be rude people. Just like being put on hold on the telephone and having your résumé ignored, rudeness is an expected part of anyone's job search. If you come to accept and deftly work around rudeness and neglect, you're paying your dues for job hunting. Like a surfer fending off errant waves, you'll work your way forward. Eventually, you'll want more than 60 percent. Bring on the people.

30

Shyness Is No Excuse

1. Many job hunters claim that shyness inhibits them from talking with people in the ways necessary for an effective job search.

2. However, there are no substitutes for these interpersonal skills; every job hunter must engage a wide variety of people at some level of effectiveness.

3. Successful job hunters learn to overcome shyness when it inhibits their progress.

4. Hence, shyness is not an acceptable excuse.

It may sound as though I'm picking on shy people. Well, yes, but only because shyness cuts directly against good job hunting, and because shy behaviors can be unlearned. Many job hunters hide behind their shyness and use it as a way to keep from doing unpleasant things.

Shyness has been widely reported to afflict 60 to 70 percent of the population. It prevents job hunters from approaching employers when they have good qualifications. Shyness may also block thousands of couples from getting together in dating, relationships, and marriages. Shyness may even be related to rabies, but we're not quite sure how.

Shyness is thus regarded as though it were genetic. They might as well wear a sticker on their foreheads saying: "Shy Person. Please Go Away." Maybe they had "Shy Baby" stamped on their heads at birth and they've been living with the burden ever since.

On the contrary, shyness is learned. Infants are not shy. Just ask their mothers who listen to them scream and negotiate for food. Somewhere along the way, people learn to behave shyly, and they can unlearn these behaviors, too.

You cannot say: "I'm shy; therefore it's okay for me to fall back on job-search methods such as writing letters and waiting for someone to notice me."

Not okay. Not effective. Shyness is an excuse for passive job hunting. As a longtime shynik, I can tell you that making hiding into an art form renders job hunting impossible. I used to get so nervous on the telephone that I'd "forget" who I was calling and hang up.

People defend or justify their shyness in various ways:

"I don't want to toot my own horn."
"I don't want to be intrusive with people."
"I feel that I should be understated about myself."
"I don't want to go where I don't belong."
"I would rather be modest than overbearing."

Many job seekers use shyness as a "reason" for not seeking face-to-face contact with people and for not selling themselves as fully as they're capable of doing. They look for methods of job hunting that will not call upon them to do much mixing with people. They hunger for ways to present themselves on paper or through other nonpersonal means, so that employers will not ask them to "sell their personalities."

This is a victim mentality. Shy people feel the whole situation is out of their control. "Don't look at me. I didn't ask to be this way. There must be other ways to get jobs."

But there are no other ways. Oh sure, there are job listings, and the Internet, and occasional pockets of activity that enable a person to enter one's name for a job without a lot of personal interaction. But these are isolated exceptions to the general rule—job hunting and career change is an activity that requires great amounts of people contact.

Shy people have had many years to entrench their shyness skills. They look shy, they act shy, they hang around other shy people, they buy shy clothing, and they wear paper bags over their heads whenever possible.

There are people who say "I can make it just fine as an engineer, or a carpenter, or a roofer, or a seamstress without talking very much." In isolated cases, maybe they're right. But for the most part, advancement and job/career mobility are directly related to the ability to talk to people, influence them, be socially engaging with them, work cooperatively with them, and otherwise demonstrate healthy measures of nonshyness. Even highly technical occupations (e.g., engineers, computer scientists) require many interpersonal skills to get ahead.

Let's look at some realities:

1. *People who talk get promoted.* People get promoted when they're able to talk about what they have accomplished—to their bosses, to their coworkers,

to their customers. This doesn't mean "tooting your own horn." It simply means helping people to understand what you have done for them. People who sit quietly and wait to be noticed are often overlooked.

2. *People who talk are good salespeople, and these days, everyone is a salesperson.* Most workers have some connection with their customers or clients. The more effectively they can find out what the customer wants, the more they help the company. Selling is about talking . . . and listening. Nonshy people are good at both.

3. Anyone who contemplates self-employment had better learn to talk. More than ever, people are turning to self-employment, one-person businesses, small businesses, etc. When you have a direct relationship with the buying public, shyness won't work. Customers want to be talked with, listened to, understood, and talked with some more.

4. *Most career advancement involves some degree of public speaking.* You don't get very far in business, government, the nonprofit world, or anywhere if you cannot stand in front of a group and say something. The formerly shy must overcome this particular fear, and when they do, they are liked, recognized, and respected. When you fade into the background, you will be bypassed.

It is not necessary for you to be overbearing, intrusive, or a braggart in order to be an effective job hunter. Such characteristics would work against you. But an unwillingness to put yourself forward will also work against you in many ways.

Of course, there is the occasional exception, the lone genius who writes papers and communicates in scientific and mathematical language without relying much on words. But what happens in professional meetings or public meetings where one's cohorts or fellow citizens want to know what you're thinking about? Einstein and other people of great brilliance were perhaps reclusive at times, but when the time came to talk, they did it well.

What is the minimum that job hunters must be able to do that requires nonshyness?

+ introduce themselves to people they don't know
+ attend professional associations or other meetings and meet new people
+ request information interviews and job interviews
+ talk about oneself comfortably during interviews
+ call to request information that may produce job leads
+ walk into businesses and other offices to request information and possible meetings

You may have ample reason to believe your shyness cannot be overcome. Your mother is shy, your father is worse. You were locked in a closet at birth. Someone stole your tricycle out from under you, and it's been a nightmare ever since.

Job hunting does not require you to have great persuasive powers, nor is it necessary or even desirable for you to be pushy or aggressive. Do not compare yourself to people you know who are wildly outgoing or "silver-tongued devils." A normal, relaxed, low-key communication style will work for you.

So, how do you overcome shyness, if this is your problem?

1. *Practice.* We've said it before, and here it is again. Practice. Let's call "talkativeness" the opposite of shyness. How do you become this way? By doing it. Again and again and again. Of course, it's uncomfortable for you. You reflexively move away from people. You abhor being in the center of a conversational group. It does not come naturally. Then do it unnaturally. Do it self-consciously. But do it. Talk, interact, mingle, express your opinion even when you don't know if you're right. It's been said that the way major leaguers learn to hit a rock-hard baseball coming eighty-five to ninety miles per hour is that they do it (nearly) millions of times—in batting cages, on practice fields, in games. If you keep talking enough, you'll become more comfortable.

2. *Do not insist on being 100 percent right.* A lot of talk is just that—talk. The speaker doesn't know if he's right about what he says—he's just talking. But he's doing so to try out ideas, see how people react, learn from their responses, and listen to what others are saying. If you have only your own thoughts, and you keep them to yourself, you have only yourself for feedback. That is the talker's great secret—he/she learns continually by trying ideas on others.

3. *Take criticism.* This may be a big reason why shy people are shy in the first place. They don't want to be exposed to other people's opinions, gibes, criticisms, and needling. It can be a lot easier just to keep to yourself. Well, it's time to get out of that particular protective shell, because criticism is the price of admission. You don't get anywhere in business, in careers, without taking your lumps. Any successful person will tell you this. If your shyness has been a wall against being knocked, it's time to bring that wall down.

4. *Put yourself in social situations that are enjoyable.* A lot of shy people believe that interacting with others is painful. Never quite knowing where the pain will come from, they avoid everything social. But some mingling situations are better than others. Choose groups, organizations, parties where it looks as though you'll have a good time. Learn that talking, socializing, mingling can be more enjoyable than you thought. On that one night that you just don't want to leave the house, go out —and you'll thank us for it later.

5. *Put yourself in difficult social situations.* See if you can reach 20 percent

beyond yourself. Choose situations where you have to talk to people you don't know. Suffer a little. Deal with people who are snotty or rude. Make conversation with people who seem only marginally interested. Remember what mothers all over the world have said to their children: "You *never know* who you might meet if you go to that party. But, if you don't go, you'll never meet them." I promise you that, no matter how demanding or unpleasant the situation you put yourself in, you will survive it. And you'll be tougher and more resilient the next time. Learn to talk in settings where previously you would have beaten a hasty retreat. You'll get a little better each time. You're becoming a social warrior.

Do all the talking, socializing, schmoozing, interacting, and public speaking that you can do, in order to become the person you want to be career-wise. Anything less than that, and you're doing yourself a disservice.

Remember, in the final analysis, the employer is on your side. Employers are always looking for capable people who can help them achieve their objectives. But you have to tell them before they'll know what you can do. If you act shyly, they will not hear your whisper.

Advantages of Shyness

Shyness itself works in negative ways, but there are characteristics shy people have that tend to work in their favor. Does that sound like a contradiction? Consider this. People who avoid contact with other people are going to lose in the job search. However, if you're shy, you probably have developed some other attributes that will work in your favor. Here are the things about you that employers like:

- you're undoubtedly tactful and diplomatic
- you're probably a good listener
- you're not so full of yourself that it turns people off
- you're well attuned to the feelings of others
- you pay attention to cues from other people
- you can probably work well on your own
- you don't mind not being the center of attention

These are valuable attributes; they make it possible for you to be an effective member of a working team and make it easy for people to approach you. So if you can shed your noninteractive behaviors, learn to mingle with people and share ideas with them often, and still retain the strong qualities noted above, you'll have an effective combination of qualities for obtaining new jobs and succeeding in them.

31

If You Believe You're Not Qualified,
Here's What to Do

This is America. You can do anything here.

—Ted Turner

If you wait until you have all the qualifications for a job, you'll stand still forever and never apply for anything. Every job candidate is an "imperfect" candidate—he or she always lacks something the employers say they're looking for. Therefore, you should not eliminate yourself even though you may lack this or that. Consider the qualifications, skills, and experiences you *do* have that are relevant, and make the best possible case for yourself.

The *biggest step* you will take in the job search is the first one—getting yourself to apply for a job. More people trip themselves up here than any other place in the job-hunting process. Deciding not to apply is so easy. You just think of some reason you're "not qualified." As Krumboltz says in *Private Rules of Career Decision Making*, "when a reason is needed, any reason will do."

Almost everyone can tell you why their backgrounds are "wrong" for the jobs that they want—or why they are working in fields they were initially "not qualified" for but got anyway, or "just lucked into," as they often say.

> *Examples:* I'm working in the finance department, but only have an English degree.
>
> I'm an editor at a book publishing house, but I was in insurance sales for three years, studied biology in school, and never wrote for the school paper.
>
> I'm head of a small historical library, but took only one history course, and used to be in the car repair business.
>
> I studied classics in college and now I'm entering the artificial intelligence field, even though I'm just learning about computers.

No doubt you can explain why you have a missing piece or two for the field of work that you want to enter. Your differences may not be as broad as those described above, but you have an image of the ideal candidate, and you don't believe you fit that profile.

People are champs at pulling themselves out of the race. More individuals disqualify themselves from job possibilities than are ever rejected through job interviews. Why does this happen? Because you do not want to apply incorrectly for a job, and then wind up looking foolish—or being embarrassed—and eventually getting rejected.

Believing yourself to be an inferior candidate, you may refuse to apply, or apply halfheartedly, or apply to only one place and forget the others, or give up halfway through the process and conclude, "I was right all along, they did not want me." Then you drop back and limit yourself to only those safe job possibilities where you know you have a good chance and will not face more rejection.

Feeling discouraged and being rejected in a job search are inevitable. You have to take your lumps with the rest of the job hunters. But, before you make the situation worse by pulling out of the hunt, consider this:

+ Job-qualification statements are written as though they descended from Mount Olympus. Human resources departments, which write the job qualifications for many job openings you hear about, are notorious for inflating the job requirements beyond what they expect to hire. They do this in order to attract the best possible candidates, knowing that the decision maker will usually settle for less, for someone who fits some of the criteria but not others. Anyone who writes a job-candidate profile likes to include everything they might want from applicants, recognizing that it will be possible to back off when they review the candidate pool.

+ Most employers will admit that job-candidate profiles are written in order to screen applicants, to keep out the driftwood, to discourage people who truly are not in the ballpark. What they are looking for is not someone who fits all the criteria on paper, but "the best possible person," "a candidate who fits *some* of the basic criteria, is highly motivated, is nice to work with, has good learning skills, and has potential for staying and growing in this field." But they can't put that description on paper, because it sounds too loose. Thus, your task is to get into the interview, based on having *some* of the right criteria, and then in person try to demonstrate that you are motivated, ambitious, willing to learn, likable, and want to be given a chance to show what you can do.

You won't have a chance to impress people in job interviews if you eliminate yourself at the front end. Deciding to apply in the first place is the biggest decision you will make in the job search. Without it, you are nowhere. As research consistently demonstrates, direct application is the single most successful method used in obtaining jobs, across the entire spectrum of the job market.

You are probably wondering whether you should pay any attention at all to job requirements when reviewing job notices or job descriptions. Of course you should. Try to choose those jobs that best fit your background and experience. However, do not make the mistake of reading "qualifications" statements too literally. There are two main areas of concern here: *education* and *experience*.

Education. Do not limit yourself to only those jobs that request your particular academic background. While in some cases the academic degree required will not be flexible (e.g., you have to show an engineering degree for an engineering job), most of these are in the technical fields. In many other cases, the degree requirements are looser than you think. For example, many liberal arts graduates are hired for business jobs and elsewhere, even though they don't have academic majors that fit the jobs. If you are not sure whether the educational requirement is strict or not, check with people who have been hired recently in that kind of job and see what degrees they have.

Experience. Do not eliminate yourself if you don't believe you have the experience called for. The experience requirement is a typical screening device used to discourage candidates who are less motivated or who truly know little about the field and don't have the capacity to learn it. In many cases you can stretch some experience you have had to be relevant to the job, or discover skills you have developed that will be useful in this job. "Relevant experience" is open to much interpretation. For example, if you want a job as a museum worker but have not ever worked in one, your experience as a library assistant (information gathering), or your theater background (set-designing skills), or your history courses can be described as related experience, at least enough to get you in the door.

Thus, in deciding whether or not you are qualified for a particular job, keep these principles in mind:

1. Go ahead and apply. Even if you lack something compared to the requirements on paper, go ahead and apply if you believe you have relevant background, and especially if you are highly motivated. The best that can happen is that they will respond well to your enthusiasm, look closely at your positive features, and give you a chance to sell yourself. The worst that can happen is that you don't match up to other candidates, but you will learn what the job is about and may be referred to other job opportunities.

2. Focus on what you do have, not on what you don't have. Concentrate on those abilities, experiences, and areas of knowledge that you believe do fit the job, and sell these as well as you can. Don't waste any time talking about what you don't have, because you'll just sound defensive and will fritter away valuable interview time. Even when they ask why you don't have certain "qualifications," answer concisely and truthfully and then use this as an opportunity to clarify your positives.

3. Don't oversell yourself. Do not be arrogant, disrespectful, or overly general in stating your attributes and qualifications. You might be tempted to say: "Just show me any job. Whatever it is, I can do it." That's going too far. Instead, pay attention to what is needed in the job, and explain patiently why you believe your skills and experiences will enable you to perform well. This shows you have respect for the job and the person who wrote its description at the same time you are displaying confidence that you are a good candidate.

4. Skills can be learned. Perhaps the biggest reason that people eliminate themselves from careers is that they cannot envision themselves learning, growing, and changing. They incorrectly assume, "This is the way I am. I only have certain skills and I'll make the best of them." But any skill can be learned.

You are not a fixed set of skills. You're more like a blank slate, upon which can be written the skills you want to acquire next. Want to be a carpenter and last time you tried to hammer a nail you bashed your thumb? Apprentice yourself to a carpenter. Give it some time. Practice, watch the professionals, practice some more. In months, you'll be doing things you never imagined.

5. Learn how to "package" yourself. Your particular combination of experiences, education, skills, interests, and knowledge can be appropriate for many different kinds of work, because they can be "packaged" and repackaged in different ways. Résumé writing is a form of packaging. So is your verbal presentation in the interview. Learn to complete the statement "I am a good candidate for this job because _____," or "I believe that I can learn this job and do it well, because _____." For one job, you will emphasize certain features of your background, for a different job you will emphasize other features. That is what packaging is all about.

Your marketability is affected greatly by how much you *believe* you are marketable for that kind of job. I am not suggesting that you apply inappropriately for jobs where your missing qualifications cannot be overcome. But give yourself the benefit of the doubt. If you have some reason for believing that you can do that job well, give yourself a chance to express that belief. Turn the Krumboltz statement on its ear: "When a [positive] reason is needed, any reason will do."

"I think I'll be a good stockbroker because I don't like money, and I want to help other people who don't want to deal with it either, but are forced to, and we can talk about how to minimize our involvement with investments, and still get good results."

Not the usual reason one might hear from a prospective stockbroker, but this person can sell it if he/she believes it and thinks that approach will appeal to prospective customers. Whatever works for you works for you. Don't be afraid to tell someone about it.

What Is Your "Wrong Set of Qualifications"?

How are you undervaluing yourself? What beliefs do you have about your marketability that are slowing you down, perhaps keeping you from making contacts or applying directly in fields where you would like to have a chance?

I am not saying that all lack of progress in job hunting is self-induced. Certainly many of the market requirements are realistic and many fields are off-limits to you. However, I would estimate that a typical job hunter disqualifies him/herself from 33 percent of the job possibilities that would be available if he/she pursued them. One-third of all job opportunities represents a lot of lost chances. Let's take a look at the main themes of self-disqualification.

"I Have the Wrong College Major"

I majored in sociology, so I can't get a job in business

I studied biology, so I guess I'll be eliminated from job possibilities in journalism, which is where I really want to work

I majored in economics, but I really think I'd like human resources work, and I suppose that's for psychology majors

College graduates unnecessarily eliminate themselves on the basis of perceived qualifications for certain jobs. Believing that college studies are like vocational training, they often assume they have missed the boat, and therefore cannot enter certain fields of work. On the contrary. For all fields except those that are technical (engineering, architecture, pharmacy, nursing, etc.), college graduates having the "wrong" majors will be considered and welcomed if they have: relevant experiences, some coursework in related fields, strong interest, or relevant skills. Many of the "wrong" graduates are hired and perform well on the job. Liberal arts graduates, though not the only examples, are often the best proof of this, in that their majors seldom denote any fields in the world of work. Yet they obtain good jobs and advance satisfactorily, often to higher levels of responsibility than those "trained" in certain vocational areas.

Many employers recognize that technical information is best learned on the job rather than in prior schooling; hence they are little concerned about a graduate's major field of study. They seek individuals who have general learning skills and high motivation, so they can provide training themselves, within the organization.

> *Examples:* Desired field: journalism; "wrong major": medieval history
>
> *Solution:* This history major applied her writing and research skills developed in many history courses to the tasks of a journalist, and recognized that her understanding of history would help her to write good news stories and features. She "packaged" herself as a person with skills relevant to newspaper/magazine journalism, and got a job with a foreign affairs newsletter in Washington, D.C., and then used that experience to become a correspondent with the *Baltimore Sun*.
>
> Desired field: social work; "wrong major": music
>
> *Solution:* This music major had been a counselor at a music camp and had volunteered in social service agencies during college, including Family Planning and the Rape Crisis Center. She applied to the local mental health clinic as a beginning caseworker and was hired on a trial basis. Her talents were evident and she was soon promoted to a job as social worker, and has used this experience to change jobs to social work positions having greater responsibility.
>
> Desired field: corporate finance; "wrong major": radio/TV/film
>
> *Solution:* This RTF major decided he did not want the communications field after all, even though he completed the degree; he took his two accounting courses and a summer job in a bank to the finance department of a large corporation. He convinced them to give him a junior financial analyst job based on his interest in the company, his high score on a company aptitude test, and his willingness to take finance courses at night from a nearby college. Obviously, he did a "sell job," but it worked. He is now Vice President for Financial Affairs in the same corporation, having proven himself through on-the-job performance.

"I Have the Wrong Combination of Experiences"

Career development is supposed to look orderly on paper. Résumés are supposed to "make sense," but often they do not. You may have an odd jumble of experiences and education, and furthermore they may differ from the field of work you now want to enter. Despite what you have done or studied in the past, you cannot predict what you will want to do in the future. Thus, the unexpected career change is born, and you are forced to justify this odd progression to future employers.

How do we account for the biology major who works successfully for a computer company (as a service representative) for several years and then goes on to start an eventually profitable music publishing company? How do we explain a stockbroker who quits her job, enrolls in law school, then quits that to become a successful director of a summer camp? Or a retailer who leaves that business behind him to become a happy leader of river-raft tours, and then leaves that field after several years to become a successful fund-raiser for his alma mater?

Careers are expected to be predictable and "logical," but they seldom are. Perhaps you know what you would like to do next, but are pessimistic that the marketplace will let you do it, based on your unlikely combination of past jobs, education, and other experiences. You may not be the ideal candidate for the job you want (hardly anyone is), but you can make a strong case for yourself if you look closely at what the job needs. Let's take a look at a few case studies.

These examples are especially relevant to (a) career changers, who want to leave one field for another; (b) liberal arts graduates, who are not in any fields of work that they can apply for; (c) anyone who has "done many different things" and is not sure how they all add up.

Examples: Goal: To be a recruiter for a major corporation

"*Unlikely Combination*" *of Experiences:* Arthur has been a librarian for ten years, has a personal interest in sailing, changed jobs to become an auto mechanic for three years, and volunteers his time at the local dog pound.

Strategy: This sounds like a tough one, doesn't it? You would not expect this guy to want to become a college recruiter. But the motivations of the individual cannot be predicted that easily. Arthur takes a job as a production assistant with a large company, then applies for a transfer to the HR department, where he becomes a pension analyst for two years, but then an opening occurs in the college relations section of personnel and he applies for the job, gets it, and becomes part of the company's college relations team. He used his library experience to show that he knows how to develop a computer system for keeping track of job candidates, offers made, trips completed, etc. He used his contact with one of his sailing buddies, a vice president in the corporation, to get the initial job in the production department.

Goal: To start a graphics design business

"*Unlikely Combination*" *of Experiences:* Ann was a secretary for a construction firm for six years, has a college degree in biology and home economics, spent three years as an insurance agent, and does community work with the Humane Society.

Strategy: Ann has some raw talent in graphics work, and believes she has a feel for magazine and book layout, for brochure design, for using graphics to dress up publications. But she has the ol' bugaboo, No Experience at All Whatsoever. So she volunteers to "apprentice" with a friend of hers for a year, discovers her instincts were pretty sound (she does have talent for graphics work), and then starts part-time in acquiring clients. How does her past experience help her? Work as an insurance agent helps her in dealing with the public, secretarial work helps her to keep the new business orderly and take care of the correspondence, and community work has given her contacts for potential clientele. Where do biology and the Humane Society come in? Who knows? But it's quite possible that one day Ann will design layouts and promotional materials for books and magazines about the animal world. And where, pray tell, could they find somebody better?

Goal: To manage a state or local program providing job training for the unemployed

"Unlikely Combination" of Experiences: Bill has a college degree in philosophy and history, six years' experience as a trust officer at a bank, is a carpenter in his spare time, and worked two years with two partners, trying to develop a new kind of hardware store (it didn't work out; the idea flopped and the partners fought).

Strategy: Bill had heard the community was trying to attract funding for helping the unemployed and school dropouts; he wanted to become involved, but had no idea who did such things or how they did it. He checked with his banking friends, one of whom is a member of the city council, and learned that a new group was forming, called the Private Industry Council. He applied to be a community representative on the P.I.C. Board, served for a year, and learned that an opening existed on the P.I.C. staff. He applied for the job and got it. How did he sell himself? Bill knew a lot about low-income housing (carpentry experience) and the unemployed people who need it; he had been a good administrator at the bank and figured those skills would transfer to coordinating employment training programs; and he said that he could figure out how to tap into federal and state moneys available for this purpose. He used his analytical skills and research skills (remember the philosophy and history majors?) to investigate the latter. He did not have nearly the ideal résumé for a P.I.C. staff member, but he reasoned that he could do the job as well as the next person, and gave it a shot.

Goal: To become a financial counselor on a private basis

"Unlikely Combination" of Experiences: Judy has an Associate of Arts degree in Textiles and Clothing. After that program, she enrolled in a paralegal school, and she works presently for a large law firm. She does gardening in her spare time and is a board member of the Y.W.C.A. Judy has been taking accounting courses at night, but finds she is bored by that field and would prefer to help people manage their money. She has no experience in the field, but reads a lot about financial decision making.

Strategy: How does a person become a financial counselor these days? Some work for banks, others are glorified stockbrokers, still others hang out a shingle and hope someone will respond. Some are certified (C.F.A.—Chartered Financial Analyst), but most are not. How can Judy get on this train with little relevant background? The same way that most people market a product or service successfully to the public—they offer it, and people vote with their dollars. Judy intensifies her reading, attends seminars, has long conversations with friends who are in related fields, reads some more, takes courses, does some mythical investment planning of her own, tries her skills with family and friends, and then finally goes public. Gathering clientele is slow at first, but some people are pleased with her ability to organize their whole financial picture and offer patient, low-key opinions about how to reallocate their money. Word of mouth begins to work for her. She quits the law firm when there is enough steady business to believe her long-term prospects are good. Her income is less steady and often lower than what it was in paralegal work, but she likes it better and sees greater earnings ahead, as the concept of "financial counselor" becomes more familiar to people and gains greater public acceptance.

Goal: To work as a lobbyist for a state education agency

"Unlikely Combination" of Experiences: Larry has a college degree in physics, worked for several years as a service representative for a firm that sells equipment to eye doctors, and then moved to Washington, D.C., to work for the National Science Foundation. He left that job to start his own company raising bees for honey production, and now is unemployed. He knows a lot of teachers who have gripes about their jobs, but what makes him think he can become one of their representatives in the state capital?

Strategy: Larry is a resourceful guy. He has had his fill of science, and figures the way to be a good lobbyist is to be good at talking to people. He takes an interim job as an equipment repairman (physics background helps), but devotes his primary energy to volunteering his time with the local teachers' union. He learns what their needs are, develops friendships with union leaders, and gets introduced to the lobbying staff. One thing leads to another, his view is confirmed that successful lobbying is getting your ideas across to people (in this case, legislators), and he applies for a job on the staff. Can a physics major find happiness on Capitol Hill? The rest is history.

What do we make of all these examples of people whose careers take new twists and turns, and yet they come up breathing and find new ways to succeed? Life's a mess and make the best of it? Are these oddball examples that really do not fit the great majority of people? Do we really want people to bounce around like this, instead of getting into a field and staying there?

These examples are real people, and any one of them could be you. Take note of the ways they have dealt with their situations, because career development is the challenge of reacting to your present circumstances and making the most of what you've got, not settling for less. If you're bored, move on. If you're unemployed, stitch together your assets and find someone who wants you. If you're looking for a new challenge, repackage yourself for a different market. The examples above reflect these key principles:

1. *Your life and career are essentially unpredictable.* You have to take what develops in your needs and the shifts of the labor market, and find something different to do, whenever circumstances change, and they will. The work that excites you today may be old hat tomorrow. The industry you are part of may lose its grip on the public. Your spouse may get an offer he/she can't refuse in another city and you can't find your present job there. Or your money needs may change, upward or downward, and that will dictate a different kind of work. Expect the unexpected, and don't fret if the work you're seeking next does not seem "logical" based on what you have done before. If careers were that predictable, we could all get our heads stamped when we take our first jobs. But they are not. The economy changes, family situations change, jobs and careers change, and perhaps most of all, so do you.

2. *Anything can be combined with anything.* Any job experiences, educational credentials, and personal interests can be combined and made useful toward a particular career goal. Now, that is a tall order, or quite a strong claim. Yet whether you have farming and calligraphy, or playing the drums and real estate, carpet cleaning and auctioneering, or auto mechanics and bird watching,

any combination of experiences in your life can be hung together to contribute toward the work that you want to do next.

The magic of combining is that, in some way, things can relate to each other if you look closely enough. This is because transferable skills underlie most jobs, and these skills can be applied in new contexts. For example, the drummer knows about pleasing people, working odd hours, and networking with others. He/she can apply these experiences to work as a real-estate salesperson. Wherever you go, you take the tools in your kit with you. You may not be the perfect candidate for the job you want, but you'll stretch every last bit of knowledge and skill to fit the new job description. And, if they give you a chance, you're a pretty good bet to show that you can learn the job and do it well.

3. Your imagination and general ability to learn are often more powerful than labor market qualifications. Now certainly there are plenty of jobs you cannot apply for, and others for which you would need formal training to enter. However, there are many other jobs where formal qualifications are less important than the desire to succeed. If you imagine that you could do the work (everyone who has never done a job before has begun by *imagining* it) and draw on your general learning skills to help you, then there are many jobs and careers available to you. I could fill this book with examples like those above, but I would prefer that you talk to friends, neighbors, and others to hear their real-life stories of how they learned *on the job*, en route to advancement and satisfaction.

4. The job market is not as rational as it claims to be. Employers are supposed to hire people with the best qualifications, but they do not always do so. For many reasons, they hire individuals with unorthodox backgrounds, people whom they like, people who happen to show up the week they really need to hire someone, people who have more promise than past performance, and people who are recommended by friends. It's almost impossible for an employer to figure out which job candidates are the best, based on paper credentials. Thus, if your qualifications for the job sound reasonable, and you're standing there in front of them, and you're pretty likable too, they say to themselves: "Why should we look any further?"

5. Technical jobs sometimes do not require technical people. A strict training requirement does not always exist, even in some technical fields. For example, William Schaffer's book *Hi-Tech Jobs for Lo-Tech People* notes that computer firms often hire people who did not complete any computer science courses. If they feel the individual has the ability, they give her/him a lot of room to learn what the firm and the industry are about and prove themselves.

Self-Disqualification Can Ruin Your Complexion

If you disqualify yourself from job possibilities, it can be dangerous to your job-hunting health. The dropout syndrome affects your job hunter's immune system. If you eliminate yourself arbitrarily, you will have less ability to fight the infection of rejection, not to mention the trauma of post-interview depression. A healthy job hunter is one who keeps exercising the exploratory muscles, and exposes his/her body to the rigors of job-market workouts. Self-disqualification is like checking into the sick bay at summer camp on the chance that you might come down with a cold. Don't do it. Keep yourself in the hunt. There is a place for your combination of experiences and ambitions.

Sometimes You Win, Sometimes You Lose

Sometimes employers hire the most qualified individuals, but other times they take whoever is available because they don't have the time and resources to look further. More important, they have imperfect judgment about who is best for a given job. Thus, sometimes you will be hired when you are not the best candidate (but you got there first), and on other occasions you *are* the best applicant but someone else got hired for some irrelevant reason. And other times you're a strong candidate and you happen to show up at the right time, and you make a good case for yourself, and it all hangs together.

Roll the dice and keep rolling, because in this game the losses do not count against you. Sure, the jobs-not-gotten cost time, energy, and sometimes money, but the standings of your wins and losses do not appear on the sports pages. An employer does not care if you have applied for thirty-eight other jobs and lost them, if you are the one he/she wants. Good things happen to people who keep their positive beliefs going in the face of uncertainty. As Tom Jackson says, job hunting is a bunch of NO's waiting for a YES.

If you disqualify yourself, you're out. If you succumb to the myth that every job has a right candidate and you're not it, then you're doubly out. But the game still goes on and all kinds of "wrong" applicants are getting jobs out there. You know some of those less-than-perfectly-qualified people yourself, don't you? They must have had "pull," you think. In some cases perhaps they did, but in most situations they just went ahead and applied and their assertiveness worked in their favor.

Don't wait around for the right job for you. Go ahead and apply for a few of the wrong jobs where your background doesn't quite fit, but what the heck—they deserve a chance to find out who you are and what you can do.

32

Overcome Telephone Torture

"I can't take your call right now. . . . Please hold for the next five days while I decide when I might come to the phone." . . . "Ms. Jones is on extended leave with regard to phone calls such as yours." . . . "If you'll leave your name and number, I'll bury it in the backyard." . . . "Please let me know where I can reach you, and I'll pass your message around so it can be ignored by everyone in this office." . . . "Note that whomever you're calling cannot ever come to the phone right now . . . at the sound of the beep, please give up."

The telephone used to be an aid in your job-search process. Now it's a series of obstacles, an array of technological blockades. Job hunters face a wall of phone-message options as they increasingly lose the battle of how to get through to a real person who will consider their qualifications.

The telephone labyrinth has to be dealt with. Your future as a successful job hunter will depend on your ability to navigate the intricate web of telephone technology without losing your cool.

Trying to contact prospective employers on the telephone has become an exercise in frustration. People are using technology to avoid having to answer their phones directly, and you're trying your best to get through. Before talking about what to say on the telephone, we must consider how to reach the real person in the first place.

Telephone turmoil can sap the spirit of the most dedicated job hunters and information seekers. It's hard enough once you get to talk with real people. But being stonewalled by the very people you're trying to meet—that's enough to make a person consider giving up this "networking" routine. If you can't get through to anyone on the phone, why mess with it?

You're entangled in the rhododendron of telephone systems where apparently no human beings ever answer their phones anymore. That is precisely where a lot of people simply give up and turn their career prospects over to fate.

The people you're trying to reach—employers, contacts, job holders whom you can information-interview—have figured out ways to screen out all but their closest friends, or their most familiar coworkers, or people who want to give them money. You don't fit, so you're leaving messages until you're blue in the face. What's a person to do? Learn to communicate effectively through voice-mail messages.

Auditions by Voice Mail

When you have perhaps as little as forty-five seconds to leave a message on voice mail that will make a good first impression, it's a daunting task. It feels much like a theatrical audition and there's no chance for a retake:

> "Hello, my name is Sylvia Dradnatz and I'm calling about a job sneezing computers, I mean a job freezing computers, I mean a job leasing confusers . . . Could I just start over again?"

There's no getting around it. People will make judgments about you based on what they hear in your phone messages. Qualities that are important include the three C's—clarity (can they hear what you're saying easily?), conciseness (you have to keep it under sixty seconds, and sometimes you're cut off after thirty seconds, in which case you have to start over, and that is awkward), and color (does your voice have enthusiasm, an inviting quality that says "this will be a pleasant person to talk with"?).

Since it's an audition, I recommend that you write down, word for word, what you want to say and practice it several times before going "live" on the phone. Let other people listen to you and tell you how effective you sound. You may run the risk of sounding a little rehearsed when you get on the phone, but that's a lot better than fumbling around nervously and conveying anxiety in your message. After a certain amount of practice, you will learn to adjust your presentation so that it does not sound prepared.

Part of your "audition" will be to maintain positive emotions. You may devote hours to reaching the right people. Then you want to convey a lot of positive energy in your messages.

Control Your Frustration

When you have no choice but to reach a person by telephone, learn to manage your emotions so that you always come out on the positive end. After a long wait, instead of being ready to explode, you must give your most upbeat, focused response: "It's certainly good to hear from you. I'd like to tell you something that you'll find interesting . . ." as though the previous ten minutes or three days of phone-mail uncertainty had never existed.

Always smile on the telephone. Remember that the other person has been juggling a lot of phone messages and she wants to hear a happy voice as much as you do. Also, they know you've been batted around the phone-mail system. They want to see how you react to frustration and pressure. If you can radiate calmness and enthusiasm after a bout with telephone torture, then you've already shown your quality and your willingness to work with the system.

What if you're still not very good at this? They put you on hold so you have to listen to Earnest Ervin and the Eccentrics, cut you off, and do everything but attach electrodes to your ears. How can you be warm and friendly when you finally get a real voice on the phone?

1. Practice. Call businesses that have voice-mail and phone menus. Sit through five minutes or so, and then practice being kind and congenial. It may be easier to do it when your livelihood is not at stake. Practice being a friendly person when you've been kept waiting. You can do it. Your mother wants you to do it.

2. Pretend that, when you finally get a live person on the phone, he/she is going to be your employer for the next five years. Be ready. You never know. It could happen.

3. You initiate your conversation cheerfully, the person wants to talk with you, they decide they want to meet you in person, you get a job offer, your life is changed forever. It won't always happen this way, but if you start the conversation with a pout, a complaint, or a harrumph, you can guarantee that the job will never be yours.

It's been widely noted that content is only a fraction of what comes across in communication. This is doubly true on the telephone. Since there are no visual cues, the listener focuses closely on vocal cues, to reveal: "How does this person feel about me? How much energy is there behind his message? How likable is this person?" The person who can communicate warmth and confidence in her telephone messages is the person who will have her messages returned.

What if you're just not that kind of live-wire person who comes across strongly on the phone? Do not fret. With practice, you can see dramatic changes. Do just this—make a forty-five-second tape of your voice leaving a phone message, and play it back five times, adjusting your message each time. You will see a noticeable difference in your vocal quality by the fifth time.

Here are some other suggestions regarding effectiveness on the telephone:

1. *Have your messages be as focused as possible.* When you must use the phone to reach someone, (a) Know the names of the people you're calling; (b) Whenever possible, use the name of someone else who referred you to the person you're calling. Even if your name is not familiar, if your referral is known to that person, it will increase your chances of getting a response; (c) Know what you're calling about and be able to state that in forty-five seconds or less.

2. *Warm up before making your important calls.* If you sound like your most agreeable voice doesn't want to come out yet, give it some opportunities to warm up. It's like warming up your muscles, except in this case, think of them as "emotional muscles." Get your voice and psyche ready by doing things that will put you in a good mood. Call a friend and laugh awhile. Talk to someone who's easy to talk with. Play some music you like. Call another friend and get your voice warmed up. Do whatever works for you. But don't make an important call if you're sleepy, you haven't used your voice yet, you're feeling grouchy, or you're otherwise not ready.

3. *Work on your vocal skills.* It doesn't seem fair to ask us regular people to do auditions! Actors and actresses practice for months to say their lines. We don't even think of rehearsing to give a telephone message, but why not? You need to be as good in that forty-five seconds as you possibly can be.

Practice listening to yourself talk. Play it back on a tape recorder. You may be upset or aghast at what you hear, but that will fuel you to change. You must get across your message clearly, quickly, and with zip. A lot of people have voices that are too slow, too fast, too dull, too muddled, not clear enough, or stiff-sounding. Vocal skill can be improved greatly through feedback and practice.

Don't Be a Stranger on the Telephone

Voice-mail messages can be an uphill battle when you are a complete unknown to the person you're calling. If the respondent says "Who *is* this calling me?" they may not call back.

If you have already met the person you're calling, you're about five times as likely to get through when you call. Even if you talked with that person only briefly, the name-voice-and-face recognition on the phone will make a big difference.

Therefore, you must continually try to create situations in which the person you're calling has some prior knowledge of you. Here are ways to do that:

1. *Find ways of meeting the person face-to-face before you call.* Even if you only meet a person at a party, a reception, a social event, a professional meeting, or somewhere else, you will be much more likely to have your call welcomed and receive a prompt response.

When they remember your name or your face, then your phone call becomes a way of *continuing* the relationship rather than your struggling attempt to start it. When you call, give the respondent some cues to help them recall your in-person meeting:

"My name is ———— and I met you at the American Society for Training and Development meeting last week. I was the one who talked with you about Totowa, New Jersey. . . ."

Professional association meetings are excellent places to meet people in career fields that interest you. This message is repeated throughout this book, because professional associations are a reliable and widely available source of help. You must get up the gumption to find out about such meetings, attend them, and then be assertive enough to speak with people. The rewards are numerous. You meet real "live" professionals who do what interests you. You get their office phone numbers, you hear what their working lives are like, and they refer you to others in this field.

When you have met someone, and then you call them, remind them in your phone message who you are and where you met. That will increase your probability of getting a return call quickly.

Walk into places of business if they are small and informal enough. Introduce yourself as someone who is interested in what they do. Smile. Dress appropriately. Talk to anyone who will talk with you. Ask for a brief tour. If you like what you see, ask if you can "shadow" them for a day or two. All they can do is say no. Maybe they'll say yes, simply because you're interested and you're there.

2. *Use the name of a referral.* If you cannot meet the person face-to-face beforehand, try your best to find someone who knows that person, who can recommend that you call:

"My name is ———— and ———— suggested that I call you, because he thought you might be able to give me some information about real-estate work in the Johnstown area. I'm looking for employment in this field, but I'm *not* asking you for a job. I simply want to get your impressions of this field and your suggestions about how I can best prepare myself."

3. *Send some information in advance, by mail or computer.* If you have done work that is relevant to the person you're calling, send something to them. It might be a brochure promoting your work, an article you've written, a brief work sample of some kind, or an article someone else has written that would be of interest to them.

Sending written material is somewhat weaker than the first two forms of introduction, because mail can be ignored or the respondent may have had no opportunity to read what you sent. Nevertheless, this is a way of gaining some "recognition" before you make telephone contact.

4. *Give them some reasons to want to talk with you.* If you cannot establish some connection to the person you're calling, and you must use the telephone before meeting them in person, ask yourself: "Why would she want to meet with me?" "What might I do for her that could possibly make her job easier?"

> "Hello, my name is _____ and I know that your photography business is always looking for ways to broaden your customer base. I have three years' experience as a commercial photographer and I'd like to tell you how I helped my previous employer—in New Orleans— expand her business."

If you have no such direct experience, then say something else that might entice the listener:

> "Hello, my name is _____ and I know that your photography business is always looking to expand its customer base. I worked in the hotel business for six years and I have some ideas about how you can attract new customers."

The listener might be just curious enough to want to talk with you. You've thrown out a "hook" for them to bite on. If you say anything suggesting you may help their business, it's worth fifteen to twenty minutes of their time to talk with you.

Don't let telephone technology get the better of you. People want to talk with you on the phone, but they have constructed barriers to make the most efficient use of their time, not because they hate you. If you speak clearly, warmly, and concisely, you will be much more likely to get through to the people you want. If you have met them in person, so much the better. Legislate impatience out of your voice. Notice how well *you* respond when a cheerful voice leaves a message for you.

The telephone can be a reason for teeth-gnashing, or it can be a place where you demonstrate your skill and sophistication in playing by the modern rules of communication. Deal successfully with the telephone. When you finally get through to your target person, and she likes what you're saying, only you will know what a special triumph it is.

Professionalism on the Telephone

Voice mail, phone menus, message machines, call waiting, and other devices are going to take up residence between you and your intended. Your ability to respond to these things with patience is a skill, even an art form. After three hours or three days of waiting, during which time you have been sinking into a pit of pessimism and despair, when the person you want finally comes on the line, it is a wonderful skill to be able to bury your frustrations and say:

"What a pleasure hearing from you! I've been looking forward to talking with you. Let me tell you briefly why I'm calling. . . ."

This is professionalism at its best. The really first-class job hunters do it well, and you will too, because you know that your respondents did not put you off on purpose. That's simply the way things are. You're not their first priority every minute, and you never will be. Or, even if they did put you off deliberately, so what? You've learned to accept these things graciously and get on with business. You've kept people at arm's length too. So you understand each other. "Gracious" is the key word. People appreciate other people who can respond calmly and respectfully under any circumstances.

The telephone has become a many-splendored thing. There are barriers between you and the person you're calling, but your job is to adapt to them. When we could reach people by telephone too easily, we took it for granted. We interrupted each other unnecessarily, just because we knew the phone was there.

Now, when we reach a person on the phone, we're abundantly grateful that life has given us this gift. We treat in-person telephone time during the business day as something special. We use the time more judiciously. We're respectful of the time that our respondents have available. Now, that isn't necessarily a bad thing, is it?

There's the phone again. Are you gonna answer it? Screen it? Ignore it? Refer it to voice mail? Put 'em on hold? Bump the call to someone else? Fine. They'll be doing the same thing to you.

You can understand why employers may evaluate you based on your telephone communication. It may seem harsh to grant you a forty-five-second audition and then reject you because you didn't come across warmly, clearly, and with grace. But the employer knows that how you are on the telephone is how you'll be with customers and suppliers and with company executives and with company guests and with everyone. It's only forty-five seconds, but it is a good sample of you. Give that forty-five seconds your best and you'll be amply rewarded.

33

Do Not Exaggerate, Inflate, or Lie

I know you don't do this, but I'm putting it here because the consequences for this kind of behavior are so severe that I want to scare you away from ever thinking of it.

This chapter could be written in a single sentence: Don't lie in job hunting; it will hurt you. But, just as it has been said that we have thousands of laws to enforce the Ten Commandments, so is it necessary to elaborate the basic message to not lie.

From the time we first spot that cookie jar all by itself, we think we can grab a few and get away with it. Who will be the wiser? And we tell fish stories about our past accomplishments. Our listeners weren't there. How will they know? The temptation to slant things in our favor is ever present.

Everyone finds out what you've done or haven't done, sooner or later. The only secrets in life are temporary. Inflating, exaggerating, and lying may feel good at the time, but they'll come back to bite you. Count on it.

People routinely expand their capabilities on résumés. Those who read résumés expect about 20 to 30 percent exaggeration. They suspect even more. The catch is that they don't know which 30 percent is inflated, so they have to suspect *all of it*. Your résumé is thus devalued currency. Just another reason to not be overly dependent on your résumé in job hunting (see chapter 28).

A lot of people lie on their résumés. The record is so permanent that you'd expect people to be more careful on these documents. But they fib away, hoping to get that "edge" in the selection process, even though it's illusory. When a résumé is all the employer knows about you, there may be a great temptation to inflate one's accomplishments. Earlier in this book (chapter 28), I recommend that you take the emphasis off the résumé as a front-end tool for marketing yourself because there are so many ways you can be eliminated based on this piece of paper.

Interviews also encourage exaggeration. In the pressure of a forty-five-minute interview, especially when the interviewer knows nothing else about you, the temptation to lie can be overwhelming. How does the interviewer know whether anything you're saying is true? But, as in card playing, there are "tells," ways of unintentionally revealing your discomfort. Some of these are involuntary or even unconscious. If you are fibbing, nonverbal cues can give you away:

+ long pauses before you speak
+ lack of eye contact
+ changing the subject abruptly
+ nervous laughter

In contrast, a person who tells the truth (a slight understatement is helpful) radiates an atmosphere of trustworthiness. And when your references support what you've said about yourself, your integrity is solidified.

Since interviewers are always on the lookout for fabrications, you want to find ways to establish your integrity. Here are some ways to reinforce that you are telling the truth about yourself:

1. Connect your statements about yourself to mini-stories regarding when you have used the skills you are citing. These stories are "evidence" that you really used those skills in concrete situations.

2. Offer to have your references call the employer.

3. Give tangible examples of your accomplishments—papers and reports you have written, project results, money saved, awards received.

4. Tell how you would plan to use your skills in the new job if it's offered to you (see chapter 24—"Show Rather Than Tell").

There is nothing more solid and valuable than integrity when you have it and more difficult to recapture when you've lost it. If you have misled a former employer, or your résumé is discovered to have puffery or lies, the interviewer will remember this more clearly than anything else about you. If you can't be trusted, then the employer has no basis on which to gauge your future value.

People often lie because they think they can get away with it, and because it seems to be so commonly done today. It's equated with political chicanery, athletes taking illegal substances to gain a competitive advantage, and people cheating in business. "Why miss out?" seems to be the prevailing view.

Lying and exaggerating are bad not only from a moral point of view; they also make little sense as job-search strategies. What makes you think you could keep information hidden indefinitely? Even if you were hired based on inflated data about yourself, sooner or later the employer would find out the truth, and then where would you be? Discredited, that's where. And any future advancement you may hope for in that company would have a dim chance indeed.

In job hunting, lying/exaggeration does at least two bad things for you: (a) It undermines your legitimate accomplishments. Once an employer knows or suspects you of lying, she cannot trust even the things you have done that are real; and (b) It follows you wherever you go. People remember the dirt, probably because they're trying to protect themselves. "If this person lied or exaggerated once before, he will probably do it again, and most likely at my expense."

Would you hire a person who could not even be truthful about the topic he knows best—himself?

Inflating, exaggerating, and lying are common in the job market because even usually honest people sometimes get desperate and think, "Well, only this once." It's a big mistake. The small and very temporary advantage you may gain from it is grossly outweighed by the perhaps permanent loss of reputation you'll suffer when you're discovered. There's more stress associated with lying, too. As if you need more stress in your life.

34

Don't Give Up Too Soon

"It's Not My Fault . . ."

Job hunters are notorious for putting the responsibility for their plight onto someone besides themselves. When this attitude is allowed to fester, the job hunter eventually concludes he has little control over the job market and you hear statements such as:

"It's all controlled by people in 'smoke-filled rooms.'"
"There's nothing much I can do about it."
"They don't want people like me."
"It's a good-old-boy, or good-old-girl, or good-old-someone network and I'm not in it."
"I've always been on the wrong side of things, so why should this be any different?"

How to Overturn the "Give Up" Syndrome

Everyone has thoughts of surrendering in the job search sooner or later. But there are ways to make this attitude merely a temporary lull. You must substitute Active behaviors for Passive ones. In this list of Active behaviors, you have a number of ways to measure that you have *not* given up.

Active: Make sure that at least 60 percent of your job-search energy is devoted to face-to-face contact with people.

> *Passive:* Write a lot of letters, and look through job-search materials and employer directories for "job openings."

Active: Meet at least three new people every week who have some connection to your fields of job and career interest.

> *Passive:* Limit yourself to the same old people, contacts, and sources you've been tapping before; don't venture out to meet anyone unfamiliar.

Active: Work hard at "needs assessment"; use information interviews to find out what your target employers are most willing to pay money for.

> *Passive:* Try to guess what the employers want; lament that you know so little about the companies where you're applying; complain a lot.

Active: Seek contract work, temporary work, volunteer work, or part-time work as ways of getting personal exposure to your target employers.

> *Passive:* Wait for the "perfect job opening" to appear; limit your contact with employers to job interviews.

Active: Be active in a professional association related to your target career field. Attend meetings, get to know professionals on a personal basis. Ask them if they know about temporary work, etc.

> *Passive:* Lament that you know hardly anyone in your target field, and wonder out loud how you can ever become an "insider."

Active: Work hard to acquire or improve a skill that will be crucial to your career advancement, especially if it is an area of "weakness" for you. Identify this key skill through information interviews.

> *Passive:* Stick with your present abilities. Don't think about how you can learn and grow to become a better candidate for the jobs you're seeking.

If you do all of these "active" things and avoid the passive attitudes, the following are likely to happen:

+ you will expand your pool of contacts
+ your optimism and confidence will grow
+ you'll discover job possibilities you would not otherwise have known about
+ you'll get job offers

Nadine thought the businesses of Cincinnati had all conspired against her. She only wanted an office job, with an emphasis on filing. But, despite her persistent information interviewing, nothing turned up. Then one day she noticed that XYZ Business Systems had sent her the wrong application form—three times. She figured maybe they had a filing problem there somewhere. Nadine called and reemphasized her "filing skills" and was granted an interview.

"Yes, we did get your file mixed up. Happens all the time here. Do you think you could help us with this?"

It was unusual for this small company to admit its problem, but they needed help. Because she was persistent, Nadine had finally arrived in "the right place at the right time."

There are many "reasons" to give up, but none of them is a good one. Staying active is the best antidote to pessimistic feelings. As Charles Kettering once said:

"No one ever stumbled across anything sitting down."

35

Treat the "Little People"
with Respect

Just in case you were wondering, there are no little people. Everyone you meet in job hunting is important. Those job hunters who think there are "little people" are going to trip over their own condescension.

You're going to meet a lot of people in your travels to workplaces, professional meetings, social occasions, and elsewhere. It's easy to slip into a "some-are-more-important-than-others" frame of mind. This becomes job-hunting snobbery. Before you know it, you're giving some people slight attention. Imagine if you were on the receiving end of that.

Of course, you're going to pay more attention to the bosses, the decision makers, the people who have the most to say about whether you're hired. That will be built into the structure of your interviews. You'll have greater access to the bosses and therefore will devote more energy to them.

But between interviews you'll see lots of people in passing. You don't really know who they are. The possibilities include:

+ staff people who work for your intended bosses
+ high-level people from other departments who don't announce themselves as such
+ people who may have roles in your target department that are unclear to you
+ people from other companies who are there for one project or another
+ suppliers or others who have a connection to the company but don't work there
+ people from other companies who are working cooperatively with your target organization

The key is, *every one* of these people may have something to say about whether you're hired. It's as simple as this: The boss sees one of the above and asks: "We had Ms. Frazoo here for interviews today. Remember, you met her in the hall. What did you think of her?" Presto. One of these seemingly "unimportant" people suddenly may have significant input in the hiring decision about you.

This kind of thing goes on all the time, because the interviewers are looking for outside opinion to either confirm or deny what they felt about you in the formal interviews. "Was she being real in the interviews, or did she show a different side of herself to someone else?"

Interviewers are aware that candidates can hide aspects of their personalities during the interview. They check with others who may have observed "the real you" in casual conversations. Furthermore, in most offices, the concept of a "working team" is crucial to the success of the organization. Thus, the more team members who like you, the better.

The people who work for the boss often have a lot to say about who gets hired—even those who have the least responsibilities. Some have worked there many years and have a shared history of who got along well in your target job and why.

I've observed job candidates who impressed the boss but lost the job because they short-shrifted the secretary or the receptionist, who said: "I don't think we'd like him here." It happens, and I'm sure you've seen it too.

+ *"You Never Know" with Whom You're Talking*
That woman who drops by to say hello and leaves a copy of a report when you're with the boss may be checking you out, because your intended position affects hers. Or the boss may have asked her to give some input. They may not tell you this because they want to catch you off your guard.

+ *If They're in the Office and They Talk to You, They're Important*
Don't play guessing games with yourself about who is important and who is not. Most people who cross your path during your interview day did not get there by accident. Many contacts that do not look "planned" to you were in fact arranged by your interviewer.

+ *Hints About the Passing Parade of Individuals*
As you try to sort out who's who and get a feeling for the big picture of how the company is organized, here are a few guidelines:

1. *If you don't know who a person is, ask her what she does.* It's OK to ask people about their responsibilities. It shows you're a good information gatherer and you have an interest in how the pieces fit together. Maybe they're waiting to see if you'll ask. It's better to ask *what* she does, rather than her title.

2. *Ask others what a person does.* If you miss your chance to ask the person herself, it's OK to ask someone else: "What kind of work does ——— do?" If they're vague about it, don't press too hard, but absorb whatever information is volunteered.

3. *Ask if there are others you might be working with whom you have not met as yet.* It never hurts to ask this. You might uncover an opportunity to meet someone they have forgotten to introduce to you, a person with whom you would have a working relationship.

4. *Listen for signs of satisfaction or discontent.* People who are not on your interview schedule may be more likely to reveal how they feel about working for the company, because they may have less stake in whether or not you're hired. Sometimes they want to "ventilate" their feelings to someone and you're perceived as relatively "safe." This is, of course, valuable information for you to have, since you're interviewing them as well as vice versa.

5. *Keep it light.* Don't start discussing serious matters in the hallway. They usually want to experience your personality in these unscheduled times, not your competence.

People who go to job interviews and treat some individuals as "little" or "less important" are courting disaster. Even the most subtle condescension is usually noticed and long remembered. All members of the "working team" are important. If you regard everyone with respect and give them the personal attention you'd like to have yourself, you can't go wrong.

36

Quit Doing Things That Will
Make Sure You'll Fail

Job hunting is hard enough without finding ways to inhibit your chances of being evaluated positively. Career counselors tell countless stories of individuals who undermine themselves by:

+ being late for interviews
+ not sending information that employers ask for
+ not following up opportunities as soon as they are made available
+ acting casually when they should be selling themselves
+ sending carelessly prepared résumés
+ failing to contact their references
+ dressing badly for interviews
+ failing to read the company literature before the interview
+ not investigating the needs of the employer
+ waiting for job opportunities to fall into their laps
+ being passive during job interviews

Any of these can be a way to get yourself eliminated from a job competition. And the importance of each of them seems obvious enough that you would expect a person to make sure they are covered well. Sometimes people don't know any better, but often they do. Despite knowing the Do's and Don't's, and having ample time to prepare, these individuals contrive to come in second place or worse every time, because they make one or more errors that could not be ignored but could have been prevented. Such people are a mystery to their career counselors, to their families and friends, and perhaps even to themselves. On the surface, they seem quite involved in their job searches, and willing to devote effort to the task, yet they have a piece missing in their puzzle and do not take full advantage of their abilities.

Self-defeating behaviors are obvious to the bystander, but maybe not obvious to you. Find some people who have been successful job hunters and compare what you do to what they do. If you're making any of the errors noted above, you're going to keep dragging yourself down. Job hunting is challenging enough without throwing rocks in your own path.

What You Can Do About This Problem

Self-defeating behavior, while it may sound ominous, is really pretty common among job seekers. We mess up and we don't know why. Sometimes it is just ignorance, and sometimes other priorities in our lives intervene, so that we cannot pay full attention to all the intricacies of job-search behavior. There *are* a lot of things to remember to do in job hunting and, just like forgetting to check the battery cells in your car, you are going to slip from time to time.

However, if you find yourself ignoring things repeatedly, or overlooking important details when you really wanted to remember them, you may have a more ongoing concern. Self-defeating behaviors can be corrected pretty easily. But first you have to figure out where they are coming from. There are four possibilities:

You have not learned how to do it. Through inexperience and general lack of advice, you may be doing things wrong without even knowing it. You may be mailing hundreds of résumés and waiting patiently by your mailbox for the job offers to come rolling in. This is self-defeating, because you will be frustrated to find nothing in your mailbox except rejections, and yet you may not know what you have done wrong. Or you may be unprepared because you never knew that employers have literature you can read before applying for jobs. Or you may not know the role of references in the job search.

Many job seekers get bad advice or little at all. If you are one of them, reading this book is a great start toward correcting the situation. I would also recommend you talk with a career counselor about your job strategy. You may find a counselor at one of your local colleges, a community career center, or a counselor who has a private practice.

As noted throughout this book, there are plenty of ways of doing job hunting wrong. If you don't know how the job search is done well, now's the time to learn.

You never had to look hard for a job before. Once again, self-defeating behavior can be sheer negligence on your part. Maybe you have been contacted by someone else for all the previous jobs you have gotten, so you did not have to exert any effort to get them; unconsciously, you are expecting the same thing to happen again. While being chosen by others without deliberate effort on your part is an ideal to be sought (see chapter 21, "Make Job Offers Come to You"), right now you will have to take more initiative. Following up job opportunities, doing research, contacting references, and all that may come as a rude awakening to you, but now is a good time to start new habits.

You may not want the job you say you want. Self-defeating behavior—inattention to the details of an effective job search—may be a sign that you are walking down the wrong trail. You may have chosen a career goal but are ambivalent about it. Your uncertainty is perhaps reflected in your lack of follow-through and your casual attitude. People don't usually sabotage themselves unless there is an underlying reason. A person who is fired up about his/her job objective will typically take care of every item without being coaxed. If you are letting things slip, take a closer look at your motivation. Is there some other kind of work that you would really prefer but have been reluctant to admit to yourself? Temporarily, try adopting a different job objective. See if you follow through on job-search tasks more efficiently. If your self-defeating behaviors disappear, then you have learned something about the work you really want.

You may have ambivalence about succeeding in general. I know this sounds terribly psychological, but it does often happen that people act in self-defeating ways because they are reluctant to succeed. In job hunting, lateness for appointments, inability to prepare, casualness of attitude, etc., can be signs that someone is setting him/herself up to fail, certainly to not get the job he or she is supposedly seeking.

If you think you have a touch of "fear of success," I encourage you to explore that theme within yourself (with the help of a counselor or psychologist if you choose) before you do yourself any more damage in job hunting. If your job search is disorganized or uneven, you will not get much benefit from it, only frustration.

Regardless of where it comes from, if you see a self-defeating pattern in your own behavior, I encourage you to break the pattern while you are aware of it. If you have to get out of the game for a while, do it. Jump back in when you can see what you did wrong before and your motivation is more clear.

Get Rid of Your Self-Defeating Beliefs

A person's job search can start with self-assessments that make progress very difficult:

+ Interviewers don't like me
+ I really don't have a sense for the business world
+ Computers scare me
+ I don't have the confidence to deal with that type of customer
+ I don't have enough class for that kind of place
+ I'm not smart enough to do that job
+ I'm too "East Coast" for that job and those people
+ People don't warm up to me easily

And, like trying to move a bale of hay with a large cow standing in your way, that is where the project both begins and ends. Self-defeating beliefs, whether they are true or not, become true when the job seeker believes them. If you say one of those statements to yourself often enough, you have a reason to get discouraged or even give up.

A self-defeating belief can override the job hunter's positive research and growing knowledge of the field of work. If people feel pessimistic, they will interpret their data to fit their expectations. Now we know what some philosophers mean when they say there is no reality, just our own perceptions of it.

Self-defeating beliefs can be lurking around any corner, ready to pounce on your good, constructive job-hunting techniques. All the king's horses and techniques in this book cannot put you back together again if you fashion a negative image of yourself based on some "reason" you believe you won't make it.

What You Can Do About This Problem

Everyone can imagine one or more disadvantages in their backgrounds if they try hard enough, even though these may not be disadvantages at all.

- ✦ too old/too young
- ✦ too little experience/too much experience
- ✦ need more large-business experience/need more small-business experience
- ✦ too many previous jobs/worked for only one employer

Before you accept your self-defeating belief as fact, do these things:

Reality Check. Test your image of the occupation against a sample of people who are doing it. Do they have the characteristics that you believe? Allow for your inexperience before judging yourself too harshly. How did recently hired people penetrate this field? Were they once in the same position you are in? Ask them how they believe you could adapt your background to the job. Look for people with your characteristics who are doing the job. If you can find someone like yourself, this could allow you to cancel your self-defeating beliefs.

Find Counter Factors. While you are reality checking, look for reasons that will *support* your presence in that kind of work. If you're going to develop a bias, it might as well be a positive one. Just as there may be areas where you lack something, so there can be ways that you will have the edge on your competitors.

Rewrite Your Self-Statements. Based on better information, write a more accurate set of self-beliefs for yourself. Give yourself the benefit of the doubt. "I have good potential for this job because of these skills: _____, and it will be even better when I work on _____."

Fill the vacuum with data that you gather firsthand, and if it looks as though you have even a decent chance of being a good candidate, give yourself a try. Yes, rejections will occur in the natural course of job hunting, but this is better than rejecting yourself.

Self-defeating beliefs make you into a "poor me." You can talk yourself into defeat and inaction, but why do it? So you can lament, complain, and curse the darkness? If that's your idea of fun, OK. Otherwise, it's better to get your beliefs going in your favor. Write some stories where you come out the winner. To a large extent, you are who you think you are:

As a person thinketh, so shall they be.
—Proverbs

38

Always Have Backup Plans

You may not like the idea of a Backup Plan, and I'm not sure I like it at first glance either. It sounds as though you might be settling for less, in case your main plan doesn't work out. Backup quarterbacks are not starting quarterbacks, so why should you take a backseat to your main career aspiration?

Lots of things can happen. There's chaos all around us. Your target industry can fall into the tank. . . . You can lose job offers to other people. . . . The salmon hatchery can overflow on your way to a job interview and, instead of making your presentation, you're spawning upstream. . . . Your family decides Shingle Springs, California, is the place to be, and there's no market for investment bankers there. . . . Twenty years is enough of running a restaurant called Herman's Halibut Hideaway, so what now?

Having a Plan B is not settling for less. It means looking at the market as having multiple opportunities for you, and being aware of these opportunities so that you make the best deal for yourself. Plan B may turn out to be better than Plan A.

Your backup career objectives can be similar to Plan A or they can be entirely different. You may decide to get "the next-best thing" to what you wanted originally, or you may decide to chuck it completely.

A backup plan can also be an "interim job" (see chapter 13), a job that you get in the meantime, while you're still nurturing opportunities for Plan A objectives.

Plan B has several purposes:

1. It demonstrates that there's more than one kind of work in this world that might capture your interest. This is important because you may have thought there was only "one right career" for you. Not true. You are "multipotential," a term coined by an early philosopher of career development, Donald

Super, which means that you're capable of being satisfied and successful in any of several different careers at the same time.

2. It gives you a concrete objective at a time when you need to stay active. Your Plan A is unattainable or out of reach for the moment, so rather than sink into a pit of despair and mumble incoherently about how unfair the world is, you can attach your energy to a different, but specific, goal. Better to be pursuing *something* than hiding in your basement.

3. Plan B opens you up to other possibilities that may have been waiting in the wings to make an appearance. In taking an interim job or simply a job that is available, you may find other abilities and motivations you were unaware of. In some cases, one's Plan B turns out to be more attractive than Plan A. Either Plan A did you a favor by turning you away, or Plan B was what your unconscious wanted to happen all along. Your unconscious or your intuition may guide you without your being aware of what's happening. Sometimes certain things are "meant to be."

When should you formulate your Plan B? There is a range of choices available to you: (a) Make your Plan B at the same time as you develop your Plan A objective; (b) Wait until the prospects for Plan A are starting to look unlikely, and then identify an alternative objective; (c) Wait until Plan A falls through completely.

Option (c) is a bit riskier. I would tend to recommend (a) or (b). However, you can choose based on the degree of plan-ahead-ness that you're comfortable with.

What does a Plan B consist of? Identifying a target area of work, a set of possible employers in your target geographical area, and a rationale for why you believe you may be a candidate for this kind of work.

You may have difficulty identifying a goal for Plan B because you have so much energy tied into Plan A; it distracts you to try thinking of anything else you might do. You may not want to feel that you're compromising yourself. Give yourself a break. Obsessiveness about a single career goal will leave you blind to other possibilities, oblivious to other parts of yourself.

It sometimes happens that Plans A and B merge to form a whole that is greater than the sum of the parts. For example, if you long to become a journalist, and your Plan B involves photography, you might find a home as a photojournalist. That one's kind of obvious, but most any combination of Plans A and B can be envisioned. Take a combination such as an accountant and a plumber. You might be in financial management for a plumbing-supplies business.

Or, if Plan A is to be an auto mechanic and Plan B is to be a mortgage loan officer, you might develop loans for an auto mechanic union, or you might run the motor pool for a large mortgage loan company.

The short-run value of a backup plan is to help you maintain a flow of earnings when your immediate objective flees the planet. However, the deeper objectives of Plans B and C are to help you recognize that, at any given moment, you have numerous opportunities for gaining employment or being self-employed.

Your transferable skills enable you to be marketable in many different places. If you believed there were only one kind of work that you were capable of, you would feel pretty frightened and alone. "Only one kind of job for me? What if it's not available?" You're not being fair to yourself if you paint yourself into the proverbial corner of one career or one kind of job. Since you are an evolving being, your Plans A, B, and C may change from year to year or even from month to month. Honor your multipotentiality.

It is healthful and stimulating to imagine that you might apply yourself to different career fields. "What if" is a fun game to play. And, as noted earlier, it's quite possible you'll develop a strategy for combining two or more career objectives that enables you to create a unique career direction.

Thus, Plan B is not so much about survival, because you'll figure out a way to survive. Plan B is about being fully engaged with the creative ways you can apply your talents to income-earning.

Successful entrepreneurs know this from experience. When one business idea drops by the wayside, they invent another . . . and another. Making a living is an ongoing parade of changing products and services. Since you're the chief executive officer in charge of yourself, every job possibility is another entrepreneurial option for you. "If you don't want my apples, then how about my bananas? Peach cobbler?"

39

Deal with Your "Bright but Scattered" Ambitions

There are many job hunters who are a pleasure to talk with, who can think of lots of possibilities, and who are clearly brimming with intelligence, yet bounce around, unable to establish themselves or perform with distinction on a job. These people have lots of potential, but that's where it stops.

If intelligence and verbal facility could be cashed like so many chips in the marketplace, these people would do fine. But ease of conversation and an engaging manner are not the same as goal-directedness and determination.

Sometimes, these bright but scattered people appear to feel "too good" for jobs they are offered, and their apparent aloofness simply adds to their problems.

What You Can Do About This Problem

We've all been scattered and uncertain at one time or another, so let's not consider this a social disease. Being restless can be a sign of constructive impatience. A certain amount of scatteredness is all right as you are roaming the fields, looking for ideas. However, if you are continually unfocused and unable to find anything, then perhaps we'd better look a little closer at what's happening in your not-yet-brilliant career.

It is possible that regular, salaried jobs won't do it for you. You may be resisting the entire working-for-someone scene. If so, imagine starting your own little business, or working with a few other people in a small business, or developing a highly portable skill (photography, word processing, graphic arts, language translation) that allows you to avoid a nine-to-five, one-office desk job.

If self-employment won't work, and you need a secure salary, then you'll have to face squarely this problem of scatteredness. If you move from job to job, or you simply fail to be focused enough in job interviews, eventually you'll be typed this way and will find it a difficult reputation to overcome.

Where does your restlessness and uncertainty come from? I can think of two strong possibilities. First, you may still be on the trail of your real ambitions. If you have done little self-assessment (see chapters 1 to 7), you may not yet know the answers to important questions such as "What do I really want? What kinds of work would be most worth doing? Where can my abilities best be used?" If this is the case, be patient with yourself and take interim jobs while you are shaping your ambitions and career dreams.

On the other hand, you may be a person who will be perpetually unsatisfied with your paid employment, and the search for a fully satisfying job will largely elude you. This happens to a lot of people. No one ever said that paid work is the answer to everyone's prayers. Many jobs will provide only partial satisfaction, no matter how motivated you are.

If this is the case, consider how you can get fired up about some activity outside your paid work. Let your outside interests be your primary involvements, if possible, and regard your paid work as simply a job to be done, nothing more. Your outside interests may also offer clues for future career possibilities.

Bright people can have a hard time with career development once they have rejected the obvious "successful" career paths (doctor, lawyer, business executive, professor, scientist). A conventional career may not be right for you. Your career may be a floating circus of involvements, some of them paid, some of them unpaid, but with the program always changing.

You may need to be very creative about shaping your career. Maybe no one else will have a career quite like yours. Your so-called scatteredness may be your effort to find all the pieces in your career jigsaw puzzle before you put them together. Don't settle for disillusionment or wallow in it. Find something good to *do*, whether it is paid or unpaid, temporary or permanent, promising or uncertain. Just talking about it leaves you deeper in the pit of inaction. Go ahead and do it.

40

Avoid Anger

No one likes an angry job hunter. Yet there they are, teeth bared, growling at people, corporations, or the world in general, feeling resentful at the ways they've been treated. We all have our unfavorite examples—canceled interviews, misrepresentations, interviewers who lie to you, discrimination—but they all add up to the same thing: you're angry, and it's getting in the way of your job hunting.

Career counselors are quick to spot people whose anger or resentment has affected their job-hunting attitudes. They say to themselves: "If I were an employer, I would be very reluctant to hire such a negative person."

Anger serves no purpose in the job search other than to slow you down. Anger is energy distracted from the task at hand. If you're angry, your goal is to exact a "payback" from those who have wronged you. Lots of luck. Those who treat us badly are usually down the road and out of sight.

If you're carrying feelings from past job hunting that you want to resolve, you're distracted. Even if your anger is subtle and you believe you're burying it, negative feelings will show up. If someone asks you about a former employer and you do a barely audible "Grrrrr," it won't play well. You can ventilate and blow off steam outside of the job-search arena, but leave it at home before walking out the door.

Anger feels good in an odd kind of way. You can feel so "justified." So "right." You can explain up one side and down the other why you're right and they're wrong.

As Scott Peck said: "Life is not fair." Or certainly not as fair all the time as you would like it to be. People will mislead you, lie to you, misunderstand you, ignore you, and not fully appreciate you. It will happen again and again. What are you supposed to do about it? Try to avoid the people and organizations that can't be trusted. And move on. Keep smiling. It's a test of your ability to handle adversity.

Sure, it's fun to complain about things, but when you do it with an interviewer, you take the risk that he/she will view *you* as the source of the problem.

Negativism of any kind—including snide remarks, "funny" stories that make someone else look bad, criticizing former bosses, or just going along with the popular cynicism ("Ain't government bureaucracy awful?")—will always be taken by the interviewer to reflect badly on you. There's no escaping a general dictum of employers: "If you're negative in the job interview, you'll be negative on the job."

When you're angry at how you've been treated in the job market, you may believe that someone should come along and make it right. That's irrational. No one watches over the job market and rights every wrong. Most wrongs slide on through and life goes on. Your belief that you "deserve better" may degenerate into: "They have it in for me."

I'm not describing some out-of-control bozos when I talk about angry people. Rage and growling—that couldn't be you, could it? Yes, it could. Yours may simmer just below the surface, and the more "justified" you feel, the less it seems like irrational anger. But what looks like "I'm right" is just a grudge in a different guise. And grudges are poor companions when you absolutely need to be positive in how you relate to others.

Think about what anger does to you as you're trying to mount a job-search campaign, or sell your services as a consultant, or start a new business. You don't smile; instead you look grim. You don't make people comfortable. Instead you invite them to share in your anger toward your former employers/villains.

How do the "learned optimists" do it, those people who take one "unfair treatment" after another, bounce right back, smile, and continue to believe that people will like them and see their value?

> Optimists believe defeat is not their fault. Circumstances, bad luck, or other people brought it about. Such people are unfazed by defeat. Confronted by a bad situation, they perceive it as a challenge and try harder.—Martin Seligman, *Learned Optimism*[1]

But anger is hard to dispense with. Underneath your anger is often the feeling that "I'm doing something wrong and I have no idea what it is." So anger is often self-anger. Anger is also raw energy. It means that you care about your work, that you want very much to do well. In that sense, anger can be a good sign. But it must be turned in a positive direction.

Let's Get Angry One Last Time

Anger hurts you more than anyone you're trying to criticize. Your anger makes you moody. You are sullen without realizing it. Does that sound like the kind of person you'd want to hire?

So let's move on. Let's talk about how you can bury your anger so you're free to mobilize your positive energy and not be fighting old battles that nobody cares about except you.

1. *Write a hundred-word statement about your anger.* In no more than a hundred words, explain "what they did to me" as vividly, clearly, and strongly as you can. Give it punch. Say it as powerfully as you can.

2. *Put it in a box and bury it.* Have a formal ceremony for burying your Anger Statement. Choose any old box, just so it's sturdy enough. No need to bury it in the backyard; bury it in a drawer somewhere.

3. *Decide to move ahead.* Commit yourself to future growth, free of anger. Nothing in the past is important enough to drag down your efforts in the present.

4. *Revisit your anger when you feel the need.* If you get a flash of the old resentment, it's OK to open the drawer and read your Anger Statement every so often, just to remind yourself of how you once felt, and that you have moved on.

Picture an angry person on the job-search trail. Head down. Looking for places to trip. Scowling at people on the bus or train. Imagining everyone cutting him off on the highway. Impatient on the telephone. Unable to muster enough natural friendliness to get a smile in return. And waiting, just waiting for the next person who has no time to talk with him. When you see such a person in an office, you make sure you don't have the time.

You have the right to feel angry about being wronged in the marketplace. But remember that you'll be misunderstood and misled again, despite your best efforts to line all the planets up in perfect order. People will also do things for you that you don't expect. Someone will occasionally discriminate in your favor. The universe throws a lot of random variation at you while you're making your way through the swamp.

As many sages have said, whatever happens to you, you always have a choice about how to react. Events are not under your control, but how you react to them (both behaviorally and emotionally) is under your influence. If you react positively, you gain. If you get angry, you lose.

Job hunting would be so much better if people would respond to you the way you feel you deserve. Here are a few examples:

♦ When your résumé arrives at the company, the secretary drops her correspondence and her coffee, rushes into the boss's office, and the boss says: "This is the woman we need to solve our problems!"

♦ The boss looks carefully at your résumé and says to herself: "I've been trying to help the company recover its lost market share for months. This woman can do it for us!"

+ The boss tells all her friends, family members, and tennis companions to withdraw their names for the job once she receives your résumé.

+ You call for an interview and the receptionist puts five other people on hold for half an hour while looking for her boss.

+ You're invited for an interview and the boss listens patiently while you explain your capabilities and your life story. She doesn't interrupt to tell you anything about her life, doesn't answer her phone, and doesn't rush to another meeting, even though her boss is waiting to discuss the $100,000 to be cut from next year's budget.

+ They call the references you gave them and they believe everything the references say about you.

Life would be immeasurably better for you if job hunting were like that, but alas, it's not. Truth to tell, job hunters are too focused on themselves. Every job candidate thinks his résumé is the most important and that they've worked so hard at job hunting that they should get immediate attention.

It doesn't work that way, and job hunters get annoyed. They get impatient. They get to feeling that any sign of being neglected is a good reason to be resentful. Hence, anger. "Don't they recognize everything I've done in my work life?" Of course they don't. Why should they? You know yourself a thousand times better than anyone else. It's your job to educate them.

And there will be slippage along the way. People will lose your résumé. . . . People will completely forget what you just told them two minutes ago. . . . People will answer your phone calls and forget you're on. . . . People will not answer your voice-mail messages even though they're interested in what you had to say. . . . People will call you by the wrong name. . . . They'll call your references at 6 A.M. because of a time-zone difference. . . . They'll leave messages with your four-year-old even though they know better. . . . They'll lose your file.

Anger Is the Last Refuge Against Living

There are people who have made a lifetime activity out of their anger. They build castles to their anger; they make it the very center of their existence. They're devoted to showing they were right. This is ridiculous and self-defeating.

There's a lot of Good Work to be done out there. If you don't do it, somebody else will. There are books to be written, houses to be built, songs to be sung, and people to be cared for.

So you take your lumps and move ahead. It's an old lesson, one that we learn again and again. Anger, resentment, disappointment, sadness, and loss. Your career will rise or fall based on how well you can dispense with anger, resolve loss, and remobilize your positive energy.

Expect to be mistreated. Don't be surprised or offended by it. Respond to everything with a smile, with a willingness to repeat yourself ten times if necessary; show the patience of Job (maybe that's how he got his name). People don't treat you neglectfully because they want to make you angry. They're focused on themselves and they're leading their own imperfect lives, just as you are. Be ready for the moment when you have their attention. Be gracious. Act with class. It will be remembered.

41

Don't Fall Back on Easy Income

This may sound like an advantage in the job search, and certainly it allows you to eat while you are developing your grand strategy, but often the availability of outside financial support works perversely against your desire to forge ahead.

It is one of the most mysterious problems in all of job hunting. How can money be a curse rather than a blessing? Many career counselors have reported that their clients are blocked or strangely unable to shape or move toward their goals when they have a steady or sizable income to keep them warm. Oddly enough, when money is there to free people to do whatever they really want most to do, they get stuck in their own trenches.

You may be having the same experience. Just when you are on the brink of doing what you really want, you seem to founder and feel unable to make up your mind. You are so taken with the idea that you can choose from the great candy store of careers that you become immersed in the process, and bog down in a morass of information, introspection, and creating still more ideas. Too much time and too much financial security can seduce you into exploring so many options that you begin to wonder: "If I make a choice, will I be over-looking something else that I would have found if I had kept looking?" We *could* look forever for careers, for marital partners, for a new car, if we had enough time. But meanwhile, life goes on.

Career counselors note that this problem is a particularly tricky one; it *looks* as though the client is working hard, investigating, etc., and seems quite moti-vated. Often these are highly capable people who *do* have a lot of skills and awareness of their potential, who should be able to get a successful career under way. Yet, as time goes on, it becomes clear that these clients cannot mount the effort it takes to find goals that fire them up, and to move assertively and deliberately toward these goals.

What You Can Do About This Problem

If this problem seems to describe you, I will first give you credit for admitting it. This is a difficult problem to recognize.

You may be a new college graduate who is being supported by your parents. Or perhaps you are married, and your spouse's income is making it possible for you to develop a career path at your own pace. Or maybe you have an inheritance or trust fund that enables you to live comfortably while you are looking for a new job.

If you have been looking for your job for only a brief time, it's premature to consider that money is the problem. However, if you have been looking for six months or more, and you still don't have a clear goal in sight, or you have been unwilling to take steps necessary to move toward your goal, then you may be subtly undermining yourself with the comfortable pillow of financial support.

It may seem ludicrous to ask someone to surrender financial comfort, but you may want to consider some variation on that theme. So far, a steady income does not seem to have worked in your favor. Why not try cutting yourself loose for a while? Suppose you gave yourself a time deadline ("I won't use the money past a certain date"), or a financial limitation ("I will only spend $_____ per month, so that I am forced to find employment by a certain time"), in order to build some urgency into your job-search plans.

The presence of income support may compromise your efforts in subtle and complex ways. You may be thinking—perhaps unconsciously—"I have to find the perfect job," believing that your choice has to be *better* than the jobs of other people, because you have the so-called luxury of time and money to decide. In general, I believe that too much time and monetary support become liabilities, because they force you to think too much. You may spend so much time dwelling on the possibilities and gathering new information that you get weighed down with data. The pile of information makes it harder for you to pay attention to your intuition, your gut feelings about the direction you should choose.

Of course, money can also tie you to the needs, preferences, and wishes of the person who is supplying it. You may feel, without even asking, that you're obligated to choose a job or career that would please him or her. You may never have had such a conversation, but the influence can be felt anyway.

Thus, in many respects, it can help you to get clear of your financial support, if that is possible or you are willing to do it. Even if you are unable or unwilling to change your financial situation, ask yourself how it might be affecting your motivation. At the very least, you should do the following:

1. Identify a career goal that represents what you think *you* most want.

2. Talk with your family, spouse, etc. about your goal and do your best to draw out their feelings about it. If they disagree or are even lukewarm about it, hear what they have to say. Sharing your disagreement openly will help you to decide what is best for you and may lead you to a firmer decision.

How long do you want to continue contemplating your choice while the world beckons you to do something? I appreciate the need for research as much as the next person, but you may need to hit or get off the plate. If you *had* to find something worth doing by tomorrow, what would it be?

If you are bogged down in your job search, and you suspect that financial support has something to do with it, decide what you have to do to build a fire under yourself. Whatever direction you take, it is important that you clarify how your financial condition may be affecting you.

If you continue falling back on easy income, and you dabble in careers rather than making a commitment, you may lose respect for yourself. Don't let the availability of money drive your career process. Create a sense of urgency for yourself. If you're overwhelmed with options, commit yourself to a career for a full year. No more research or endlessly weighing alternatives. Take a wild guess. Let your unconscious rule.

Don't Be Defensive About
Your Liberal Education

I Tell Them I'm a Liberal Arts Major

And then, of course they say:
"How quaint; and what are you going to *do* with that?"
. . .
Well, I thought perhaps I'd put it in a cage
to see if it multiplies or does tricks or something
so I could enter it in a circus
and realize a sound dollar-for-dollar return
on my investment.
Then, too, I am exploring the possibility of
whipping it out like a folding chair
at V.F.W. parades and Kiwanis picnics.
I might have it shipped and drive it through Italy.
Or sand it down and sail it.
What am I going to *do* with it?

. . .
You don't understand—
I'm using every breath to tread water
in all-night swimming competitions
with Hegel, Marx, and Wittgenstein;
I am a reckless diver fondling the bottom of civilization
for ropes of pearls

. . .
What am I going to *do* with it?
I'm going to sneak it away from my family
gathered for my commencement
and roam the high desert
making love to it.

—Carol Jin Evans[1]

Many readers are people whose education is general rather than specific vocational preparation. You are relying on your generic learning skills to help you get a job. You may either have chosen "liberal arts" (this is a term I will use to apply to any nonvocational general education) deliberately, or you may have completed a specialized program but now are seeking work in a different field. All of you have contemplated how your general education will help you in your pursuit of a career.

There is a pervasive misunderstanding about the relationship between education and jobs, and it goes something like this: Many people believe that the main purpose of going to school is to become trained for a vocation or a career. Thus, those who direct their schooling toward this end, and choose the "right" fields of study (those that have good job markets), are the presumed winners of the labor market game. Those who miss the boat either studied the "wrong" fields, or chose liberal arts education and therefore never got themselves "trained" for anything.

Following this reasoning, it seems ludicrous that anyone would consciously choose liberal education, because they would seem to have no chance of success in the labor market. But colleges of liberal arts (both private colleges, which have *only* liberal arts, and universities with large liberal arts colleges) continue to enroll thousands of students. In fact, approximately 1 million college graduates receive liberal arts degrees every year. You may be one of these graduates or may expect to become one. Thus, you would wonder: "What *does* a person do with a general education in the job market?"

How Do Liberally Educated People Get into All Those Careers?

In the face of schooling that purports to "train" an individual for certain careers, the interesting question remains: "How *do* the 'untrained' but generally educated compete effectively for these jobs?" If you are one of these, what do you have that you can throw on the table that can compete with the person who has an academic credential in management, journalism, marketing, radio/television/film, or some other field that you hope to enter?

In fact, the liberally educated graduates have many assets they can call upon other than specialized academic credentials.

I call this the "Tools in Your Kit" approach to marketing yourself, and it looks like this:

"Tool Kit" of the Generally Educated Who Seek Jobs and Careers

General Learning Skills. The ability to become competent in a wide variety of jobs, through having learned how to learn. Courses that emphasize analytical thinking, research, writing, and communication skills are valued because they can be applied to any new learning situation.

Specific Academic Courses. While a person may not have an academic degree relevant to the career he/she desires, it is possible to have taken certain job-related courses, such as accounting, computer systems, statistics, expository writing, etc.

Experience. General exposure to a field of work outside of the classroom can include internships, work experience during summers, volunteer or part-time experience during the school year, etc. Such experience often provides greater knowledge of a field of work than what can be gained from academic courses.

Motivation. Your sheer desire to succeed, drive to become involved in a given field, and level of enthusiasm will contribute greatly to your overall job and career potential. Often motivation is the factor that distinguishes one good job candidate from another, because such drive colors everything that you will do on the job.

Skill. Employers seek generic skills to enable a person to perform well. Such skills—which can be acquired in either academic courses or outside the classroom—include research, writing, planning, supervising, organizing people or data, budget management, and many others.

Interpersonal Skills. Often referred to as "getting along with people," this set of skills can be acquired anywhere, and is highly valued. The ability to engage people, work cooperatively with them, motivate them, and deal well with conflicts can be demonstrated in the job interview itself, or by reference to past jobs, campus activities, community work, or leadership experiences.

Thus, we can begin to understand why the liberally educated find places in the job market, even though their academic credentials do not show any "training." While the "tools" noted above do not provide you any guarantee of being hired for the jobs you may want, these factors enable you to compete effectively with others having "vocational" majors.

It is often said that the "ability to work effectively with a wide variety of people" is one of the hallmarks of a liberal arts graduate. Courses in anthropology, languages, political systems, history, literature, and others help make you more sensitive to the reality that the world is filled with people very much unlike yourself. You soon learn that much of your success in a career will depend upon your ability to work productively with people who think differently from you, value different things, have different backgrounds, and often speak different languages. A liberal education encourages this sensitivity, so don't try to tune it out. As Lee Iacocca notes in his autobiography:

> In addition to all the engineering and business courses, I also studied four years of psychology at Lehigh. I'm not being facetious when I say that these psychology courses were probably the most valuable courses of my college career. . . . I've applied more of these courses when dealing with the "nuts" I've met in the corporate world than all the engineering courses in dealing with the nuts (and bolts) of automobiles.[2]

A Liberal Education Is Important for the Vocationally Trained, Too

If you think you're going to gain entry to a career simply because you have an academic degree that says you learned all about it, guess again. Employers do not hire academic transcripts; they hire people who have the greatest potential to become productive in their organizations. They have learned that workers are productive for a variety of reasons, among them, general learning skills. Employers know you cannot be trained in school to face every problem that you will encounter on the job. So they want your mind to be as well trained as possible.

Those who study career-oriented curricula cannot afford to ignore liberal learning. If they concentrate only on their career-preparation courses, and believe mistakenly that knowledge of a career and its technical concepts are what matters, they will suffer from a lack of analytical, writing, research, and other generic skills. Perhaps even more important, a career-focused student may ignore the importance of interpersonal skills, of understanding other cultures, or of learning to think imaginatively. The short-run, "bottom line" mentality of business school graduates is a deficiency in present and future business leaders.

The vocational courses may look good on the transcript, but they are long forgotten once an organization looks to you for leadership of people, strength of ideas, and the breadth of thinking to be able to manage an organizational ship in uncertain waters.

Career-focused courses *can* be taught with general learning skills in mind. However, you must look closely at your courses to see what skills are emphasized. Does the course require you to express your ideas in writing? Do you have to handle abstract concepts and think broadly about problems? Are you required to express your ideas in class and be challenged by others? Do you have to exercise your research skills? Does the course sensitize you to different cultures? Move toward schooling that emphasizes these broader skills, because you will need them in whatever job or career you enter.

The Long-Run Advantage and Leadership Potential of the Liberally Educated

Most liberal arts graduates do not know at the time they graduate—at age twenty-one without any work history—the benefits they will get from their education as they progress through their careers. The virtues of general education do not unfold until after some years have passed, jobs have changed, and the graduate can reflect upon the skills and attitudes that made a difference in his/her career. Such insights are not available to the new graduate, nor should we expect them to be.

Nonetheless, it is becoming increasingly clear that the liberal education provides a critical base for those who desire to advance to positions of leadership in their careers, whether in small organizations or large ones, in the profit or nonprofit sectors.

The higher one's level of responsibility in a career, the more important are the generic learning skills and interpersonal skills that tend to characterize a liberal education. The ability to solve complex problems for which you have not been "trained," to communicate effectively, and to understand different views are going to be crucial qualities for any organizational leader.

Executives are frustrated by new graduates of business schools and other career-focused programs who cannot function well beyond the level of mere technicians, and who communicate poorly within their organizations. A senior vice president of First Atlanta Corporation says, "If I could choose one degree for the people I hire it would be English. . . . You can teach a pack of Cub Scouts to do portfolio analysis."[3]

Furthermore, several research studies have demonstrated the long-run merits of a general education, and the leadership qualities evidenced by liberal arts graduates:

+ AT&T, the largest employer of college graduates in the United States, studied the college backgrounds of employees who, after twenty years, had advanced to senior management positions. It was found that 43 percent of liberal arts graduates advanced to senior management, compared to 34 percent of the business school graduates and 28 percent of the engineering graduates. In a highly technical company such as AT&T, one might have expected the reverse. The president of AT&T, Charles Brown, offered an explanation: "The humanities and social science majors were most suitable to change—the leading feature of this kind of high-speed, high-pressure, high-tech world we now occupy."[4]

✦ Chase Manhattan studied the effectiveness of its people as "relationship managers" and learned that 60 percent of the liberal arts graduates were regarded as high performers, while 60 percent of the MBA graduates were evaluated as "low performers."[5]

Questions Asked by Liberal Arts Graduates

As they embark on the job search, liberal arts graduates seem to have certain questions that stump them and make it difficult for them to express full confidence in themselves:

1. "How do I answer 'Why did you study liberal arts and not business'?"

"I felt that I would get a better set of learning skills in liberal arts, and that I could demonstrate my interest in business in other ways, through my part-time work experience and membership in business clubs on campus. I learned (in my liberal arts courses) the analytical, writing, and research skills that I'll need to be a good financial analyst, and have also taken a few business courses so that I am familiar with the problems that occur. I am confident I can do this job."

Any variation on these themes will express your confidence in yourself, your education, and your career goals. Employers want to know that you take your career goals seriously, and want to hear your rationale for your educational background. It would also help to identify any experiences you have had that reveal potential for a career in business.

2. "Must I go to graduate school?"

Liberal arts graduates often enroll in graduate and professional school programs, but they can also get many jobs without additional education. In fact, the majority find employment immediately after graduation, rather than continue their schooling.

There are many fields of work that have corresponding graduate programs but can also be entered with a bachelor's degree, such as business, social work, journalism, public administration, city planning, and many others. Does that mean that people with the advanced degrees will get the better positions? In some cases, perhaps that is true, but in others it is not. For example, a Bachelor of Arts graduate can go just as far on a newspaper as a Master's of Journalism. Or, as the Chase Manhattan study demonstrated, Bachelor of Arts graduates have often done even better than the MBA's in their company. So before you decide that a graduate degree is necessary or preferred, talk with managers in the field of work itself, to see what their experiences have been with bachelor's and advanced-degree holders.

3. "How important are my grades?"

Much less important than you think. While grades are a good measure of your performance as a student, they tell an employer little about how you will function on the job. If your grades are low, don't be defensive about them. Your best response is something like: "I am proud of my degree, and would have made better grades, except that I chose to be involved in other activities, such as _____, which enabled me to develop skills that will help me on this job, such as _____." Draw some advantage from your grades if they are good, but don't ever depend on a grade average to sell yourself as a job candidate.

4. "How do I compete with a 'trained' graduate?"

If, for example, you want a job in business and you are competing with people who have BBA degrees, (a) Show some evidence that you have had business-related experience, such as a part-time job, or business-related skills you have developed in a campus activity; (b) Do enough research that you know what these business jobs are about; (c) Show evidence of your leadership capabilities; (d) Be enthusiastic about the jobs you are applying for; and (e) Point out the business-related courses you have taken in your academic program.

This approach toward job hunting emphasizes that your college major is just one of many tools that you have to offer in the marketplace, and that you should be sure to make all of your assets known rather than relying only on your academic transcript.

5. "How much should I know about computers?"

Know as much about them as seems advisable, in terms of your specific job goals. Since most jobs today have some involvement with hardware and software, you probably ought to have had a computer course or two or gained some exposure in other ways. You probably don't plan to be a computer specialist, but you will be working closely with computer people on your job and will need to know what the equipment can accomplish for you. It is not necessary for you to major in computer science, unless you plan to be a specialist. However, you should understand the computer terminology that is widely used, regardless of what career you plan to enter. You will acquire much of your computer literacy after you are employed. Be prepared to learn a lot about computer capabilities. Many of the decisions you make in your job will depend on the tasks a computer can perform that will help your operation function more smoothly and productively.

✦ *Computer Jobs Available for Liberal Arts Graduates*

> The commonly held idea that the high-tech industry is for technical people . . . nothing could be farther from the truth. For those who have a background in the liberal arts . . . I have a really good piece of news. The high-tech industry needs people like you! . . . I have met pianists who became programmers, and reporters who became salesmen, artists who became advertising managers . . . historians who are now product managers, and a woman who ran a gift shop for several years who is now an internal management consultant. . . . I've become absolutely convinced that the high-tech industry is the most democratic there is.[6]

6. "Why do liberal arts graduates get paid so little?"

Starting salaries for liberal arts graduates average lower than those for engineers, business graduates, and others because employers are willing to pay more for technical skills at the entry level. The potential for a liberal arts graduate is more uncertain at the start; therefore the employer prefers to give raises after he/she has shown some productivity. Also, certain industries that are popular with this group (publishing, banking, insurance, advertising, and others) are known for starting new college graduates at low pay; this applies to both LAGs and other graduates.

The pay increases as graduates advance through their organizational hierarchies. To the extent that a liberal arts graduate attains positions of leadership (which they often do), he/she will have earnings that exceed those of other graduates. Thus, the liberal arts graduate will often start lower in terms of pay and responsibility, but become higher over time. In general, starting salary is a poor predictor of future earnings because the employer has no evidence yet of the graduate's ability to perform.

How to Deal with Personal Flaws

Hidden somewhere in many of us is the fear *"something about me* will slow down or halt my job-search progress, even if I do everything right." Maybe you have felt this before. You were qualified for the job, you applied correctly, had all your paperwork in order, presented yourself well in the interviews, but they still didn't hire you, and you suspected you were boomed because of— how you looked, how you spoke, your personality, your size, or something else that should have nothing whatsoever to do with the hiring decision. You don't really know why you were rejected, but you fear discrimination nonetheless. And these factors, of course, are never mentioned in the interview or afterward in any evaluation or feedback you may receive.

Physical Appearance

Physical appearance is a major concern of a lot of job hunters. Imperfect diamonds that we are, there is usually something that we worry will detract from our marketability. What should you do about it, if you feel you are at a disadvantage in this respect?

1. Leave Well Enough Alone

The first strategy is to do nothing at all—that is, nothing different from the rest of your job-search strategy. Recognize that there are many physical attributes you can do nothing about, and just sit back and appreciate the way you are, trusting that others will too. Qualities such as:

Shape of body, height, size of body
Facial features, body features (nose, ears, eyes, elbows, skin, etc.)

Type and amount of hair, complexion, ways you walk
Speech pattern, accent, vocal qualities

All of these are things that define you; you've been living with them for a while and will have many more years to carry them around. Don't get obsessed with trying to change these, because you probably cannot do much about them and will only create frustration for yourself when you say: "If only I were a little taller." It's better to focus on things that you can change and want to change, because there are certainly enough of those to occupy your attention.

If you are concerned that an employer is judging you on one of these physical attributes, and you would like to say something about it, you may consider doing so, but don't feel that you must. There is room for you to make comments such as the following, if you feel they are necessary:

> *Example:* You may be wondering about the fact that I am very small, and may think I look immature for this job, but I can assure you that I will present a strong image to the customers, and that I will do as good a job as anyone—probably better.
> ▶ I know that my speech is a little different and that sometimes I talk too slowly, but I am effective at getting my points across and can handle myself in any situation.
> ▶ People sometimes comment on the fact that I walk funny, and think that I can't keep up, but it's not a problem for me, and I'm sure you'll see that if you hire me to work here.

Letitia was never a "looker." She was scrawny, wire-haired, bookish, and inclined to withdraw from personal contact. As an adolescent she suffered the criticism you would expect. Eventually she learned that her feeling of presumed "inferiority" had to be dealt with. She decided: "I can't let my body keep me from doing what I want to do." She made the unlikely metamorphosis from withdrawn scarecrow to salesperson of computer equipment and eventual computer manager, because she wanted to make it big in the world of technology. Letitia grew more attractive with her business successes and learned that her so-called physical liability was minor indeed.

2. Things You Might Do Something About, But You Would Prefer to Leave Alone

This is another do-nothing strategy concerning physical attributes that you might change if you wanted to, but you prefer to leave intact. There are hundreds of big and little physical qualities you might alter if you chose. They include:

Body weight, style of clothing, grooming, hairstyle
Clarity of speech, vocal qualities, personal habits (smoking, etc.)
Speaking vocabulary, casualness of dress

Looking at those aspects you might change, but prefer not to, is a way of looking at the hiring equation: "How much do I believe that weight/dress/ speech, etc. are considered in the hiring decisions?" Are your other attributes— job competence, personality, previous experience, etc.—enough to compensate for the physical aspects that might be considered? In most cases, physical attributes will not matter as much as experience, skills, motivation, and credentials. You will decide that your appearance is plenty good enough, and that even though some competitors may be a little better looking than you, you have qualities they don't that will beat them out in other ways.

3. Situations in Which You Can Change, You Want to Change, and You Should Change

Now we're left with the situations where you feel you're going to be one down in a selection process because of one or more physical attributes, and you would like to do something about it. There are several situations in which you should probably consider some changes:

1. *You feel bad about it yourself:* Bad results in job hunting sometimes come from the feelings you carry around inside you. If you feel that being over-weight—or talking differently, or dressing differently from others, or your unusual laugh—or other physical factors are casting you in a bad light, and your self-belief is undermining your general confidence, then you should consider some changes.

2. *The norms of that job setting call for you to change:* If you have done enough investigation of the job and the organization where you want to work to see that most of the people there look different from you, and you would like to fit in better, then you ought to consider some changes. Perhaps they wear different clothing, or everyone in the office is trim and fit, or they all have better diction than you do, or they speak more forcefully. Egad! The stereotype of this profession is coming true, and your physical qualities are going to put you at a disadvantage. Yet you would like to work there very much. There *are* jobs where appearance is important. Sometimes this factor is openly stated, and

sometimes it isn't. If your research reveals that physical attributes are important, you'd better do whatever you can about them.

Personality Traits

This is another reason many people are rejected from jobs without knowing why. Some people with personality flaws will approach this section and move on, thinking that it could not possibly apply to them.

Evaluation of personality characteristics is highly subjective. One person's ogre is another's hard-driving hero. However, there is still room to say that certain personality characteristics will tend to work against a job candidate in many situations. These traits are common enough and amenable enough to change. You may want to consider whether any of these may be hurting your success in the job market: overbearing behavior, timidity, sneakiness, rigidity, negativeness, aloofness, faultfinding, or talkativeness.

While we can think of situations in which such traits would be useful (for example, the aggressive personality can certainly pay off in courts of law; as a newspaper reporter; to sell certain products), in other job-hunting situations such traits are going to subtract from one's overall effectiveness.

We are not talking here about the wonderful variety of personality differences that make people interesting. There is great room for individual styles, senses of humor, ways of interacting, personal mannerisms, etc., in life as well as in job hunting. Here we are concerned about those traits that will most often be perceived as negative, because they will make you a less effective worker. Often the interviewers will not tell you that you have exhibited one or more of these but will proceed to "ding" you, "boom" you, or otherwise short-circuit your job prospects because of them.

What should you do?

1. Identify Specific Behaviors That You Can Try to Change

The more specific you can be about a personality trait, the more likely you are to be able to change it.

> *Examples:* I need to learn not to interrupt people when they're talking. I want to learn how to talk about my good qualities clearly and concisely. I must learn not to make negative comments about my previous jobs.

2. Hold Mock Job Interviews

Eventually you must put into practice what you are learning and changing. Practice job interviews give you a good opportunity to hear yourself talk and interact, and allow you to get feedback without the pressure of knowing you're being evaluated for a job. Mock interviews can be arranged with college career-planning offices, high school counselors, professional counselors or psychologists, your friends, or people in the working world who may be willing to role-play situations with you.

In a mock interview:

+ Prepare yourself to answer the questions you would find most difficult.

+ Tell the "interviewer" in advance about the personality traits that concern you, and ask him/her to test you firmly on these, even try to trap you into showing some of those traits you've had trouble with before.

+ Allow enough time to get feedback immediately after the practice interview.

+ Choose "interviewers" who are not particularly easy, so that you have to face pressure similar to that of a real job interview.

Personality Traits Are Touchy Business

Nobody likes to have anyone else mess with their personality, least of all, perhaps, a job interviewer or author of a job-search book. Telling you that you don't act right is an invitation for "Same to you, buddy." Nonetheless, interpersonal skills are critical in hiring decisions. If you're doing something that makes you less likable than other job candidates, or interviewers are concluding that you may not get along well with others, then you need to change your behavior enough to show the best sides of your personality and your most positive potential for the job.

Taking Advantage of Your Disadvantages

We all know people who are overweight, rude, look funny, or act oddly but seem to benefit from their differences rather than suffer from them. Some are covering up their difficulties, but others truly use their ways or features as departure points for making their lives work. You can be one of them too. If you decided long ago "This is the way I am," then you can go forward with confidence.

Certain attributes, such as rudeness, I do not advise you to maintain. But others—casual style of dress, little attention to fitness and body image, talkativeness, brashness, low-keyness, and others—may work well for you.

Examples: I know I dress differently from others, but that won't stop me from doing a good job as a graphic artist for you.

I talk a lot, but I believe that is necessary in this field of fund-raising.

I'm an overweight "Big Daddy," but I'm happy with myself and I know you'll be happy with me as your insurance agent.

Unusualness can often be turned to your advantage. As long as you are comfortable with yourself, you can use your individual features as your "calling cards."

44

How to Jump-Start Your Job Search

"Hi, ho, hi, ho. It's off to job hunt we go!!!" Now, doesn't that sound ridiculous? Who could ever muster that kind of enthusiasm about job hunting? You want the job search to be over and done with as soon as possible.

Things have not been going well for you. You're discouraged. Your energy is sapped. You can hardly rouse yourself for one more day of telephone calls, networking, chasing job leads, and worrying in between about what you're supposed to do next. And the more eager you are to see the finish line, the more the process seems to drag out. Criminal activity is looking like an option.

A Transformation

Job hunters fall into a trap of believing that "every minute I don't have a job means I'm failing." They have an oversimplified win-loss criterion that says: "No job = I'm no good."

It's all in how you see things. Suppose you transformed your daily job-search adventures into "Every minute I am learning something" rather than "How have I failed today?"

"Boo, hiss!" you say? You want results and you're impatient with learning? Just give it a try here. Desperation, frustration, anger, and "woe is me" have not worked for you so far, so what do you have to lose? Try this view:

1. *Take your eye off the ball.* Don't aim at the job. When you keep trying to lunge for the job, all you convey is your desperation. In *Zen in the Art of Archery*, Eugen Herrigel says we aim at the target by not aiming. Successful job hunting is thus becoming one with the process, not obsessing about the results.

2. *Set intermediate goals* that fit your situation, preferably some that are attainable pretty quickly—five information interviews within a week, an "interim job" within two weeks, temporary work within two weeks, etc.

3. *Decide what you want to learn this week and bend every effort to do it.* Ask yourself: "What can I learn that will make me better prepared for the kinds of work I think I want?"

Paul desperately wanted a job in advertising as a copywriter, but none of the agencies liked his work samples. "Good but not good enough . . . very competitive field. Get some experience . . . then try us later, much later." Paul heard that until he was nauseous. He decided to get off the Desperation Track and onto the Learning Track.

Paul wrote some free ads for his church newspaper and his softball recreation newsletter. He took a small "interim job" as a copywriter for a poor little newspaper that barely paid him, but it "paid" him in experience. Paul ran ads in the paper saying: "Copywriter. Will work for shelled peanuts. If I get results for you, tell your friends."

Paul's mantra was "Every day I will write copy and ask for feedback so I learn how to make my ads better."

4. *Give up the long-range goal for the moment.* Pour your energy into the intermediate goals. Paul saw that he needed success experiences to build a bridge between himself and the ad agency job he coveted.

5. *Think of every day as a complete job in itself.* What kind of work can you find to do that will test yourself and give you opportunities to learn, every day? Employers would prefer to hire based upon observing your work rather than trying to guess from your résumé or your interview. They want to "watch what you do, rather than what you say." So give them something to look at. Find work. Do it. Do it as well as you can. Learn to do it better. Let people observe you.

Every day you work eight hours as a temporary worker or otherwise, that's like an eight-hour interview to anyone who observes what you're doing. Temp work, part-time work, volunteer work, contract work, interim jobs allow you to show who you are, well beyond the strict confines of a forty-five-minute job interview.

The All-or-Nothing Criterion

Job hunters get discouraged because they feel they haven't done anything. No job, no results. Like singles, looking for love in all the wrong places, they feel defeated and wonder "What am I supposed to do next?" The deck seems stacked against them. Every possible action feels as though "Why bother?"

There *are* ways to feel successful before you land job offers. You need these ways, because if you maintain an all-or-nothing attitude, you will hide deeper and deeper in your closet with each passing day.

1. *More is less and less is more.* Concentrate your attention on fewer people in the world of work, rather than more. It's a "success" if you get to know someone's work well, if you make a friend whom you know you can return to. Success is the beginning of a relationship with someone who knows about you and respects your abilities, not a fleeting encounter of fifteen minutes while you race on to the next "contact." Focus your energies on people who interest you the most, rather than trying to cast your net over as many unsuspecting bodies as possible.

2. *There is strength in weak ties.* This principle was validated by the studies of Mark Granovetter, author of *Getting a Job*. It means that you should look for new contacts (some of which may grow into relationships) among people you know less well than others. Don't travel only in the circles most familiar to you. Look up the names of people you've met only once and seek those who seem intriguing to you. Widen your exploration to as many outer circles as possible.

3. *Measure your progress by the numbers of new people you've met and gotten to know. Do not measure yourself by the number of job interviews.* Every in-person contact is an "interview." Everyone who comes to know you has the opportunity to connect you with job possibilities, if they choose. They won't always choose, but then, not everybody loves you, either. If you measure yourself by job interviews, you're continually straining to reach for the brass ring. By doing so, you hurt your emotional muscles and you get fatigued.

45

In Conclusion

This book is nominally about job hunting, but it is really about finding your place in the world. There is a place for you, and there is a place for everyone. You have something special to give, and you deserve to be rewarded for it.

Don't let yourself get swallowed or intimidated by bureaucratic trappings in the job search. Behind those concrete walls and telephone menus, there really are human beings. They appreciate what you're going through, and they'll pay attention to you if you give them some reasons to be interested in you.

You will find a job that is creative and rewarding, if you give yourself permission to do that. Don't settle for simply earning a living. Look for work where you believe you're making a difference. You don't necessarily have to save the world, but you do have to save yourself from boredom.

If you look on a job as just finding employment, it will remain just that, a pedestrian exercise of getting hired. However, if you see job searching as finding a place to be of value, you will approach employers with a sense of purpose.

Work can be a heaven or hell. You're pretty much in charge of which bus you want to take. When your work is rewarding, it spills over to everything and everyone else in your life.

People who feel a sense of purpose in their work have a strong sense of connectedness to others. They don't walk around grousing about their jobs. They don't commit crime in the streets. They don't get angry on the highways. And they don't turn to entertainment to rescue them from feelings of emptiness. Everyone can have purpose in their work. Why not you?

Job hunting is straightforward, but you have to do it right whenever your career takes a new turn. This book is simply about putting yourself out there, letting people know the good you have to offer, and not getting discouraged by the usual knocks in finding where you belong. There are people in the working world just waiting to meet you. Don't disappoint them.

Notes

Chapter 1: Express Your Values

1. Gail Sheehy, *Pathfinders* (New York: Bantam, 1981), p. 15.
2. Ralph Mattson and Arthur Miller, eds. *The Truth About You* (Old Tappan, NJ: Revell Press, 1977), pp. 34–46.

Chapter 2: Decide About Money

1. Jacob Needleman, *Money and the Meaning of Life* (New York: Doubleday, 1991) p. 112.
2. *1998–1999 Occupational Outlook Handbook.*

Chapter 3: Trust Your Intuition

1. Daisetz T. Suzuki, *Essays in Zen Buddhism* (New York: Grove Press, 1949), p. 19.
2. Ibid.
3. Daisetz T. Suzuki, *Zen and Japanese Culture* (New York: Pantheon, 1959), p. 13.
4. W. Timothy Gallwey, *The Inner Game of Tennis* (New York: Random House, 1974), p. 138.
5. Daisetz T. Suzuki, foreword to Eugen Herrigel, *Zen in the Art of Archery* (New York: Random House, 1971).
6. Gallwey, *The Inner Game of Tennis*, p. 31.
7. Ibid., p. 135.
8. Rudolph Flesch, *The Art of Clear Thinking* (New York: Barnes and Noble, 1951), p. 146.
9. Bill Harper, quoted in Bil Gilbert, "Play," *Sports Illustrated*, October 13, 1975, p. 90.

Chapter 4: Take Advantage of Your Skills

1. Joseph Luft, *Of Human Interaction* (Palo Alto: National Press Books, 1969), p. 13. The Johari Window gets its name from the first names of its inventors, Joseph Luft and Harry Ingham.

2. Sidney A. Fine, "Nature of Skill: Implications for Education and Training," Proceedings, 75th Annual Convention, American Psychological Association, 1967.

3. Ibid., pp. 365–366.

Chapter 5: Use Your Career Imagination

1. Michael Ray and Rochelle Myers, *Creativity in Business* (New York: Doubleday, 1986).

2. Edward DeBono, *Lateral Thinking* (New York: Harper and Row, 1970), p. 14.

3. Alex F. Osborn, *Your Creative Power* (New York: Scribner's, 1972), p. 269.

4. Alex F. Osborn, *Applied Imagination* (New York: Scribner's, 1953), p. 284.

5. Adapted from DeBono, *Lateral Thinking*, pp. 91–99, 131–140, 167–174, 193–205; and from Osborn, *Applied Imagination*, pp. 212–214, 217, 261–262.

Chapter 8: Jobs Are Everywhere

1. Richard Bolles, *1999 What Color Is Your Parachute?* (Berkeley, CA: Ten Speed Press, 1999), p. 43.

Chapter 9: Build a Network of Relationships

1. John C. Crystal and Richard N. Bolles, *Where Do I Go From Here With My Life?* (New York: Seabury Press, 1974), p. 188.

2. Mark Granovetter, *Getting a Job* (Chicago: University of Chicago Press, 1995).

3. Stanley Milgram, "The Small-World Problem," *Psychology Today*, May 1967, pp. 290–299.

4. Kirby Stanat, "How to Make An Interviewer Want You," in *Careers Without Reschooling*, Dick Goldberg, ed. (New York: Continuum, 1985), p. 46.

Chapter 10: Information Interviewing

1. Richard N. Bolles, *1999 What Color Is Your Parachute?* (Berkeley, CA: Ten Speed Press, 1999), p. 118.

Chapter 13: Take Advantage of Interim Jobs

1. Adapted from Howard Figler, *PATH*, 3rd edition (Cranston, RI: Carroll Press, 1993), p. 122.

Chapter 14: Use the Library and the Internet

1. Richard Bolles, "The Internet and the Job Hunt, Part II," *Career Planning and Adult Development Network Newsletter*, June 1996, p. 6.

2. Richard Bolles, "The Internet and the Job Hunt, Part III," *Career Planning and Adult Development Network Newsletter*, September 1996, p. 2.

Chapter 15: Listen Before You Talk

1. Theodore Reik, *Listening with the Third Ear* (Moonachie, NJ: Pyramid Publications, 1972).

2. Lawrence Brammer, *The Helping Relationship* (Englewood Cliffs, NJ: Prentice-Hall, 1973), pp. 81–82.

3. Gerard Egan, *The Skilled Helper* (Monterey, CA: Brooks/Cole, 1975), pp. 65–66.

4. Paul J. Moses, *The Voice of Neurosis* (New York: Grune & Stratton, 1957).

Chapter 16: How to Ask Questions

1. Alfred Benjamin, *The Helping Interview*, 3rd edition (Boston: Houghton Mifflin, 1981).

2. Ibid.

Chapter 17: Be the Initiator

1. Gordon Bower and Sharon Bower, *Asserting Yourself* (Reading, MA: Addison-Wesley, 1976), p. 60.

Chapter 18: Use Writing Effectively

1. Natalie Goldberg, *Writing Down the Bones* (Boston: Shambala, 1986), p. 134.

2. Ernst Jacobi, *Writing at Work* (Rochelle Park, NJ: Hayden, 1976), p. 4.

3. J. Mitchell Morse, "The Age of Logophobia," *Chronicle of Higher Education*, May 16, 1977, p. 40.

3. Thomas S. Franco, "In answer to your ad . . . ," *Public Relations Journal*, February, 1977, p. 24.

Chapter 20: How to Sell Yourself with Dignity

1. Jack Falvey, "Developing Party Skills," *Managing Your Career* (New York: Dow Jones and Co., Fall 1986), p. 39.

2. Ibid., p. 40.

Chapter 21: Make Job Offers Come to You

1. Adele Scheele, *Skills for Success* (New York: William Morrow, 1979), pp. 28–33.

2. Robert Wegmann, Robert Chapman, and Miriam Johnson, *Looking for Work in the New Economy* (Salt Lake City: Olympus, 1985), p. 113.

3. Bob Weinstein, *"I'll Work For Free"* (New York: Henry Holt and Co., 1994).

Chapter 24: Show Rather Than Tell

1. Nicholas Corcodilos, *The New Interview Instruction Book* (Lebanon, NJ: North Bridge Press, 1994), p. 23.

2. Ibid., p. 126.

Chapter 27: The Eight Factors of a Successful Job Interview

1. John L. Lafevre, "A Peek Inside the Recruiter's Briefcase," *Managing Your Career* (New York: Dow Jones Co., Fall, 1986), p. 32.

Chapter 40: Avoid Anger

1. Martin Seligman, *Learned Optimism* (New York: Alfred A. Knopf, 1991), p. 5.

Chapter 42: Don't Be Defensive About Your Liberal Education

1. Carol Jin Evans, "I Tell Them I'm a Liberal Arts Major," *Chronicle of Higher Education*, June 9, 1980 (20), 15, p. 48.

2. Lee Iacocca, with William Novak, *Iacocca: An Autobiography* (New York: Bantam, 1985).

3. "The Money Chase," *Time*, May 4, 1981, p. 61.

4. Robert E. Beck, *The Liberal Arts Major in the Bell System Management* (Washington, DC: Association of American Colleges), p. 13.

5. Stanley Burns, *From Student to Banker: Observations from the Chase Bank* (Washington, DC: Association of American Colleges, 1983), p. 16.

6. William A. Schaffer, *Hi-Tech Jobs for Lo-Tech People* (New York: American Management Association, 1994), pp. 2–3.

Selected, Annotated Bibliography

Chapter 1: Express Your Values

Figler, Howard E. *PATH: A Career Workbook for Liberal Arts Students*, 3rd edition. Cranston, RI: Carroll Press, 1993.

Offers an integrated sequence of exercises for assessing your work-related values, attitudes toward work, and ways that play correlates with work.

Green, Thomas F. *Work, Leisure, and the American Schools*. New York: Random House, 1948.

A philosopher's keen understanding of the definitions of job, career, labor, work, and leisure. Green helps us understand when a job is not a career, what "good work" is about, and why leisure is not simply recreation.

Miller, Arthur and Mattson, Ralph. *The Truth About You*. Old Tappan, NJ: Revell Press, 1977.

States the importance of key motivating factors in your career and explains how they can be detected and defined through close scrutiny of your patterns of life experiences.

Sher, Barbara, with Gottleib, Annie. *Wishcraft: How to Get What You Really Want*. New York: Ballantine, 1983.

A thorough and entertaining look at the emotions that inhibit people from aiming for their highest values in work, and ways that creative forces can be tapped in the job search.

Chapter 2: Decide About Money

Slater, Philip. *Wealth Addiction*. New York: E. P. Dutton, 1983.

A provocative look at the ways in which money affects and often rules people's lives. Once money is given a favored position in a person's values hierarchy, other values are slighted or distorted. The author explains how such choices occur unconsciously and what the individual can do about them, if desired.

Needleman, Jacob. *Money and the Meaning of Life*. New York: Doubleday, 1991.

A philosopher's thoughtful exploration of the meaning that money has in everyone's life and how broader, deeper values can be reflected upon. The "real" and "unreal" aspects of money are explored.

Chapter 3: Trust Your Intuition

Ray, Michael and Myers, Rochelle. *Creativity in Business*. New York: Doubleday, 1986.

A detailed exploration of the ways in which intuition is so powerful in making business decisions and personal decisions. Explanation of how Eastern philosophy overlies one's understanding of intuition.

Chapter 4: Take Advantage of Your Skills

Bolles, Richard N. *1999 What Color Is Your Parachute?* Berkeley: Ten Speed Press, 1999.

The leading, best-selling philosophy of the self-initiated job search, in which you learn that identifying your main skills is the central strategic element. The better you know and can talk about your skills, the more effective your job search will be.

Chapter 5: Use Your Career Imagination

Figler, Howard. *PATH: A Career Workbook for Liberal Arts Students*, 3rd edition. Cranston, RI: Carroll Press, 1993.

Explains and gives many examples of how your values and skills can be creatively combined into numerous career options.

Osborn, Alex F. *Applied Imagination*, 3rd revised edition. New York: Scribner's, 1953.

Gives hundreds of examples of creative thinkers and how they developed their ideas; includes an outline of the nine fundamental creative processes and demonstrates how you can nurture them.

DeBono, Edward. *Serious Creativity*. New York: HarperBusiness, 1992.

Tells how to use "lateral thinking" to create new ideas; a comprehensive study of numerous methods for stimulating one's creative powers.

Chapter 8: Jobs Are Everywhere

Bolles, Richard N. *1999 What Color Is Your Parachute?* Berkeley: Ten Speed Press, 1999.

An explanation of the philosophy of "the hidden job market" and ways to tap into it; a philosophy of creative job searching.

Chapter 9: Build a Network of Relationships

Granovetter, Mark. *Getting a Job: A Study of Contacts and Careers*, 2nd edition. Chicago: University of Chicago Press, 1995.

A sociologist's careful study and explanation of how people get jobs through informal networks.

Chapter 10: Information Interviewing

Bolles, Richard N. *1999 What Color Is Your Parachute?* Berkeley: Ten Speed Press, 1999.

Gives a detailed rationale for using the field-survey method and information interviewing in a job search and explains how to use them most productively in all stages of your search.

Chapter 14: Use the Library and the Internet

Riley, Margaret, Roehm, Frances, and Oserman, Steve. *The Guide to Internet Job Searching*. Lincolnwood, IL: VGM Career Horizons, 1995.

A comprehensive guide to ways that you can use the Internet to identify career information and a wide variety of career resources.

Chapter 15: Listen Before You Talk

Egan, Gerard. *The Skilled Helper*, 6th edition. Pacific Grove, CA.: Thompson Publishing, 1997.

Clarifies the essential qualities of a good listener—the verbal, nonverbal, and emotional components of fully attending to the messages of another person. You can use these listening skills to improve your communication in any formal or informal career-related interview.

Chapter 16: How to Ask Questions

Benjamin, Alfred. *The Helping Interview*, 3rd edition. Boston: Houghton Mifflin, 1981.

Explains how to ask effective questions and how questions can be misused. You can learn ways to use questioning to maximum advantage in your career search, types of questioning, and common errors.

Chapter 18: Use Writing Effectively

Goldberg, Natalie. *Writing Down the Bones: Freeing the Writer Within*. Boston: Shambala, 1986.

A most inspirational guide to discovering the writer that lies within everyone; a down-to-earth examination of the feelings associated with writing and how to develop them to your advantage.

Strunk, William Jr., and White, E. B. *The Elements of Style*, 3rd edition. Englewood Cliffs, NJ: Prentice-Hall, 1995.

Offers the last word on the written word and gives rules and advice regarding syntax, grammar, composition, style, usage, and form. You should always consult this reference when you're unsure about anything you have just written.

Zinsser, William K. *On Writing Well*, 6th edition. New York: HarperCollins, 1998.

A superb set of guidelines for clear writing. This book demonstrates and explains the simplicity and power of saying what you have in mind without excess words to muddy it. The book, which is its own best example, warns against the overuse of verbs, adverbs, adjectives, and other parts of speech.

Chapter 21: Make Job Offers Come to You

Weinstein, Bob. *"I'll Work for Free."* New York: Henry Holt and Company, 1994.

A rationale for doing free work as a highly useful strategy for entering and advancing one's career. Gives numerous examples of career success that began with volunteer work.

Chapter 24: Show Rather Than Tell

Corcodilos, Nicholas. *The New Interview Instruction Book*. Lebanon, NJ: North Bridge Press, 1994.

A guide to winning job offers using proven techniques developed by headhunters. The author develops his philosophy of getting the job by "doing it" during job interviews, rather than talking about it.

Chapter 27: The Eight Factors of a Successful Job Interview

Medley, H. Anthony. *Sweaty Palms: The Neglected Art of Being Interviewed*. Berkeley: Ten Speed Press, 1992.

A most insightful guide to the art of being effective in job interviews. This book examines every aspect of the interview in detail and illuminates each topic clearly and with great understanding.

Chapter 37: Get Rid of Your Self-Defeating Beliefs

Seligman, Martin. *Learned Optimism*. New York: Alfred A. Knopf, 1991.

The author carefully defines what distinguishes "optimists" from others and shows how this constructive attitude can be cultivated and applied to daily living.

Chapter 42: Don't Be Defensive About Your Liberal Education

Schaffer, William A., *Hi-Tech Jobs for Lo-Tech People*. New York: American Management Association, 1994.

A detailed explanation of how and why many liberal arts graduates and other nontechnical people gain access to the computer industry and other technical jobs, and why they are given many degrees of freedom to prosper there.

Figler, Howard. *Liberal Education and Careers Today*. Chicago: Ferguson Publishing, 1989.

A summary of research indicating the advancement of liberal arts graduates across the world of work. Explanations from business leaders and others regarding the merits of liberal education. Skills that derive from a liberal education and how they apply to career progress.

Index

Corcodilos, Nicholas, 232, 233, 236
counterpuncher, 247–48
creativity, 63–72
  defined, 63–64
  nine processes of, 67–69, 71–72
  stimulating, 65–67, 69–72
Creativity in Business (Ray and Myers), 40
criticism, 282
Crystal, John C., 109
cues from others, 283

data
  blabbermouth, 248
  irrelevant, 66
DeBono, Edward, 47, 66, 70
De Mille, Agnes, 85
detective work, 9–10, 97–100, 162, 201
dignity, 8, 185–96
diplomacy, 283
direction, by indirection, 44–47
Directory of American Scholars, 140
divergent thinking, 69
Doyle, Arthur Conan, 130–31
dream career, 22
dreamer, arrogance of, 67
dress, 340, 342
  and interview, 253–54, 312
  and walk-in, 128
dropout syndrome, 295

earnings, potential, 37–38. *See also* money; salary
ease, and likability, 256
education
  and grades, 336
  and job qualifications statement, 286
  liberal arts, 288–89, 290, 330–37
  and "wrong" major, 288–89, 330
effort
  "effortless," 44–45
  wasted, 15
Egan, Gerard, 149
Einstein, Albert, 281
electronic communication, 218–19
elimination, by résumé, 272
e-mail, 215
emotions
  anger, 322–26

and benefits of job, 21, 24
and hiring, 239–41
and voice-mail messages, 297–98
employer(s)
  getting to see, 276–77
  giving reason to want you, 220, 227
  and least-reliable data, 99–100
  list of prospective, 218
  needs and priorities of, 226–31
  perspective of, 99–100
  and practice interviews, 247
  and referrals, 107
  and relevant experience, 227
  researching specific, 138–39
  time pressure of, 99
employment agencies, 89, 93
encouragement, lack of, 15
Encyclopedia of Associations, 96–97, 137
enthusiasm
  and getting hired, 240, 257–58
  and voice-mail, 297
  see also motivation
Evans, Carol Jin, 330
exaggerating
  experiences and qualifications, 303–5
  to stimulate creativity, 71
excuses for not searching for job, 12–15
  alternative as worse, 14
  can't do anything else, 12–13
  complainer, 14
  doesn't hurt enough yet, 14
  don't like rejection, 13
  don't want to shake things up, 14–15
  fate, 13–14
  financially set in present job, 15
  hang on to what I've got, 13
  no encouragement, 15
  nothing may turn up, 15
  present job takes all my time, 13
  too old, 12
experience
  ease of getting, 91–92
  firsthand, 79
  and liberal arts graduates, 332
  vs. opinion, 74–75, 80
  and qualifications statement, 286
  and résumé, 272–73
  and self-defeating beliefs, 316
  "wrong" or varied, 289–93

DATE DUE

DEMCO, INC. 38-3012